THE GREEKS
LIFE & CUSTOMS

THE GREEKS
LIFE & CUSTOMS

E. GUHL & W. KONER

KONECKY&KONECKY

Konecky & Konecky
72 Ayers Point Rd.
Old Saybrook, CT 06475

10 digit ISBN: 1-56852-743-8
13 digit ISBN: 978-1-56852-743-7

Printed in the USA

CONTENTS

THE GREEKS

THE GREEKS
LIFE & CUSTOMS

THE GREEKS

1. IN undertaking to describe the life of the Greeks in its distinct external appearance, we have first of all to direct our attention to the products of architecture. For of all the creations designed by man's ingenuity and executed by his hand, these produce the grandest and most powerful impression, and give the most distinguishable character to the life of a nation.

Originated by the free creative phantasy of man, they have to serve at the same time certain purposes and demands of life. They therefore open a view into the genius of their creators, giving at the same time a picture of the real existence in which these creators moved. If this is true of nations in general, it is particularly the case with the Greeks, because they were enabled and gifted more than any other nation to render the innermost nature of their genius in external works of art. It being the task of all investigations of antique Greece to make us understand the spirit and mode of thinking and living of this people, we shall scarcely be able to attain this aim without considering, together with the creations of their poetry and philosophy, with the legal institutions of the State and the doctrines of their religion, also the numerous and variegated productions of their architecture. In these, no less than in the others, Greek genius and Greek culture find their expression, with all the greater distinctness as these introduce us into the varied phases of real existence, and tend to show a distinct character common to all their different peculiarities.

For whatever part of Greek life we may consider—be it public acts of religion or social intercourse, public feasts and games, or the more quiet scenes of home and family—we find that for all these their ingenious mind has created works of architecture, which, through being regulated by these various demands, give

B

us a much more vivid idea of this life than the mostly isolated written testimonials in our possession are able to do. Indeed, the materials which these latter offer to our investigation can only be completed and invested with full life by an accurate knowledge of the monuments.

To do this in a manner as complete and comprehensive of all the phases of life as possible is the task of " the architectural remnants of the Greeks," with which we begin our description of antique life. It is not our intention to give an æsthetical reason for the forms, or a history of their development, which belong to a different science. We only wish to show how the Greeks supplied the various demands of religion, and of public and private life, in their edifices. For this reason also our division of the abundant material cannot but be a purely practical one ; beginning, quite in accordance with Greek notions, with a description of the temples, and adding afterwards the various kinds of profane buildings. For it was the custom of the Greeks to begin with divine things, even in the works of daily life, and of all their creations none are so apt to bring home to us this connection between the celestial and terrestrial as those belonging to the domain of the fine arts.

Poetry begins simultaneously with the narration of human feats of valour and the praise of the immortal gods. The fine arts are developed from the ornamentation of the various appliances of daily life, combined with the desire of giving distinct form to the image of the deity. In this manner architecture serves a material want in affording shelter to human beings, but no less it meets the ideal want of the religious mind in erecting the temple as the protecting dwelling of the divine image. A firm house was prepared for the god to testify his protecting presence, and a centre was created, round which the exercises of various arts grouped themselves. In building and adorning temples architecture has become a fine art, and the images of the gods dwelling therein, combined with the symbolical representation of their deeds and history, have raised sculpture to its highest perfection. Moreover, in the same manner, as within the holy precinct the peace-offering was celebrated, the temple became likewise the centre of festival and dignified events which were so frequent in the life of the Greeks, and endowed it throughout with an artistically beautiful and harmonious impression. In front of the temples were heard the songs of the god-inspired poet; it was there that the processions of Greek virgins moved in measured grace, that the powerful beauty of youths strengthened by athletic sports showed itself. In the shadow of the temples walked the sages and leaders of the people, and round them gathered the wide circle of free and honest citizens, rejoicing in the enjoyment of a life ennobled by art and culture, and justly proud in the consciousness of being Greeks. In this way the temple became the rallying-point of everything good, noble, and beautiful, which we still consider as the glory of Greek culture and refinement. To the temple, therefore, we must first of all devote our attention, in order to revive our consciousness of the spirit and essence of classical antiquity.

2. But not at all times were there amongst the Greeks such temples connected with the veneration of certain gods. Not to speak of the earliest periods of Greek history, during which the gods were adored as nameless and impersonal powers, as, for instance, by the Pelasgi, it also happened at much later times that the divine principle was considered as present in certain phenomena of nature. Fountains and trees, caves and mountains, were considered as seats of the gods, and revered accordingly, even without being changed into divine habitations by the art of man. So it happened that offerings and gifts were devoted to certain trees believed to be the symbols and seats of certain gods; nay, sometimes such trees were adorned with garlands, and altars were erected in front of them. Representations from later periods testify this in various ways. Fig. 1, for instance, shows a sacred pine, to which are attached peculiarly tied wreaths and sounding brasses (κρόταλον), as they were used in the service of Dionysos, the altar in front being destined for the reception of offerings.

Fig. 1.

Amongst mountains, particularly Parnassos and Olympos were considered as favourite seats of the gods. We also find not unfrequently that certain religious rites were connected with natural caves; these being naturally considered as the seats of superhuman powers, because of the strong impression made by

their mysterious darkness on the human mind. Pausanias, for instance, tells us that a cave in a cliff near Bura in Achaia was dedicated to the Herakles Buraïkos, and that in it there was an oracle which disclosed the future by means of dice. Recent travellers believe that they have rediscovered this oracu-

Fig. 2.

lar cave of Herakles in the cliff represented by Fig. 2. They allege that the natural rock has been shaped purposely into a certain form, and that, at the top of the rock, the rudely worked likeness of a head is recognisable.

These and other similar usages point back to a time when the gods were considered in the light of indefinite powers; the want of temples, properly speaking, seems to have become more urgent only when the gods began to be imagined and represented under distinct human forms. Only then it became of importance to find for the representative image of the god a certain protected dwelling-place. But here again it was originally the custom to make use of natural objects which were considered as connected

with the nature of the god, and the same places which formerly were considered as the habitations of divine beings now were in reality used or prepared for the reception of the idol. We know, for instance, that the oldest image of Artemis, at Ephesos, was placed in the hollow stem of an elm-tree: even Pausanias saw in his own time the image of Artemis Kedreatis in a large cedar at Orchomenos. Later sculptors

Fig. 3.

often show divine images of smaller size placed on the stem or branches of protecting trees, as is the case in a relief (Fig. 3).

3. The above-mentioned appliances for the protection of

divine images may be considered as preparatory stages of the
temple properly so called. In the same degree as architecture in
its attempts at constructing and securing human dwellings became
more and more developed (see § 21), the desire became apparent
of procuring to the god a dwelling at once firm and lasting
in accordance with his eternal nature. With the progress of
architecture, which made this possible, the development of
sculpture went hand in hand; and as, in the poems of the Greeks,
the gods became more and more humanised, we notice in the same
degree a change in the fine arts from the bare and simple outline
to a more and more perfect human representation of the gods.
And the nearer god approached man, the closer also the primitive
protection of the image began to resemble the house. A lucky
accident has preserved in Euboea several specimens of the oldest
temple-buildings in the shape of simple stone houses. In this
island, not far from the town of Karystos, rises the steep mountain
of Ocha (called at present Hagios Elias). At a considerable
height there is a narrow plateau, to which there is only one
access, and over which the rock rises still a little higher. On
this plateau modern travellers (first Hawkins) have discovered

a stone house, from
which there is a splen-
did view over the sea
and the island (see
Fig. 4). According
to the measurement of
Ulrich, it forms an
oblong from west to
east of forty feet in
outer length, by

Fig. 4.

twenty-four in width. The walls, four feet deep and formed
of irregular pieces of slate, rise to seven feet in the interior. In
the southern wall there is a gate covered with a slab thirteen feet
long by one and a half feet thick, and two small windows which
remind one of the gates in old Kyklopic or Pelasgic walls
(see § 18). The roof of this house consists of hewn stone slabs,
which, resting on the thickness of the wall, are pushed one over
the other towards the inside—a mode of covering which has also
been used in the buildings of the earliest period of Greek archi-

tecture, as, for instance, in the treasure-houses of the old royal palaces. It ought also to be noticed, that in the middle of the roof there has been left an opening nineteen feet long by

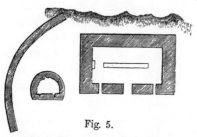

Fig. 5.

one and a half wide, the first beginning of the *hypœthral* formation (see plan, Fig. 5, and interior, Fig. 6). In the interior there protrudes from the western wall a stone, which most likely was destined for the reception of the idol or of other holy objects. In the temples of later periods the holy statues also stood generally nearest to the western wall, looking to the east, where the entrance usually was. That this is not the case here is explained by the situation of the holy edifice, for close to the eastern wall the rock falls steep into the sea. For this

Fig. 6.

reason the gate could be placed only on the southern side, up to which winds the rocky path which forms the only approach. To the west of the temple there are remnants of a wall which either served as an enclosure (peribolos), or may also have belonged to a treasure-house. Notwithstanding the objections of some archæologists, we are entitled to consider this building as a temple, perhaps dedicated to Hera, who was particularly worshipped in the island of Eubœa. This opinion is further confirmed by the myth, that, on this very Mount Ocha, the goddess celebrated her wedding with Zeus; we may indeed assume, almost with certainty, that the described temple was erected in commemoration of that mythical event, on the very spot where it was said to have taken place. Of similar construction are three other stone buildings in Eubœa lying close to each other north-east of the village of Stura, two of which are oblong, while the third and middle one is a square in form, covered with a hypæthral roof like a cupola, formed by protruding slabs.

4. From the simple form of the quadrangular house surrounded by smooth walls, as we have seen it in the just-mentioned primitive temple, there took place a gradual progress towards more beautiful and varied formations. These embellishments consisted chiefly in the addition of columns. Columns are isolated props used to carry the ceiling and the roof, and applied in a particular artistic form and order. Such props are mentioned in the Homeric poems ; they were used chiefly in the interiors of the royal palaces described therein, where, for instance, the courts are surrounded by colonnades, and where the ceilings of the lordly halls are supported by columns. All the later forms of Greek temples arose from the connection of these props with the holy edifice, and from their different uses in the exteriors and interiors.

Before we describe the temples we have to consider the different kinds of columns. Not to speak of the gradual transformation which the column underwent in the course of time, the consideration of which belongs to the history of art, we have to distinguish two chief kinds, the knowledge of which is required in order to form a notion of the different species of the temples themselves.

These two species of columns, which are generally denominated the orders of columns, are the Doric and Ionic. A third, the Corinthian order, belongs to a later period of Greek art. The Doric column has its name from the Greek tribe of the Dorians, by whom it was invented and most frequently used, and with whose serious and dignified character its whole formation corresponds. It is divided into two parts, the shaft and the capital. The shaft consists of a stem of circular form, which up to a third of its height slightly increases in circumference (ἔντασις), and decreases again more or less towards the top. The bottom part rests immediately on the stereobaton or base of the temple. Only in rare cases the column was monolithic ; usually it consisted of several pieces or "drums" (σπόνδυλοι), composed without mortar, which were fastened to each other by dowels of cedar wood, such as have been discovered on the columns of the Parthenon and the temple of Theseus at Athens. Lengthways the shaft was broken by parallel indentures (ῥάβδωσις), now called flutings, the edges of which formed sharp angles, and which, as we can see from several unfinished temples, were chiselled into the columns after they had been put into their places. On the shaft rests the second part of the column, the head or capital, which the Greeks, in analogy to the human head, called κεφάλαιον, the Romans *capitulum.* The capital of the Doric order consists of three parts.

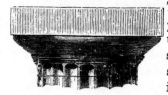

Fig. 8.

The first is called ὑποτρα-χήλιον, neck, and forms the continuation of the shaft, from which it is separated by one or more indentures. In its upper part it widens, and is generally adorned by several horizontal stripes called by the Romans rings, *annuli*. After this follows the chief portion of the capital, a ledge also, of circular formation, and strongly projecting all round. It was called by the Greeks ἐχῖνος, and comprised the supporting power of the column, under the weight of the beams and the roof resting on it. The third part consists of a square piece with square edges, which is called the bearer (ἄβαξ, whence the Latin *abacus*), and is destined for the reception of the chief beam or architrave (ἐπιστύλιον) resting on the column (see page 12).

Fig. 7.

The artistic (æsthetic and static) import of all these parts must not occupy us here, any more than the changes which they underwent in the gradual development of Greek art. We must confine ourselves to the general remark, that the older the building, the heavier and more compressed is the formation of the whole column, as is particularly shown by the few still-existing columns of a temple at Korinth, which perhaps belongs to the sixth century B.C. As an example of the most beautiful form, we add (Fig. 7) the reproduction of a column of the Parthenon belonging to the acme of Greek architecture; its capital is shown on a larger scale in Fig. 8.

The Doric order expresses artistically the spirit and the

serious tendency of the Doric tribe ; the lighter and more versatile mind of the Ionic tribe finds its expression in the more ornamental order of columns called after it. About the time of its origin we will say nothing here. May it suffice to state, that as early as

Fig. 9.

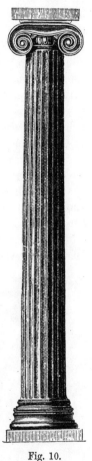

Fig. 10.

the thirtieth Olympiad (656 B.C.) the Ionic order of columns was in use, together with the Doric. At that time Myron, tyrant of Sikyon, is said to have devoted to the gods a treasure-house at Olympia which contained two rooms, one of them showing the Doric, the other the Ionic, order of columns.

The Ionic column differed from the Doric first of all by its greater slenderness. Its height in the average was equal to eight diameters at the bottom of the column, while the Doric column amounted usually only to four or five. The column is divided into three parts, a foot or base being added to the shaft and capital. The base consists of several prominences (*torus*) like bolsters, separated from each other by indentures (τρόχιλος) which rest on a square slab (πλίνθος), and in a manner raise the column from the earth. The shaft shows the same cylindric form as that of the Doric column, but the decrease in size towards the upper part is less considerable, and the fluting also differs from the Doric in so far as the deep parts are more excavated, and between them there are small flat parts called ridges (*scamillus*). The capital shows, instead of a simple and severe formation, a greater variety and elegance of form.   The neck is embellished by sculptural ornaments, the echinus is less prominent, and shows a sculptural ornament called ovolo.   The richest and most striking characteristic of the Ionic capital is the part which, somewhat like the abacus of the Doric capital, droops, as it were, under the weight of the architrave, and leans in an elastic curvature over the echinus; both in front and at the back it shows a double spiral ornamentation usually called the volute; at the sides it forms a bolster called by the Romans *pulvinar*.   Above this lies a small slab, also adorned with sculptures, and destined to receive the beam.   Fig. 10 shows a simple Ionic column which belonged to the no longer existing temple on the Ilissos at Athens; Fig. 9, a rich capital from the Erechtheion at Athens.

The third or Korinthian order of columns (the independent development of which does not seem to date back before the end of the fourth century B.C.) resembles, in the formation of the basis and the shaft, the Ionic order.   The capital, on the other hand, has the form of an open chalice formed of acanthus leaves, over which rises from the same basis a second higher row of leaves. In the interstices of this mass of leaves we see stems, with smaller

Fig. 11.

chalices at their tops, rising upwards, and from the tops of these there are again developed stalks divided into two, the tops of which are bent like volutes under the weight of the abacus, which in a manner rests on them. The beams are generally borrowed from the Ionic order.   Vitruvius (iv. 1, 9) tells a pretty story, according to which the celebrated architect and engraver (το-ρευτής) Kallimachos, of Athens, was the inventor of

this capital; perhaps he was the first to use it artistically.   In any case, the perfection of the Korinthian capital (as we know it from

its simplest beginnings in the temple of Apollo at Phigalia, up to
its noblest development in the capitals of the temple of the Didy-
maic Apollo near Miletos, and in those of the mausoleum of
Halikarnassos, and on the choragic monument of Lysikrates at
Athens, Fig. 11 (see Fig. 152), belongs to the time after Perikles.
Perhaps the first attempts at an ornamentation which was taken
from plants, and might easily be reproduced in clay, were
made at Korinth, the seat of clay potteries, and in that case the
Korinthian capital would have received its name from its first
home.

5. The simplest and most natural way of connecting the
columns with the temple itself, was to leave out the smallest
of the four walls in which the entrance was placed, and to erect
instead of it two columns, which thus formed a stately and
beautiful ingress, and also carried the beams and the roof of the
temple.   The Greeks called a temple of this kind ἐν παράστασιν,
the Romans a *templum in antis*, because in it the columns were
placed between the front pillars of the side walls, which latter
were called by the Greeks παράσταδες, and by the Romans *antæ*.
But this change of design could not be made without consequences
for the arrangement of the temple itself.   By opening in this way
the temple on the one—generally the eastern—side, there was
certainly gained an appropriate ornamentation of the chief
façade ; but, on the other hand, the regard for the holiness of the
image required a further seclusion of the room in which it was
placed : for the house of the god was sacred, separated from the
profane world, and accessible only after a previous purification.
In consequence, the space of the temple-cella was divided by a
wall into two parts, of which the one, the νάος proper, contained
the image of the god, the other
being used as an outer court or
outer temple, and therefore called
by the Greeks πρόναος or πρόδομος.

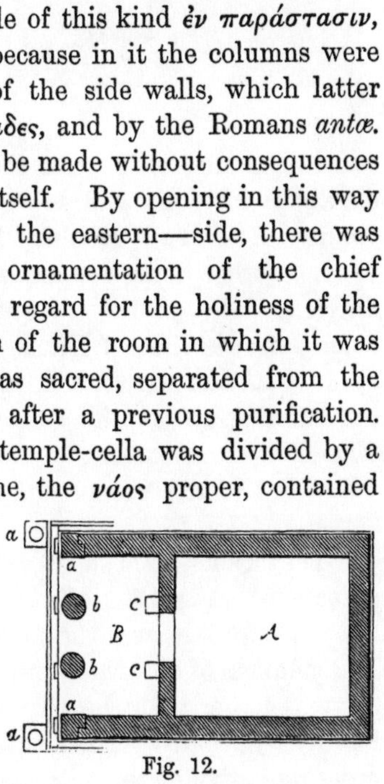

An example of this most primitive and simple design is preserved in a small temple at Rham-

Fig. 12.

nos, in Attika, which is generally designated as the temple of
Themis.   Its plan (see Fig. 12) shows an oblong form similar to

that of the temple on Mount Ocha, but that on the east side the wall has been omitted, and between the two ends of the side walls or *antæ* (*a a*) two columns (*b b*) have been erected. Passing through these columns we enter the pronaos (*B*), against the back wall of which, built of polygonal stones, stand two marble chairs (*c c*), dedicated, the one to Nemesis, the other to Themis,

Fig. 13.

as the inscriptions on them indicate (see Fig. 13). Perhaps they contained originally the statues of these goddesses; the statue of one goddess at least, in an antiquated style, has been discovered in the pronaos. The temple is small, and stands in a very irregular position by the side of a larger one, which is usually considered as that of Nemesis. For this was the goddess particularly venerated by the inhabitants of Rhamnos, and her affinity to Themis, the goddess of justice, the violations of which Nemesis had to revenge, would account for the close vicinity of the two temples; their irregular position with regard to each other finds its explanation in the circumstance of the different dates of their erection. For the temple of Nemesis belongs to the time of Kimon, while that of Themis was erected at an ante-Persian period, most likely contemporaneously with the building of the ante-Persian Parthenon and the ante-Persian Propylæa, as is shown by the polygonal structure of the walls of the cella and the use of the porous stone for the columns and antæ.

The façade which shows us the further peculiarities of the Doric order we see, Fig. 13. We observe, first of all, that the temple rests on some steps, as was the universal custom amongst the Greeks. The columns of the Doric order, as described in the last paragraph, carry, together with the two antæ, the upper part of the whole building, generally called the beams. The beams of the Doric order are divided into three parts—architrave, frieze, and cornice. The architrave consists of four-edged, smoothly hewn stone beams, which are placed from column to column (hence the Greek

name ἐπιστύλιον, *i.e.* on the columns), and are equally continued
beyond the wall of the temple. Over this follows a second layer of
a similar kind, but that here certain prominent parts, adorned with
vertical stripes and called triglyphs (τρίγλυφος), occur alternately
with square pieces called by the Greeks μέτωπον, and usually
adorned with images, *i.e.* reliefs. After these representations
(ζῶα) the Greeks called this part of the beams ζωφόρος. The
completion of the beams was formed by the cornice called by the
Greeks γεῖσον, and consisting of a prominent rafter cut obliquely
downwards. Over these beams rises on the two smaller sides of
the temple a pediment, *i.e.* a triangular structure, as necessitated by
the sloping position of the roof; it was formed by a stone wall
and surrounded by a cornice similar to the geison of the beams.
The Greeks called this gable ἀετός or ἀέτωμα, perhaps owing to
its similarity to an eagle with extended wings. The gable front
surrounded by the cornice was called by the
Greeks τύμπανον; it was generally adorned with
sculptures, such as we shall see on several of
the larger Greek temples. The ridge of the
roof as well as the corners of the gable were
provided in most of the temples with ornaments
(ἀκρωτήριον), which generally, similar to those
on the sarcophagi and στῆλαι, were formed like
anthemia (Fig. 14). Instead of these we also

Fig. 14.

find not unfrequently on the corners of the ætos pedestals,
destined to carry statues or holy implements like tripods and
vases.

6. There is still another kind of the *templum in antis*
described in our last chapter, which seems not to have been called
by the Greeks by a separate name, neither is it mentioned separately by Vitruvius, to whom we owe the classification of the
different forms of the temple. Nevertheless it deserves our particular attention, as showing the strictly logical process followed
by the Greeks in this matter.

For, after the one smaller side of the temple had received
columns instead of a wall, it was natural to do the same on the
opposite side. This was indeed only in accordance with the
feeling of symmetry shown by the Greeks, to which we shall
have to refer in considering another form of the temple.

A beautiful example of this form of the *templum in antis* we find in a temple discovered at Eleusis, of which Fig. 15 shows the plan.   It was dedicated to Artemis Propylæa, and the position of the ruins close by the propylæa of the sacred precinct of the

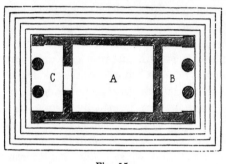

Fig. 15.

temple at Eleusis shows beyond doubt that it is really the temple seen and called by that name, by Pausanias; it is indeed one of the rare cases where the name of a Greek temple can be proved with certainty.   The temple, of which little more than the foundations remain, but which can be easily reconstructed with the help of these foundations and of some fragments of Pentelic marble,[1] is divided into three parts, of which the cella (A) and the pronaos (C) are formed exactly as we have seen in the temple of Themis.

Beyond the back wall of the cella the side walls of the temple have been continued, and between their antæ two columns have been erected; in this way a space (B) has been formed, which, although perhaps not equal in dimension, corresponds exactly with the pronaos or prodomos, and is therefore called by the Greeks ὀπισθόδομος.   In the same way as the pronaos was the front hall, the opisthodomos was the back hall, of the temple, and therefore by the Romans appropriately called a posticum.

This arrangement assists us in understanding the use of the spaces thus gained in front and back of the cella; for they must be considered not only as casual extensions of the temple, but they have a distinct significance for the religious service and its usages, as it was always the habit of the Greeks to combine artistic and religious considerations.   The openness of both spaces indicates sufficiently that they were not properly holy or conse-

---

[1] This was the case at least at the time of the first investigation.   At present the ruins found at that time have (with the exception of a few almost unrecognisable remnants) disappeared, that is, they have been used for the houses of the insignificant modern Eleusis.

crated places. They were, on the contrary, as Bötticher justly remarks of the pronaos, " show-rooms." The pronaos, which formed the entrance and as it were preparation hall of the holy room, was furnished accordingly. Sculptures and other ornaments alluded to the god and his myths; in the temple of Themis we recognised the two chairs as being most likely the seats of divine images. There were also implements placed here to prepare for the entrance into the sacred room proper. The basin with consecrated water had its place here, with which everybody sprinkled himself or was sprinkled by the priest, before entering into the immediate presence of the god, whose image always stood fronting the entrance-door. These rooms were frequently secured and closed by railings, traces of which are preserved in several temples, and in this way, although open to the eye, they could be used for the reception of the treasures with which pious custom richly endowed the temples, as is distinctly told us of the festive temples at Athens, Delphi, Olympia, and elsewhere.

A similar ornamentation, by means of statues referring to the god of the temple, or anathemata devoted to him, must have been in the opisthodomos. It must, however, be added that in some temples the opisthodomos occurs as a separate chamber behind the cella. In that case it was used for the keeping of that property of the god which was not shown in public, such as old sacred implements or perhaps old images; in some cases also money and public or private documents were kept in it because of the greater security of the place. This, for instance, was done at the Parthenon, where even a list of objects kept in the opisthodomos has been discovered. In this case the back hall of the temple (posticum) remained the show-room, adorned with sculptures, anathemes, and pictures in a similar manner as the pronaos on the opposite side of the temple.

7. In his sketch of the different forms of the temple Vitruvius mentions after the antæ-temple the prostylos. This name already indicates a temple in which the columns ($\sigma\tau\hat{v}\lambda o\iota$) protrude on one side, and which naturally forms in this way a further step in the development of the temple. In the antæ-temple the columns as it were replaced the one smaller wall of the temple-house, which had been omitted in order to give the outer part of the temple a certain public character. But after this significance of the column

---

as a separate and "room-opening" (Bötticher) prop had once been recognised, it became impossible to abide by this form, and it is quite in accordance with the steady and gradual progress always observable in Greek

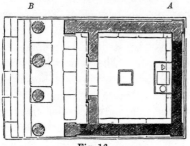

Fig. 16.

art that the columns were also advanced quite independently on the open side of the temple which required ornamentation. The general design was not modified hereby, and could remain exactly the same as in the antæ-temple.

An example of this design is offered by the small Ionic temple near the large temple at Selinus (see Fig. 16). Selinus, on the south-western coast of Sicily, was a colony of the Doric town of Megara, by whose inhabitants a great many towns were founded. Their attention was particularly directed towards Sicily, where, after founding several other colonies, they built, about the thirty-seventh Olympiad, the town of Selinus, perhaps on the site of an old Phœnician colony. The fertility of the soil and the favourable situation of the town made it soon a considerable emporium, and with its growing wealth was combined an artistic culture to which we owe several still existing ruins in the Doric style. Besides these ruins of the Doric order (see Figs. 21, 23, 33), there has been discovered a small sanctuary which shows a peculiar combination of the Doric and Ionic styles, and has lately been reproduced and described at great length as the temple of Empedokles, with the restoration of its original colours. On a base of steps about 2½ feet in height rises the little temple about 15 feet high, and resembling in its design exactly the temple of Themis. We have the cella (A) and the pronaos (B), with the only difference that the columns adorning the latter stand, not between the antæ, but protrude beyond them. The columns grow considerably slighter upwards, in analogy to the Doric order, but they have a base and an Ionic capital; their flutings resemble more the Doric than the Ionic order. The beams also are in the Doric order; on the architrave three layers are indicated by colours; the frieze has triglyphs and metopa, which were also painted; the pediment shows the form we have met with in the temple of Themis.

The connection of the portico with the cella is brought about by a continuation of the architrave from the pillar of the antæ to the column, by means of which the beams and the roof in front form a strong projection carried by the columns. This is an evident gain for the design of the temple; for in this way both the portico and the pronaos are increased in size, and the column now fulfils much better its task as an independent and "room-opening" prop.

8. Although the prostylos marks a progress in the development of the column-edifice, it cannot be denied that it shows a certain want of symmetry and proportion in its design. The back part does not correspond with the façade, indeed the strong projection carried by the columns seems to require a similar arrangement on the opposite side of the temple. There is something imperfect in the look of such a temple, particularly if one imagines its position open on all sides. This want could not but become apparent to the Greeks, who in almost all their artistic doings have shown a particular predilection for symmetrical proportions. Greek orators weighed carefully the measure of their periods, and symmetry was the principle of strophe and antistrophe in their lyrical poetry. The same care has been noticed in the plastic or pictorial ornamentation of rooms and of certain objects, in which the Greek artists always tried to carry out a perfect symmetry and parallelism of the grouping. This feeling it could not satisfy to see the front part of the temple developed in such a striking manner, and it was only natural that the Greeks should have added before long a portico to the opposite side of the temple. From this, as we have seen, quite natural and essentially Greek proceeding, arose a new form, called by the Greeks very appropriately ναὸς ἀμφιπρόστυλος, *i.e.* a temple with projecting porticoes on both sides. The amphiprostylos is, indeed, the necessary supplement or rather completion of the prostylos, a completion which was the more natural as through the double antæ-temple (see § 6) (which might appropriately be designated as *amphiparastatic*) one was accustomed to an opistho-domos or posticum, corresponding with the pronaos. The posticum, which was wanting in the prostylos, is gained in the amphi-

prostylos by means of the back hall, and became available in the
same manner as we have seen in the developed form of the antæ-
temple (see § 6). Altogether the amphiprostylos stands in the
same relation to the prostylos as the double to the single antæ-
temple, and we notice here again the steady and equal progress
which has given to all Greek creations their harmony and organic
necessity, or, which is essentially the same, their beauty. As an
example of this not very frequent form of the temple, of which
Vitruvius does not name an instance, we mention the temple of
Nike Apteros, the wingless goddess of victory, in the Akropolis at
Athens [1] (see Fig. 17). This elegant Ionic structure crowns, like
a votive offering, the front part of the wall which Kimon had
erected as at once a protection and ornament of the Akropolis.

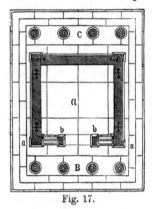

Fig. 17.

It was taken off by the Turks and used
for the building of a bastion, but was
restored to its original form from the
remnants found in the destroyed bastion,
during the first decennium of the revived
kingdom of Greece (see the sketch of
the side view, Fig. 18). From the right-
hand side of the great staircase, which
leads up to the propylæa, a small flight
of steps ascends to the temple of
Nike Apteros. It stands pretty close
to the right wing of the propylæa,
and is for this reason shorter than in

other cases, for instance in the temple on the Ilissos, which otherwise corresponds with it exactly. It is said that its dedication to
the wingless goddess of victory signified the retaining of victory
for Athens; according to earlier statements it was erected by
Kimon after the completion of the above-mentioned wall in order
to commemorate his double victory over the Persians on the
Eurymedon (Ol. 77, 3 = 470 B.C.); Bursian, on the other hand,
places its completion, or at least that of its upper parts, in the
time of Perikles. The dimensions of the temple are but small

---

[1] Of temples of this class without colonnades we also mention one, the ruins of
which have been discovered by Stuart on the Ilissos, not far from Athens. The
amphiprostylos is more frequently applied where the cella is surrounded by a
colonnade. (See § 9, *d*.)

(18¼ feet in width, 27 feet in length), but its style is beautiful and elegant.   It consists of a simple cella A (Fig. 17), with an outer hall B on the eastern side towards the propylæa, and a postico C, on the western side towards the staircase.   The opening of the cella towards the east is not, as in most cases, effected by a door in the

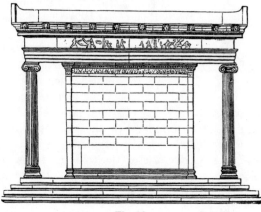

Fig. 18.

wall, but by two slender pillars (*b b*) between the antæ (*a a*), which afford an open view of the interior and of the statue placed therein.   Against the outer hall the cella was as usual closed by means of railings, the fastenings of which are still observable on the pillars and antæ.

The columns have bases and beautiful capitals in the form of volutes; their slightly heavy proportions remind one of the Doric order; the beams, on the other hand, are strictly Ionic.   Accordingly, the architrave (which in the Doric order (see § 5) consists of a simple smooth stone) is divided into three horizontal stripes (*fasciæ*), over the uppermost of which there is a thin ledge.   The frieze no more exhibits the division into metopa and triglyphs, but consists of an uninterrupted plane, equal in height to the architrave, and adorned with bas-reliefs which represent battles between Greeks and Persians.   Afteɪ this follows the cornice (γεῖσον), which, unlike the simplicity and heaviness of the Doric cornice, consists of several pieces composed in an easy and graceful manner.

The pediments both at the back and in front are similar to those of the Doric temple, but that they rise a little higher, and the cornices round them correspond with the geison of the beams.   Fig. 19

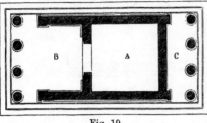

shows the plan of the above-mentioned temple, which Stuart has discovered on the southern bank of the Ilissos, not far from the well Enneakrunos ; this temple was used in Stuart's time as a Christian church, but has now entirely disappeared.

Fig. 19.

It was an amphiprostylos of the Ionic order, the division of which into cella A, pronaos B, and posticum C, agrees exactly with the above-stated principles. It was $40\frac{1}{2}$ feet in length, by $19\frac{1}{2}$ in width.

9. The most extensive use of the columns takes place when they are placed not only before and behind the temple, as in the amphiprostylos, but when they are ranged round the four sides of the building.

This is the last and most perfect form to which the combination of the columns with the temple-house could lead, and it must be considered as the necessary development of the different preparatory stages mentioned in the above.[1]   Here we have, at last, a temple-house surrounded by columns on all sides, beautifully variegated, and yet not wanting in organic unity.   In consequence, this form was used by the Greeks more frequently than any other, and most of the remaining temples, particularly those of the Doric style, belong to it.

Concerning the mode of its erection, we must imagine that the columns were placed at equal distances round the cella, so that one might walk round it, barring such cases where statues or partition walls prevented it.   For the distance of the columns from the wall of the cella there is no certain rule ; on the longer sides it was generally equal to the distance of the columns from

[1] An historic proof of this gradual growth cannot be given, seeing that already the oldest monuments known to us show the complete surrounding by columns.   With the sole exception of that on Mount Ocha, the above-mentioned temples must not be considered as actually older than those to be described in the following pages. They are only specimens of a pre-historic period of architecture, the single forms and stages of which were continued even after the completion of the peripteral temple.

each other, in front and at the back (*i.e.* on the two smaller sides)
it was considerably larger than this. The beams rested on the
columns (see Figs. 13 and 18), as in the prostylos and amphiprostylos; they surrounded the cella in an uninterrupted line,
the walls of the former being built up to an equal height, and
afterwards connected with the beams by means of cross-beams
made of stone. Stone slabs adorned with so-called caskets, that
is, square indentures (*lacunaria*), were placed on these cross-beams,
and formed the so-called lacunaria-ceiling. In this way a protecting roof was gained for the colonnade, and at the same time
the organic unity of the temple was obtained by means of the
connection of the columns with the cella. Fig. 20, showing the
section of a temple of this kind, will serve to illustrate this
arrangement. A signifies the interior of the cella, B the colon-

Fig. 20.

nades on both sides, *a b* the columns, *b c* the beams, connected with
the wall of the cella by means of the lacunaria-ceiling. (About
the interior, see Fig. 30.) The ceiling of the colonnade protruding
in this way from the cella to right and left was called by the
Greeks (in analogy with the name of the gable ἀετός, as mentioned above) πτερόν, wing, and from this expression the name
ναὸς περίπτερος was derived, viz., a temple surrounded on all sides
by a protruding wing of this kind. In the same way as this

name refers to the ceiling of the colonnade, another is taken from
the columns themselves, and according to the latter a temple of
this kind is called a ναός or οἶκος περίστυλος, that is, a temple
surrounded by columns, the colonnade itself being called τὸ πε-
ρίστυλον. The name peripteros was always, and has remained,
the most common one.

After having described the structure of the peripteros, so as
to give a distinct notion of the pteron, and of the construction of
this kind of temple in general, we must now turn to the consideration of the plan in order to learn the division and arrangement of the different rooms. This division is more complicated
in the peripteros than in any other class of temples; we find
indeed the different kinds of divisions as numerous as the classes
of temples we have hitherto met with. It will be remembered

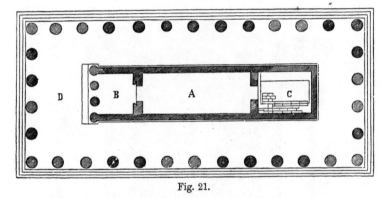

Fig. 21.

that in these latter there was only one arrangement of the
interior peculiar to each; but as it is the chief purpose of the
peripteros to surround the temple-house with a colonnade, this
house itself may have any of the described forms; it may be, in
other words, an antæ-temple, a prostylos, or an amphiprostylos.
These possible variations in the plan of the peripteros have
hitherto, perhaps, not been sufficiently noticed. Vitruvius does
not mention them, and the rules laid down by him comprise only
the smallest portion of the preserved monuments.

a. The temple-house surrounded by the colonnade may first
be an antæ-temple, as described by us in § 4. An example of
this design is offered by one of the older temples at Selinus (see

Fig. 21). It is situated, with two other similar ones, on a hill, in the western part of the town; the colonnade D is formed by six columns on the small, and thirteen on the long, sides; the cella is an antæ-temple with two columns between the walls, which latter do not end in common antæ, but take the form of columns. Through these columns one ascends the pronaos (B) on two steps; after it follows, raised again by one step, the cella proper (A), from which a staircase of five steps leads into the opistho-domos (C); this is walled in on all sides, and forms a completely closed room, inaccessible except from the cella.

b. The antæ-temple might also have columns between the antæ of the two small sides, as, for instance, in the temple of Artemis Propylæa at Eleusis (Fig. 15). This kind of temple-house may also become the centre of a peripteros by being surrounded by columns. This is the case in the Theseion, one of the finest and best-preserved temples of Athens (Fig. 22).

This temple lies on a small hill north-west of the Akropolis, and is, in all probability, identical with that devoted by the Athenians to the memory of their national hero Theseus, to whose appearance in the battle of Marathon they owed the victory. In memory of this event they afterwards resolved to

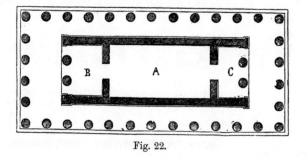

Fig. 22.

transfer the remains of Theseus from the island of Skyros (con-quered by Kimon) to Athens, and to bury them in a manner worthy of the hero. This was done by Kimon, the son of Miltiades, Olympiad 76, 1 (476 B.C.), and on the same occasion our temple was erected, and called, after the hero, Theseion.[1] The building is of Pentelic marble; thirty-four columns, in the most

---

[1] More recently it has also been declared to be a temple of Ares.

beautiful Doric style, in its freer and more elegant Attic modification, surround the temple-house, so that six columns stand on each of the small, and thirteen on each of the large, sides. The temple-house itself has the form of a double antæ-temple; in the middle lies the cella proper A,[1] joined on the eastern side by the pronaos B, on the western by the opisthodomos C, the latter forming, like the pronaos, an open hall. Beams and ceiling of the peristylos show traces of rich polychromatic painting. The temple, formerly richly decorated with statues on the gable and the metopa, has for a long time been used as a church of St. George, to which circumstance its good preservation is most likely due. At present the antique remnants found at Athens are kept in it.

    c. In another form of the peripteros, the temple-house consists of a prostylos surrounded by columns. It is, however, rarely met with, the just-mentioned arrangement (*b*) being the most usual. As an example of this third style, we mention one of the older temples on the western hill of the town of Selinunt, in Sicily (see Fig. 23). Inside of the colonnade lies the oblong temple-house, which shows a portico of four columns. It contains, besides the cella proper (A), a peculiarly shaped pronaos (B), and an opisthodomos (C), the latter being walled in on all sides.

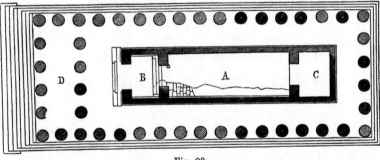

Fig. 23.

    d. The highest development of the peripteros is reached when the cella is formed by an amphiprostylos (the complement of the

---

[1] The width of the interior of the cella is 20 ft. 4 in. (English measure).

prostylos, see § 8), being at the same time surrounded by a colonnade.

As an example, we quote the temple of Athene Parthenos in the Akropolis at Athens, which altogether must be considered as one of the most perfect, if not *the* most perfect, monument of Greek architecture.[1] Being dedicated to the highest protecting goddess of Athens and of the Attic country, it occupied the most important site of the Akropolis, and evinced, both by the grandeur of its dimensions and its artistic splendour, the culture of the nation itself, which, under Perikles, had reached the acme of its power. On the same spot where had stood the older Athene-temple, destroyed by the Persians, Perikles erected this new one. The two architects, Iktinos and Kallikrates, completed the gigantic work in about ten years, in 438 B.C. The sculptural decoration of the gables and metopa was supervised and no doubt partly executed by Phidias, an intimate friend of Perikles, and equally supreme in art as the other in politics. On a strong base of Piræic stonework, surrounded by three high steps of Pentelic marble (the upper one being $101\frac{1}{4}$ ft. wide by 228 ft. long), rose the peripteros, formed by forty-six Doric columns, of which eight stood on each of the smaller, and seventeen on each of the longer sides (see plan, Fig. 24, and view, Fig. 25). The architrave was adorned with golden shields and inscriptions, while the metopa of the frieze showed the more lasting ornamentations of reliefs, representing the myths of Athene and the heroes renowned in her service. On the gables were enthroned the sublime forms, by means of which Phidias and his disciples had celebrated two important events from the cycle of myths relating to Athene. The one showed the first appearance of the goddess amongst the Olympians after her birth from the head of Zeus; the other represented the contest in which the victorious goddess had gained the supremacy of the Attic land from Poseidon. Everywhere the splendour of the Pentelic marble (of which the columns, the beams, the walls of the cella, and even the tiles of the roof, were made) was discreetly modified by the application of colours.

During the Middle Ages it was transformed into a Christian church, of which Spon and Wheler have seen as late as 1676, and afterwards described, the altar-niche on the east side and the

---

[1] See the plan of the Akropolis, Fig. 52, B.

whole interior arrangement;[1] and, owing to this circumstance, the Parthenon, like the temple of Theseus, had been well preserved, until the siege of Athens by the Venetians under Morosini, in 1687, caused the deplorable destruction of this unique building. The besieged had placed a powder magazine in the cella, and when this was hit by a shell of the besieging artillery, a dreadful explosion took place, which destroyed almost the whole building, with the exception of the two pediments.

It must be considered as a fortunate circumstance in this disaster that the ruins, although poor and scanty, if compared with the former splendour of the building, still are sufficient to allow of a tolerably accurate reconstruction of its general features. Moreover, the very ruins show a dignity and beauty of form which baffle description: a proof of the excellence of Greek architecture, which even without the passing splendour of outer ornaments, and deprived of the imposing effect of the whole building, still preserves its overpowering impression.

The design of the temple, with regard to its principal rooms, does not now seem doubtful; the previous investigations of architects and archæologists concerning the cella and the opisthodomos seem completed by the excavations in the Acropolis of C. Bötticher, during the early summer of 1862.

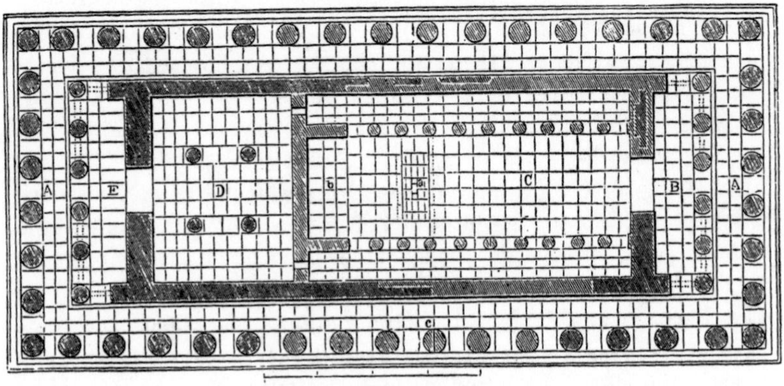

Fig. 24.

Fig. 24 shows the plan of the Parthenon after the design of Using, which is founded on a thorough investigation of the

[1] The bottom part of this niche exists still at the present time.

different opinions ; we are not prepared to vouch for *all* its details,
neither can we enter upon our own notions with regard to single
parts, gained by personal study of the remnants. Passing
through the columns of the colonnade (A), one encounters a
second row of six columns, forming the portico of the pronaos (B).
The pronaos is raised by two steps over the level of the peristylos,
and was used for the keeping of the precious offerings, which
were brought from far and near to celebrate the holiness of the
temple and of its protecting goddess. They were kept safely
behind iron railings, and carefully locked up by the Tamiai,[1] but
might be seen from the outside. In an inscription, a list of the
objects kept here has been preserved to us. The entrance to the
pronaos, which formerly had been blocked up by the 6 ft.
thick wall of the apsis of the church built into the Parthenon,
was re-opened by Bötticher.

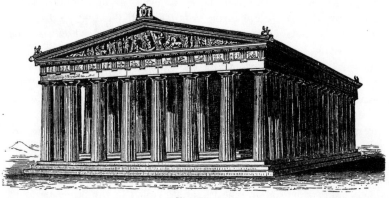

Fig. 25.

These parts of the building were also decorated with
sculptures. Beginning from the portico, the frieze round the
whole cella was covered with the marvellous representation of the
festive procession of the Panathenæa, or, according to Bötticher's
opinion, the preparations for this procession. These reliefs,
3 ft. 4 in. in height, extended originally over 528 ft.; 456 ft.
have since been recovered from the ruins, and transferred to
England, with a great many other sculptures from the Akropolis,

[1] The holes for fastening these railings were discovered by Bötticher, from bottom
to capital, in all the columns of the pronaos and posticum.

by Lord Elgin.   At present they are in the British Museum, but
other parts of the frieze found later have been kept at Athens.
Over the entrance to the pronaos, and therefore to the cella
proper, there is an ingenious representation of an assembly of the
gods looking at the approaching processions of youths and
maidens.   They are seated in arm-chairs, simply and beautifully
grouped, and amongst them the forms of the god Poseidon, of the
hero Erechtheus, and of the goddess Aphrodite with Peitho and
Eros, are recognisable.   A large door in the back wall of the
pronaos forms the entrance to the cella proper (C), which is a
hundred feet long, and therefore called hekatompedon.   Two
rows of columns, each nine in number, divided this room into
three naves, and above these there was a second row of Doric
columns forming an upper story, up to which led staircases from
the said naves.   At the end of the middle stoa, which we must
imagine as hypæthral, stood, closed in by a bar and protected by
a canopy, the chryselephantine Agalma of Pallas (*b*); in front of
it was the daïs of the prœdria (*a*), the site of which is still
recognisable by a piece of Piræic stone pavement in the middle of
the marble floor.   Concerning the masterly statue of Athene by
Phidias, we can only say a few words illustrating its artistic
arrangement.   The base on which the figure stood was ornamented by a representation of the birth of Pandora, and by the
forms of twenty gods.   On this pedestal stood the statue of the
goddess herself, in a simple but majestic posture, 26 yards[1] in
height; face, neck, arms, hands, and feet were made of ivory; the
drapery (which Phidias had fortunately made removable) was of
pure gold, which noble metal also prevailed in the other parts of
the figure.   Combined with the splendour of the material and the
imposing impression of the whole figure, the careful ornamental
treatment of the details added to the total effect.   There were,
for instance, the helmet with a sphinx and other ornaments, and
the shield standing at the feet of the goddess, with a battle of the
Amazons on the outer side; nay, even the edges of the high
sandals showed a Kentauromachia with numerous figures, amongst
which, it is said, there were portraits of Perikles and Phidias, the
last mentioned being afterwards made the grounds of accusa-

---

[1] German *Ellen*. The measurements are throughout on the German scale,
unless stated otherwise.

tions of impiety against the great statesman and his artistic friend.

Behind the cella with the statue in it was the opisthodomos, a closed room connected with the cella by means of two little doors at the northern and southern ends of the intervening wall. Remnants of these doors, destined only for the business purposes of the treasure officials, were also found amongst the ruins in 1862. The ceiling of the opisthodomos was carried by four columns ; many articles of value, documents, and anathemata not meant for public exhibition, were here kept by certain officials, who had to render strict account of them. From the opisthodomos another door, secured by a double railing, led into the back hall, similar in form to the pronaos, and used, like it, for placing works of art and pious offerings (E).

10. After the description of the ναὸς περίπτερος, which we have now considered in all its varieties, we pass over to the pseudo-peripteros treated by Vitruvius, together with the peripteros. As the name indicated (ψεῦδος, deception, appearance), this temple is not in reality surrounded by a pteron, but only appears to be. A pteron, as we have seen, consists of the wing-like protrusion of beams and ceiling, supported by separate columns. If the idea of the pteron is done away with, the beams and ceiling may remain, but they no more form an independent protrusion round the cella ; that is, they are no more supported by independent columns, but by a firm wall, which on its part may supply the columns by semi-columns or pilasters. This form is very rare in Greek architecture, which was founded on truth, but the Romans have applied it more frequently (see § 63). It is true that one Greek specimen of the pseudo-peripteros is known to us, but in it the purpose of producing the illusion of columns has evidently been absent, the arrangement having become necessary by the large dimensions of the building and the nature of its material. This temple was at Akragas. Akragas, " the splendour-loving noble city, of all the most beautiful," as Pindar calls it, was founded at the beginning of the sixth century by Gela, a Doric colony on the south coast of Sicily, and, by its favourable position and fertile soil, had acquired considerable wealth. The numerous remnants of its former artistic splendour are, together with those of Selinus, amongst the finest specimens

of the older Doric style. Not far from the well-preserved so-called temples of Juno and Concordia the foundations have been discovered of an enormous temple dedicated to Zeus, and finished, all but the roof, after the victory of the Carthaginians over the Agrigentines (Ol. 93, 3 = 406 B.C.) Diodor, who gives a detailed description of the temple with measurements, admired, after so many centuries, the grandeur of its remnants. According to later measurements the length of the temple, steps included, is 359 ft., its width $175\frac{1}{2}$ ft.; its height must have been 120 to the top of the gable, as may be calculated from the remaining fragments of the beams and columns; its site was therefore almost three times as large as that of the Parthenon. The columns, being almost 62 ft. in height, stood so widely apart that, to cover the intervening spaces by means of free architraves, slabs of stone almost 26 ft. long, and over 10 ft. thick, would have been required. But the use of such the nature of the material would not permit, the buildings of Agrigent being not of marble but of a soft crumbling kind of chalk (*Muschelkalk*), which grows firmer in the course of time, but is wholly unavailable for the covering of open spaces of considerable extension. In consequence, the Agrigentines were obliged to erect solid walls between the columns as high as the beams, and to place on them an architrave and frieze of single smaller blocks of stone. Instead of a free colonnade, the temple-house was therefore surrounded by a solid wall, with columns protruding by one-half of their circumference on the outer side, the corresponding places on the inner side being marked by pilasters. Whether the lighting of the building was hypæthral, or (as some archæologists have rather rashly conjectured) was effected by means of windows in the upper part of the wall between the half-columns, must be left undecided. The cella is long and narrow, as is frequent in Sicilian monuments (see Figs. 21 and 23), and its walls were also adorned by pilasters. The place of the door is difficult to define, because of the quite unusual uneven number of seven columns at the façade. Kockerell thinks there must have been two doors, one on each side of the façade; a native archæologist, Politi, on the other hand, accepts one large door in the middle, but this divided into two entrances by the colossal statue of a giant instead of a pillar.[1]

---

[1] This statue is still in existence; it consists of several enormous blocks of stone,

11. In our description of the Parthenon (see page 28) we
noticed that the middle part of the cella was entirely open to the
sky. This leads to a new form of the temple often used in larger
designs, and called by Vitruvius the hypæthros. His description
(leaving alone the prescriptions for the numbers of columns and
other arrangements, which in this, as in most cases, by no means
tally with the Greek monuments) is couched in the following
terms :—" In the inside (of the cella) there are colonnades, with
double rows of columns, separate from the walls, so that one may
walk round them just as in the outer colonnades. Only the
middle nave is open to the sky, and there are doors at both ends
leading to the back house and front house. Specimens of this
kind there are none in Rome, but at Athens there are the eight-
columned temple of Minerva, and the ten-columned one of the
Olympian Jupiter." The former of these is none other than the
Parthenon ; the latter we shall refer to in our description of
Roman temples.

We cannot enter upon the literary feud about the existence
or non-existence of the hypæthral temple, considering (with
Bötticher) the question settled in the affirmative. For not even
to mention the opinion that the services of certain gods required
uncovered rooms, it seems natural that large buildings without
windows, or even large doors, for lighting purposes, had an open
space in the middle, which, moreover, was quite in accordance
with the open court of the dwelling-house. Analogies between
these two were frequent. In this way architectural necessity
tallies perfectly with the statement of Vitruvius, which, moreover,
is confirmed by a thorough investigation of genuine Greek
monuments. There are distinguishable even several species of
the hypæthros, which show that it had become necessary by the
conditions of peculiar rites at an early period, and that its form
and size might be modified in various ways. The simplest form
of the hypæthros, we have seen in the small temple on Mount
Ocha (Fig. 6), where the small opening in the roof was most

which have been found amongst the ruins, and arranged on the ground, forming a
complete figure. It is generally supposed that a whole row of such statues used to
carry the ceiling of the cella. But in that case, most likely other fragments would
have been found, which, at least during my own prolonged stay at Girgenti, has not
been the case.

likely required by the nature of Zeus and Hera, as divinities
of the ether and sky. Amongst the peripteros-temples the
examples of hypæthral cellæ are not unfrequent.[1]   We mention
first the temple of Apollo Epikurios, near the town of Phigalia in
Arkadia.   On the side of one of the mountain ranges which
surround Phigalia in a wide circle, lies the village of Bassæ.
Here, near the summit of Mount Kotilios, we find the ruins of a
temple, which, barring a slight difference in the distances and the
nature of the material, seems to agree perfectly with the description in Pausanias of a sanctuary of Apollo Epikurios.   According
to him the temple was built by Iktinos, the architect of the
Parthenon, and was surpassed in beauty amongst the temples of
the Peloponnesos only by that of Athene Alea, near Tegea;
a remark which is the more important as Pausanias only in rare
cases mentions the artistic value of a building.   The remnants of
the temple, which have been examined carefully for the first time
in 1818, fully confirm this opinion, although a great part of the
building had been purposely destroyed, most likely in order to
obtain the bronze rivets joining the stones to each other.   The
original plan is, however, easily recognisable.   The design
(Fig. 26) shows a colonnade of thirty-eight columns (AA); six on
each of the narrow, and fifteen on each of the long, sides (inclusive
of the corner columns of the façades); all of these are preserved
standing erect.   The pronaos (B) is formed by the walls of the
cella and two columns *in antis*.   The cella is divided into a
covered space (D) and an uncovered one (C), the latter enclosed
by strongly projecting pilasters.   The fronts of the pilasters
resemble Ionic half-columns, and show above the capitals a frieze
representing battles of the Amazons in excellent bas-reliefs.   The
middle part of the space was open, and formed as it were a court
surrounded by niches, adapted for the keeping of votive offerings
by the frieze which protected their contents.   The back part of
the cella (D) was covered by a ceiling carried by two of the above-
mentioned pilasters, which protruded obliquely from the wall of
the cella, and besides by a single column, the latter serving at the

---

[1] For the same reason we mention the hypæthros here, differing in this from
the arrangement of Vitruvius, who goes by the position of the outer columns.   But
the nature of a great number of peristylos-temples cannot be clearly understood
without a previous knowledge of the hypæthros.

same time as a specimen of the Korinthian order in its most simple
form.   Behind this was placed, according to Blouet's opinion, the
statue of a god (*b*).   There seems to
have been a door in the back wall
of the cella ; possibly there may
have been a door in the place marked
c leading to the colonnade at the side.
Behind the cella follows the opisthodomos (E), enclosed by the wall
of the former and two columns *in
antis*.   As a peculiarity of this temple,
caused most likely by its locality,
it is mentioned that the chief façade
looked almost due north, instead of
east, as was usually the case.

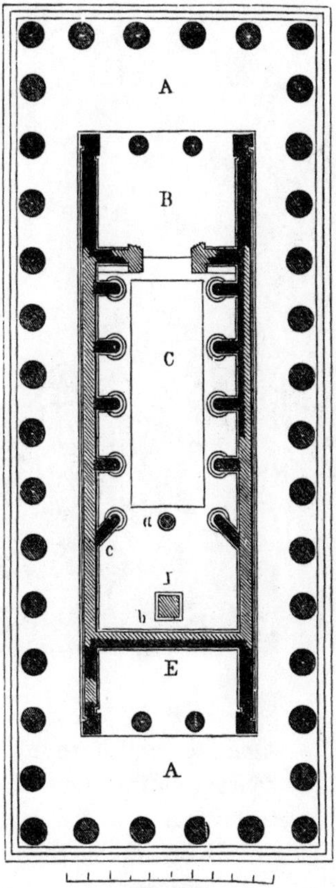

One of the remaining temples
at Pæstum corresponds still more
exactly with Vitruvius's description.
Amongst the remnants there, which
represent the severity and noble
simplicity of the early Doric style,
one temple is prominent, which,
because of its size, is considered as
the chief temple of the town ; and,
for the same reason, is generally
supposed to have been dedicated to
the protecting deity, Poseidon.   It
consists of a peripteros of six
columns on each of the narrow,
and fourteen on each of the long,

Fig. 26.

sides ; the cella, surrounded by colonnades, has both in front and
at the back two columns *in antis*.   Through the pronaos one enters
the cella, both sides of which show double rows of columns, as
described by Vitruvius.   On the back wall of the cella there are
staircases, which can be distinctly recognised, nay, even used, at
the present day.   They lead to the hyperoon or upper gallery,
and between them is the entrance-door to the opisthodomos.
Fig. 27 shows the interior of the temple in its present condition.
It is 193 feet long by $81\frac{1}{2}$ wide.

D

To conclude, we mention the temple of Zeus at Olympia. Amongst the ruins of this sacred place (situated in the plain of

Fig. 27.

the Alpheios, and forming a brilliant centre of Greek national life), for some time remnants had been noticed which showed a better material than the bricks commonly used.   After the liberation of Greece from the Turks a French exploring expedition closely investigated the place, and came to the conclusion that amongst these ruins the remnants of the celebrated temple of Zeus Olympios were preserved; nay, it was even found possible to form from these a sufficient clear notion of the sacred edifice which once enclosed the most sublime image of the father of the gods, the pride and joy of Greece.   We shall have to consider further on the splendid festivities celebrated by the nation, as it were in the presence of the God; here we must limit ourselves to the temple itself, which, next to the Parthenon, may be considered as the climax of artistic perfection, in the same way as in the statue of the God, by Phidias, it possessed the only work of sculpture which rivalled and in some respects surpassed the excellence of Athene Parthenos. "The style of the temple," Pausanias says, in his simple description (V. 10), "is Doric; with regard to the exterior, it is a peristylos. The material is porous stone found on the spot. Its height, up to the top of the gable, is 68 feet, its width 95 feet, its length 230 feet. The architect was a local man named Libon. The tiles of the roof are not of burnt clay, but of Pentelic marble, resembling bricks in their shape. At the two corners of the gable there are gilt receptacles, and on the top of each of them there is a gilt figure of Nike." The occasion of building the temple was a victory of the Olympians over the inhabitants of the neighbouring city of Pisa (Ol. 52); but the completion of the sculptures on the metopa and gables, by Phidias and his pupils, did not take place till Olympiad 86. Of the

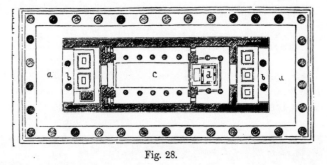

Fig. 28.

surrounding colonnade *a* (see Fig. 28) only nine columns have been found in different places, besides parts of the wall of the cella with the antæ, between the latter of which there were two columns both in front and at the back. In the pronaos *b* there has been found, underneath a Roman pavement which consists of marble and oriental alabaster, a roughly composed mosaic of pebbles, such as are found in the Alpheios, which represents sea-gods and goddesses, and which undoubtedly was the original floor. Close by this was the base of a statue, also mentioned by Pausanias, such as are frequently met with in the entrance-halls of temples. The cella was divided into different parts, the middle one (*e*) being uncovered and surrounded by two colonnades in two stories; in connection with it there was a smaller covered compartment (*d*), which contained the statue of the god. Zeus was represented as sitting

on a throne, which is described as an elaborate structure of cedar
wood, laid in with ebony and richly adorned with valuable stones
and sculptures.   The base was also richly decorated in accordance
with the figure itself.   The face, the chest, the naked upper part
of the body, and the feet, were of ivory ; the eyes consisted of
brilliant stones.   The waving hair and beard were of solid gold,
as was also the figure of Nike which the god held in his extended
right hand ; the sceptre in his other hand was composed of different precious metals.   The drapery covering the lower part of
the body was also of gold, with flowers in a kind of enamel.   But
all this splendour of valuable materials was as nothing compared
with the grandeur of the divine form.   In this Phidias had em-
bodied the description of those wonderful lines of the Iliad
(I. 528) which lived in the memory of every Greek—

> ῏Η, καὶ κυανέῃσιν επ' ὀφρύσι νεῦσε Κρονίων·
> ἀμβρόσιαι δ' ἄρα χαῖται ἐπερρώσαντο ἄνακτος
> κρατὸς ἀπ' ἀθανάτοιο· μέγαν δ'ἐλέλιξεν Ὄλυμπον.

So he sat, sublime and inapproachable, and yet mildly inclining
towards the spectator, perhaps the most perfect realisation of
the Greek ideal of godhead, and therefore the goal of every one's

Fig. 29.

longing ; not to have seen the Olympian Zeus was considered as
a misfortune.   The height of the statue was 40 feet, almost too
colossal, in proportion to the surrounding architecture, so that the
Greeks themselves used to say that if the god rose from his seat
he would knock in the roof overhead.   On both sides of the room
containing the statue there were steps leading to the upper

gallery and most likely open to the spectators for a closer view
of the statue and the single ornaments. In front of the statue
a piece of black marble pavement has been discovered, which quite

Fig. 30.

tallies with a statement of Pausanias; for, according to him, a piece
of the floor immediately before the statue was paved with black
marble, instead of white stone ; this piece was surrounded with an
enclosure of white Parian marble, and into it oil was poured so
as to preserve the statue from the dampness of the soil, in the
same way as the evaporation of water was considered beneficial to
the statue of Athene in the dry atmosphere of the Akropolis.
Behind the back wall of the cella was the opisthodomos, which
again, through the columns between the antæ, opened into the
peristylos. Fig. 29 shows the length, Fig. 30, on a little larger
scale, the width, of the temple.

12. The peripteros, *i.e.* the temple-house wholly surrounded
by columns, marks the ultimate completion of Greek architecture.
There were certainly a great many varieties of the form so gained,
as, for instance, the formation of the cella as antæ-temple, prostylos, and amphiprostylos, and many modifications of the interior
arrangement ; still, the idea of a temple-house surrounded by
colonnades is common to all of them. But this idea itself might
be enlarged by adding to the first row of columns a second one,
so as to form a double colonnade or pteron. This temple was

called by the Greeks, very appropriately, ναὸς δίπτερος,[1] *i.e.* a temple with a double pteron. "The dipteros," Vitruvius says, "has eight columns both in front and at the back, but round the cella it has a double colonnade. Of this order are the Doric temple of Quirinus, and the Ionic one of Diana built by Ktesiphon."

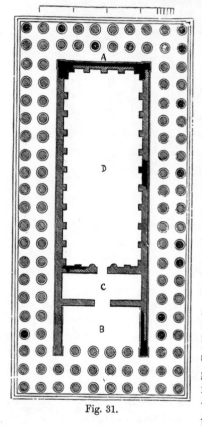

Fig. 31.

This rule of Vitruvius does, as is often the case, not tally with the remaining monuments, the number of the columns in the façades being occasionally ten, instead of eight as prescribed by him. Of the two mentioned specimens, the temple of Quirinus was at Rome, erected by Augustus; the other one is one of the most brilliant examples of this order, which seems to have been used chiefly by the luxurious Greeks of the colonies in Asia Minor. The temple of Artemis at Ephesos (see § 2) was built at a very early period, and always considered as the earliest and at the same time one of the grandest and most perfect specimens of the Ionic style (see § 4). It was afterwards considerably enlarged, but the original plan was not essentially modified. For a long time it was mentioned as the absolute perfection of the rich Ionic style, and counted by the ancients themselves amongst the seven

[1] To be quite complete we ought to add, that denominations of this kind were also derived from the number of the columns of the façades. A temple, the façade of which had four columns, was called a tetrastylos (see Figs. 16-19); one with six was called a hexastylos (see Figs. 21-23); the Parthenon with its eight columns was an oktastylos (see Figs. 24, 25); the ten-columned temple of Apollo of Miletos (Fig. 31) a dekastylos; and the votive temple at Eleusis a dodekastylos, because of the twelve columns of its portico (see Fig. 39).

wonders of the world. Remnants of the building have quite lately been discovered by English excavations, but accounts have not yet been published; we, therefore, cannot enter into a detailed description, although the plan of the temple may be guessed with tolerable certainty from the accounts of the ancients themselves. We add, instead, the design of a temple (Fig. 31), which, with regard to both size and splendour, might vie with that of Artemis, and which must be considered as an equally important specimen of the dipteros. It is the temple of Apollo Didymæos at Miletos. Miletos was one of the richest and most important colonies of the Ionians on the coast of Asia Minor. According to tradition, it had been originally inhabited by the Karians, from whom it was taken by the Kretans; afterwards the Ionians chose it as a colony; they increased it and raised it to one of the most important commercial cities, whose ships sailed to all parts of the Mediterranean and beyond the Columns of Herkules, and, on the other side, carried their wares into the Pontus Euxinus. The names of the philosophers Thales and Anaximander, and of the historians Kadmos and Hekatæos, prove the existence of scientific culture combined with commercial industry. The same may be said of the fine arts, and particularly of architecture, the high development of which is shown in the remnants of the once-celebrated temple of Apollo.

Connected with an oracle revered in this place ever since the time of the Kretan colony there had been built, at an early date, a temple of Apollo, the service in which had been, also for a long time, in the family of the Branchides. This older temple disappeared in the general destruction of Miletos by the Persians (Olympiad 71, 3), but after the independence of the city was restored, in more splendid style, by the Milesian architects Pæonios and Daphnis; it seems, however, never to have been quite finished. The plan was on the grandest scale; the façade, consisting of ten columns, was longer almost by two-thirds than that of the Parthenon of Athens; the columns were $6\frac{1}{4}$ feet in diameter by 63 feet in height, and were slenderer than those of the Artemisin at Ephesos and of other Ionic temples. Accordingly, the beams were lighter and weaker, as is shown in the design of the façade (Fig. 32). Through the double colonnade (Fig. 31, A) one enters, first, the pronaos B, which was bounded towards the peristylos by four columns *in antis*, and the walls of which were adorned by pilasters with very rich Korinthian

Fig. 32.

capitals. Through a small room (C), destined either for the keeping of treasures or for staircases, one entered the cella (D), most likely open in the middle, and enclosed at the sides by colonnades. There seems to have been no opisthodomos surrounded by walls.

13. The dipteros, as we have seen, was only an enlargement of the peripteros; the pseudo-dipteros, on the other hand (the last temple with a square cella in the list of Vitruvius), is a kind of medium between peripteros and dipteros, and is, therefore, mentioned by Vitruvius between the two. The explanation of the name is similar to that of the pseudo-peripteros; it means a temple which has the appearance of a dipteros without being one in reality, *i.e.* the pseudo-dipteros seems to have two colonnades without having them; or, to say the same in different words, its external plan is exactly like that of a dipteros, but that the second row of columns between the exterior one and the wall of the cella has been omitted. "Pseudo-dipteros," Vitruvius says, "is called a temple which has eight columns in front and at the back, there being fifteen columns on each of the longer sides inclusive of the corner columns. But the walls of the cella, both in front and at the back, are exactly opposite the four middle columns. The interval between the exterior columns and the walls is, therefore, all round, equal to two interstices and one diameter of the bottom part of a column." Evidently this order,

which is approved of by Vitruvius on account of its picturesque-
ness and of the saving of the interior colonnade, is a thing
between a dipteros and a peripteros. With the latter it has
in common the one colonnade round the whole cella; with the
former the circumstance of this colonnade being wide enough to
give room for an imaginary interior row of columns. It is said to
have been invented by Hermogenes about the time of Alexander
the Great, but one does not see why it should not have occurred
before. At Selinus, at least, the largest of the temples on the
eastern hill of the city is built in this style. It is, like the other
buildings of that city, in the Doric style, but approaching the
Attic by the gracefulness of its proportions. Fig. 33 shows the
plan of this temple. The colonnade *A* surrounding the temple
has exactly the width of two interstices and one bottom diameter
of the columns. The pronaos B is formed by the projecting

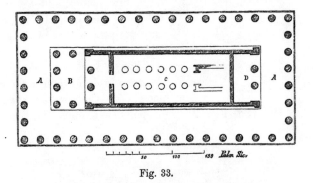

Fig. 33.

antæ-walls and six detached columns. The cella (C) seems to
have been open and surrounded by colonnades; behind it follows
the opisthodomos D.

There were several Ionic temples of this order; Hermogenes,
named by Vitruvius as its inventor, is indeed the architect who
for the first time treated the Ionic style according to a scientific
system, in opposition to the Doric style, to which he objects on
the ground of several irregularities. The temple of Artemis
Leukophryne at Magnesia on the Mæandros, cited by Vitruvius,
was, to judge from the discovered remnants, of the Ionic order,
as was also, most probably, the temple of Apollo at Alabanda,
the native city of Hermogenes, also mentioned by Vitruvius.

We quote, as an example of the Ionic pseudo-dipteros, the temple at Aphrodisias in Karia, which was built in the early times of the

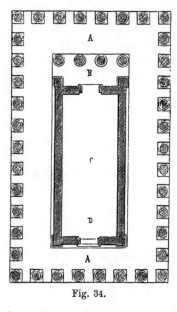

empire, and the ruins of which are exceptionally well preserved. The protecting goddess of Aphrodisias was Aphrodite, as indicated by this name being substituted for the original Ninoë, and her service was celebrated with a splendour evidently influenced by the worship of similar Asiatic deities. This was often the case in Asia Minor. For these reasons it is not unlikely that the mentioned temple was dedicated to Aphrodite. It is of large dimensions, and easy graceful proportions, quite in accordance with the nature of the goddess and her service.

Fig. 34 shows the plan [1] of the temple divided into the colonnade (A), the pronaos (B), and the cella (C, D); Fig. 35 represents a sketch of the façade,

Fig. 34.

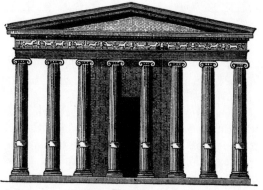

Fig. 35.

elegant and graceful in its proportions. Peculiar to it are the

[1] The width of the inside of the cella is about 22 ft. 6 in. English measure.

little tablets on the shafts of the columns with Greek votive inscriptions, which interrupt the flutings.

14. Hitherto we have discovered as the fundamental idea of the most widely different temples, the oblong square cella, the house of the god, surrounded by columns in various ways, and divided for the purposes of the service into pronaos, cella, and opisthodomos. This was, indeed, the prevalent form of all Greek sacred edifices, even of the chapels (ναΐσκοι).

There are, however, some exceptions to this rule. First, with regard to shape, there are the round temples. But, besides this, there may be different arrangements of the interior, or even of the whole plan of the building, caused by the peculiar requirements of the service. A specimen of the former variation was the double temple; one of the latter the votive temple.

a. The round temple we can mention but briefly. Vitruvius, it is true, mentions it in his list of different temples, but without reference to Greek specimens, as has been the case with regard to those hitherto considered. The only specimen of the round temple in existence is, as far as my knowledge goes, the tholos of Polykleitos, in the hieron of Asklepios near Epidauros; the foundation walls, together with some remnants of the geison, are preserved. There are, however, some analogous buildings mentioned in the records of the ancients. In the agora of Sparta, not far from the Skias, stood a circular building containing the statues of Zeus and Aphrodite, surnamed the "Olympian" (Paus. III. 12, 11). The expression, tholos (Θόλος), applied by Pausanias to the building near the Buleuterion at Athens, where the prytanes used to sacrifice, also seems to indicate a circular form. Small figures of silver, and the statues of the heroes presiding over the single tribes (φύλαι), were placed in them. Some temples at Platææ and Delphi, seem also to have been of a round form; we know, however, nothing else about their plans. A round house, οἴκημα περιφερές, stood in the Altis grove at Olympia. It was erected by Philip, king of the Makedonians, after the battle of Chæronea (Ol. 110, 3), and was called, after him, the Philippeum. It was made of burnt bricks, there were columns round it (peripteros), and on the top there was a brass decoration in the form of a poppy-head, which served, at the same time, to fasten the beams of the roof. In the interior were placed the statues of Philip, his father Amyntas, his son Alexander the Great, and those of Olympia and Eurydike, wrought in gold and ivory by Leochares. Whether or not the

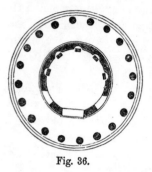

Fig. 36.

Philippeum had the significance of a temple, it may, in any case, be considered as analogous to the round temple, for which reason we have added (Fig. 36) the original plan of the building as designed by Hirt.

That form of the round temple which Vitruvius designates as monopteros, consisting of an open circle of columns with beams and a roof placed on them, is specified by the analogous Choragic monument of Lysikrates at Athens. To this we shall have to return in speaking of profane architecture (§ 24, Fig. 152).

d. The double temple. Several temples are mentioned by the ancients in which two deities were adored, each in a separate room. In this case the cella had to be divided, whence the expression ναὸς διπλοῦς; and this seems to have been done in various ways. The one least in use seems to have been that of putting the rooms of the different gods one on the top of the other. Of this, Pausanias knows only one example, viz., an old temple at Sparta dedicated to the "armed Aphrodite," whose image was placed in it. This temple had an upper story dedicated to Morpho. Morpho, however, was, according to Pausanias, only a surname of Aphrodite. Her image in the upper temple was, unlike the other, without arms. The goddess was represented with her feet in fetters and veiled, most likely in allusion to her significance as the goddess of death.

More frequent was the division of the cella into two level rooms, one by the side or at the back of the other. The separation of the cella by a wall built parallel to the length of the temple (such as it might be found in an Egyptian temple at Ombos) seems not to have been used by the Greeks. The double temple of Asklepios and Leto at Mantinea, cited by Hirt as a specimen of this division, may (according to the statement of Pausanias, VIII. 9, 1) just as well have been divided by a cross-wall right in the middle of the cella.

The last-mentioned division of the cella is proved by several other temples. At Sikyon, for instance, Hypnos, the god of sleep, and Apollo, surnamed Karneios, were adored in a double temple. The image of Hypnos was in the front compartment, while the interior was dedicated to Apollo; the latter, only priests were allowed to enter (Pausanias, II. 10, 2).

Another double temple at Mantinea was dedicated to Aphrodite and Ares. Pausanias remarks that the entrance to the room of Aphrodite was on the eastern, that to the apartment of Ares on the western, side.

Of a partition of the temple by a cross-wall we have an instructive example in the sanctuary of the old Attic deities Athene Polias, Poseidon and Erechtheus, and the daughter of Kekrops, Pandrosos, situated in the Akropolis of Athens, and called promiscuously temple of Athene Polias, Erechtheion, or Pandroseion. At a very early period there was, opposite the long northern side of the Parthenon, a temple which, according to Herodot, was dedicated jointly to Athene Polias and the Attic hero, Erechtheus. (Ol. 68, 1.) King Kleomenes of Sparta, who had expelled Klisthenes from Athens, was refused the entrance into this temple, because in it were placed the national deities of the Athenians (Ol. 75, 1); this temple was destroyed by fire while the Persians held the city. Not unlikely the rebuilding of the Erechtheion was begun by Perikles together with that of the other destroyed temples of the Akropolis; but as it was not finished by him, it is generally not mentioned amongst his works. From the fourth year of Olympiad 92 we have a special account of the state of the building. From a public document, in which the architects give an account of their work, we gather that, at that time the walls and columns of the temple were finished, only the roof and the working out of details remaining undone. This temple was renowned amongst the ancients as one of the most beautiful and perfect in existence, and seems to have remained almost intact down to the time of the Turks. The siege of Athens by the Venetians in 1687 seems to have been fatal to the Erechtheion, as it was to the Parthenon. Stuart found the walls and columns still erect, but part of the architrave, half of the frieze, and almost the whole cornice, were destroyed; stones, rubbish, and the ruins of the roof, covered the floor; in the northern entrance-hall was a powder magazine.   At present the temple has been restored as far as possible.

The plan of this building, which represents the Attic-Ionic style in its highest development, is, for various reasons connected with the divine service, one of the most complicated we know of during the Greek period (Fig. 37 [1]).   The chief part of it we must

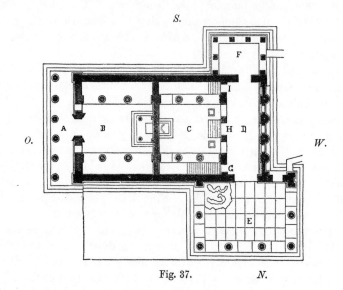

S.

O.   *W.*

Fig. 37.   *N.*

consider as a cella stretching from west to east; the masonry is 73 feet in length by 37 in width; on the eastern side a pronaos is formed by a portico of six Ionic columns.   A door led from this pronaos into the cella (B) dedicated to Athene Polias, which could be entered only from this eastern side; it was separated from the cella (C) of Poseidon Erechtheus by an uninterrupted cross-wall.   Another wall, interrupted by three entrances (I H G), separated the Erechtheion proper from the cella of Pandrosos—a small apartment, not unlike a corridor (D), which finished the building towards the west.   The western outer wall was adorned with columns, between the intercolumnia of which there were windows, but it had no entrance corresponding to that on the eastern side.   The entrance into the Pandroseion—

[1] Compare the plan of the Akropolis, Fig. 52, B.

and through it into the middle room of the Erechtheion—consisted
of a pronaos (E) carried by six slender and richly decorated Ionic
columns (compare Fig. 10), and situated at the western end of the
northern long side; from it a beautiful and still-preserved door
led into the sanctuary.   Corresponding to this pronaos we discover,
at the western end of the southern long side, a small graceful hall
(F), the ceiling of which is carried, instead of columns, by six
caryatides, representing Athenian maidens (compare Fig. 214);
a small postern led from this hall down into the Pandroseion.
Thus much about the plan and arrangement of the interior of the
temple, as gathered from Bötticher's clever researches. A conjectural reconstruction of this beautiful edifice is shown, Fig. 38;
it is the more authentic as the remaining portions, although partly
displaced and damaged, still give a distinct notion of the former
state, even with regard to ornamental details.

Fig. 38.

c. We will conclude our survey of the exceptional forms of
Greek temples with a description of the great votive temple at
Eleusis.   The sanctuaries hitherto considered were habitations of
the deity represented by its image.   Greek temples, as a rule,
were not destined for the reception of crowds with a view to
common religious ceremonies.   Individuals might enter to pray
and offer, or to gaze at the divine images; but the great religious

festivities took place outside the temple.   There were, however,
a few holy edifices for the purpose of common prayer ; which, therefore, were not only houses of the gods, but also places for religious
meetings.   These were the so-called votive temples (τελεστήρια,
μέγαρα), destined for the celebration of mysteries ; and therefore
constructed on an entirely different plan from other temples.
The great importance of the mysteries for antique life is well
known ; they date from early Pelasgic times, but their symbolic
celebration, relating to the divinities of the earth and its culture,
was in the acme of Greek development combined with artistic
energy of every kind.   The original import of their mystical
doctrine was rendered in mimico-dramatic representations, and
formed at the same time the subject of choral hymns.   For this
purpose large rooms were required, and the only building of this
kind known to us, viz., the Megaron at Eleusis, is indeed unique
in its arrangements.   It has at present disappeared almost trace-
lessly, but former excavations throw a sufficiently distinct light on
various important points of its interior arrangements (Fig. 39).
The temple was quadrangular in form, from 212 to 216 feet long by
178 wide ; in front was a portico of twelve columns which formed
the pronaos (A).   The second compartment, which one entered

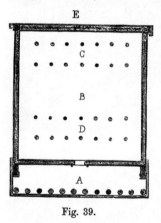

Fig. 39.

by a door from the pronaos, formed an
almost perfect square ; it was divided
into five parallel naves by four rows of
columns.   The columns, some of which
have been found, carried galleries, as
in the hypæthral temple, but that
in this case they were broader, and
rested on two rows of columns respectively (C and D).   The space in the
middle (B) extended through both
stories, and formed a kind of central
nave of increased height.   Plutarch
mentions the history of the building in
his life of Perikles, its originator.

According to him, Koroibos, most likely under the supervision of
Iktinos, began the Telesterium ; he also erected the columns of the
first story, and covered them with their architraves.   After his death,
Metagenes added the frieze and erected the upper columns (*i.e.* the

columns of the upper story); the opening over the anaktoron
(viz. the centre nave B) was covered by Xenokles. Underneath
the floor was a kind of crypt, supported by short cylindrical props
(*Cylinderspitzen*), and used, perhaps, for preparing the above-
mentioned mimical representations. On the side opposite the
entrance a raised terrace was added to
the temple, to which led, through a
narrow square courtyard, an entrance
decorated with columns. Most likely
there was a door also on this side, destined for the conductors of the mysteries (mystagogoi), while the large door
in the façade gave entrance to the
initiated, into the holy chambers. Fig.

Fig. 40.

40 shows a rich Corinthian capital of a pilaster found amongst
the ruins, and belonging, most likely, to the decorations of the
pronaos.

15. In looking back on the interior arrangements and the
surroundings of the temples, we are struck again by their rich and
solemn appearance. Wherever the situation made it possible, the
temple was secluded from the current of profane life; it stood in
a peribolos, which, at the same time, served to receive the votive
offerings less appropriate for the interior. Here were symbols of
the gods, trees, rocks, and fountains, frequently with holy traditions attaching to them; here were statues sometimes wholly
exposed to the air, or else protected by elegant small roofs; heroa,
or small chapels (ναΐσκοι), and altars used for the reception of
offerings, and often dedicated to several deities; nay, even groves
and gardens were comprised in these enclosures.

The most important were the altars (βωμός, θυτήριον) on
which burnt-offerings were devoted to the deity of the temple.
Burnt-offerings of the flesh of living creatures did not take
place in the interior of the temple (see § 59). They were
performed on the thymele before the pronaos, the doors being
open at the time, so that the image of the god celebrated could
look on the altar. It need not be mentioned that in large temples
these altars were decorated with great splendour. Originally they
were only natural hillocks which gradually increased in size
by the ashes and horns of the burnt animals, and soon became

E

capable of architectural and sculptural development. Pausanias describes (V. 13) the altar of the Olympian Zeus as an artificial structure, the base (κρηπίς or πρόθυσις) of which was 125 feet in circumference. On this stood the altar proper, 22 feet in height; stone steps led to the prothysis, and thence to the uppermost platform of the altar, to which women had no access. The altar, Pausanias adds, consisted of the ashes of the thighs of the killed animals, as was also the case with an altar of Hera of Samos; the altars of the Olympian Hera, of the Olympian Gaia, and of Apollo Spodios at Thebes, also consisted of ashes; while an altar near the large temple of Apollo Didymæos, at Miletos, was composed of the blood of the slaughtered animals. We also hear of altars of wood; at Olympia there was one of unburnt tiles which once every Olympiad was rubbed with chalk. For the greater part, however, the larger and more elaborate altars were made of stone, the inside being possibly filled up with earth. An altar at Pergamon is distinctly stated to have consisted of marble; the shape was usually quadrangular.

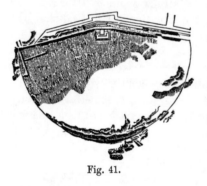

Fig. 41.

Pausanias (V. 14, 5) calls the altar of Artemis of Olympia square, and gradually rising upwards; square was, also, the colossal altar at Parion, said to have been one stadium (600 feet) in length and width. A specimen of an altar in the form of a terrace we have in that devoted to Zeus Hypatos, or Hypistos, at Athens (Fig. 41). It was cut from the living rock and formed partly by nature, partly by the hand of man, into a terrace, visible from afar, up to which led steps and well-constructed paths. Professor E. Curtius has proved this structure to be an altar, and not the Pnyx, or place of public assembly, as was formerly supposed. It was one of those places of oldest Athenian worship, connected with the " highest Jove; " which, with the increase of the city, was raised and enlarged proportionally. (See the perspective view, Fig. 42.)

Facing the altar for burnt-offerings rises the façade of the temple, consisting of beautiful marble; or, if made of lesser

material, clad with delicate stucco, discreetly coloured, a modification of the glaring whiteness, also occasionally applied to the
protruding details of a marble erection. Now and then votive
offerings are fastened to the façade, in addition to the sculptures
of the frieze and pediment. Tripods and statues crown the top
of the gable, golden tripods or other statuary ornaments are placed
on its edges, and golden shields were often hung up on the
architrave, as, for instance, in the Parthenon. Statues of priests
and priestesses stand at the sides of the entrance ; the number
and value of the offerings and statues increase on entering the
pronaos ; frequently valuable plate was kept here, partly for the
purposes of the service, as, for instance, basins for washing, partly

Fig. 42.

with a view to alluding to sacred events, as in the case of the
couch of Hera in the pronaos of the Heræon, near Mykenæ ; in
its vicinity was also placed, as an anathema, the shield which
Menelaos had snatched from Euphorbos before Troy. The cella
was fitted up in a similar but still more splendid style. The
divine image is enthroned in a carefully secluded space, frequently
in a separate niche, but always under a shelter from above. The
images of friendly deities (ἁ ρεδροι) were frequently placed in its
vicinity, surrounded at a greater distance by statues and offerings
of various kinds. Very important was the oblation-table (ἱερὰ or
θυωρὸς τράπεζα) placed before the image, and corresponding to the

burnt-offering altar outside, but destined only for bloodless offerings.

Even in their homes the Greeks had such sacred tables, near or on which were placed statues of the gods, and dishes with the first portions of the food.   Where one and the same cella was

devoted to several divinities, each of them had a separate τράπεζα inside, and an altar of burnt-offerings outside, of the temple.   The thymele in front of the pronaos and the trapeza before the image are the chief criteria of what Bötticher calls the *cultus*-temple, *i.e.* of a temple which served for the performance of *sacra* and other devotional acts of the people represented by the priests.   Both were wanting in another

Fig. 43.

class of temples, viz., the agonal or festive temples.   In these the trapeza was supplanted by the bema, from the top of which the prizes gained in the agon were distributed.   Although occasionally portable, the altars were generally made of stone.   Some of them are known from pictures, others have been rediscovered.   On an earthen vessel found at Athens an altar is depicted with a fire burning on it in honour of Zeus, whom we discover standing by the side of it, together with Nike.   On a low

Fig. 44.

pedestal is raised a small erection with ornaments like volutes (Fig. 43).   Stuart has found, at Athens, an octagonal altar adorned with garlands, skulls of bulls, and knives (Fig. 44).   A round altar of white marble, with similar ornaments, and a small erection, have been found in the island of Delos (Fig. 45).   Valuable implements of the service, like candlesticks, basins, or small votive offerings, were placed on tables, as is shown, for instance, in a terra-cotta reproduction (see Fig. 46).

16. The highest splendour of Greek architecture was shown where several temples were placed together in one particular

space devoted to the gods. Of such centres of Greek life and religious worship several are known to us; as, for instance, the grove Altis at Olympia, where an abundance of architectural monuments were crowded together, and where the agility and beauty displayed by the youth in the games, celebrated in honour of Zeus, offered plentiful suggestions to the sculptor. At other places competitions in music and poetry were added to the display of gymnastic skill, which formed the prominent feature of Olympian festivals. But even where no such games took place several sanctuaries were frequently built together. At Girgenti, even at the present day, a row of temples is discoverable on a height overlooking the sea;

Fig. 45.   Fig. 46.

at Selinunt there are two groups of buildings on two hills, and the remaining three ruins of temples at Pæstum seem also to have belonged to a group.

The entrances to such holy enclosures were always decorated with a splendour corresponding to their sanctity and beauty; the largeness and beauty of the entrance-gate, or portal, indeed, seemed to indicate in advance the corresponding importance of the place. The simplest kind consisted of a gate rising in commanding dimensions over the wall of the peribolos. Perhaps an entrance-portal of this kind must be recognised in a separate gate of beautiful stone which has been discovered standing erect in

the small island of Palatia, near Naxos (Fig. 47); its inner width
is 3,45 metres.   Palatia was connected with the larger Naxos by
means of a bridge, and had a temple, near which the mentioned
portal has been found; it consists of a threshold, which origin-

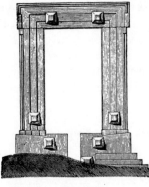

ally seems to have been level with
the ground, over which it is raised
at the present time; it is also possible that there were steps leading
up to it; the posts and the lintel
are divided into three parallel stripes
like an Ionic architrave, and surrounded with a simple cornice.

Where the entrance-structure
was developed more richly it was
natural to conform its appearance to
the chief model of Greek architecture,
the temple itself.   The simplest
kind of this conformity is displayed

Fig. 47.

in the beautiful portal leading to the peribolos of the temple of
Athene, at Sunion, on the southern point of Attika.   To this
building (see the plan, Fig. 48) the name propylæa may be applied,
which was the general denomination of portal-erections.   The
propylæa of Sunion resemble in their design a temple with

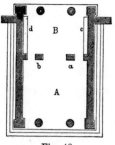

two columns *in antis* on the two small sides,
and with the cross-wall of the cella left
out.   When the plan of this building was
first made public, it was thought that in
the space covered by the roof no cross-wall
had been intended, but Blouet has since
discovered that the actual gates, formed
by two pillars (*a b*), were in this cross-wall.
These pillars, or shall we call it a broken
wall, divided the whole space into two
halves, of which the outer one (A) forms a

Fig. 48.

kind of portico, while the second division (B) is turned towards
the inside of the peribolos and the temple itself.   In the latter
stood marble benches (*c d*) against both the side walls.

Richer forms and developments are shown by the propylæa
of the two temple-enclosures best known to us, viz., at Eleusis

and in the Akropolis of Athens. The former was destined to enclose the large votive temple described above (§ 14, Fig. 39). In the plan (Fig. 49) the walls of both an outer (A) and inner

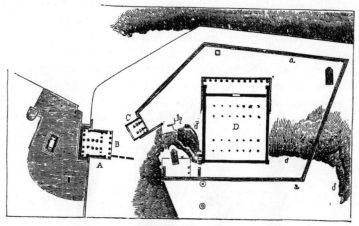

Fig. 49.

(*a a*) peribolos are recognisable. The entrance is formed by the large propylæa (B), near which the above-mentioned temple of Artemis Propylæa is situated (see Fig. 15). These propylæa

Fig. 50.

form a square space, enclosed by a wall on each side, and by a portico of six Doric columns, both in front and at the back. Inside, there is a cross-wall (Fig. 50), interrupted by five doors corresponding to the intercolumnia of the portico; it divides the whole space into two compartments, in the larger of which there are two rows of three Ionic columns each. The same arrangement we shall have to mention again in the propylæa of Athens, after which those of Eleusis were fashioned. On entering the outer peribolos, through this beautiful building, one encounters a second smaller erection of propylæa (C), which leads into the inner peribolos. The latter lies higher than the other parts, and is also surrounded by a wall (*a a*). It surrounds the votive temple (D) at a moderate distance. The plan of the smaller propylæa is shown, Fig. 51. They also are enclosed by walls on the two long

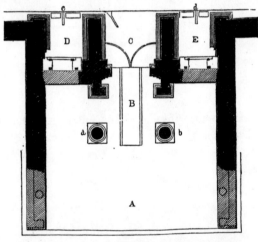

Fig. 51.

sides; a cross-wall divides the whole space into two halves. The side where the entrance lay was open in front, and had columns which supported the roof. By the walls, to right and left, are raised steps (*a b*); the part in front of the columns (A) had an even pavement, while in part B the pavement rises gradually to the amount of about sixteen inches. Into the well-preserved floor grooves have been cut, seemingly destined for the wheels of vehicles, or for rollers. The small inner space (C) was separated from the last-mentioned one by a door, the leaves of which opened inside, as is still recognisable by marks on the floor. On the right and left sides, the passage (C) is joined towards the interior by two smaller rooms, like niches, in which, most likely, statues were placed; in front of these are some holes (*c d*) carefully worked out, and evidently connected with the exhibitions which here took place. Altogether, the mentioned details seem to indicate that this entrance was used to prepare the visitors for the ceremonies in the votive temple, by arrangements or exhibitions of some kind.

The greatest splendour of antique art, however, was displayed in the propylæa which formed the entrance to the Athenian Akropolis. The Akropolis is situated on a table-land 1150 feet in length, and 500 broad in the widest places; being 160 feet high, and of steep ascent, except where it slopes towards the town. The Akropolis, in a manner, marks the beginning of Athens, both as a state and a city, having been, at a very early period, surrounded by walls, and containing the oldest national sacred monuments. The old temples were destroyed by fire during the Persian occupation, but when liberty and prosperity were restored they once more rose from their ashes with renewed splendour (see plan of the Akropolis, Fig. 52); the temple of the wingless Nike (Figs. 17, 18, and 52, D) was erected here, so as to attach the goddess of victory to Athens; here rose in majestic severity the Parthenon (A), and the graceful structure devoted to Athene Polias and Erechtheus (B), while between both stood the imposing form of Athene Promachos (E) as in defence of the castle. Numerous holy statues, altars, architectural groups, and other ornaments, stood around these splendid monuments; and it was but natural that the entrance to this beautiful and hallowed spot should be adorned with splendour. For this purpose the propylæa (C) were erected by Mnesikles on the side looking towards the city; the building of it took from 437 till 432 (B.C.), and the expense amounted to 2012 talents. The chief part of the building consisted of a large square, enclosed by walls on the right and left, but opening towards both the city and the Akropolis by means of porticoes. Nearest to the inner portico, which was slightly raised, a wall went right across the space, being interrupted by five doors corresponding to the intercolumnia of the former (see Fig. 50); these doors formed the entrance proper. Between this wall and the outer portico lay a space of not inconsiderable dimensions, which was divided into three naves by means of two rows of Ionic columns, each row consisting of three columns.

The unevenness of the soil was equalised by means of steps, but between the mentioned centre columns a gently ascending road was hewn into the rock, so as to effect a commodious entrance for the carts laden with the splendid peplos of Athene, which formed a feature of the procession of the Panathenæa. The whole space was covered with slender marble cross-pieces, which spanned the naves and carried a rich and graceful casket-work (*Cassetten-werk*). Two lower side-wings with porticoes joined the chief

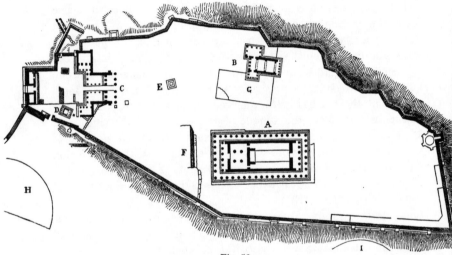

Fig. 52.

A. Parthenon.	D. Temple of Nike Apteros.	G. Terrace of Polygons.
B. Erechtheion.	E. Pedestal of Athene Promachos.	H. Theatre of Herodes.
C. Propylæa.	F. Steps in the rock.	I. Theatre of Dionysos.

façade, so as to add to its impression. The northern one, which is still well preserved, contained in its interior the celebrated paintings by Polygnotos from the Iliad and Odyssey; and even at the present day its walls are covered with the smooth marble slabs which once served as the frames of these pictures. The other wing was of similar construction, but of lesser width; during the Middle Ages the materials of this building have been used for a watch-tower of the castle, which was inhabited by the Franconian dukes of Athens. Between these two buildings, which were in beautiful proportion with the great façade of the propylæa, ended the splendid marble steps placed in the slanting rock of the Akropolis; their length was equal to the width of the propylæa; some of the steps are still in existence. Between these steps lay a wide carriage-road, paved with large slabs of marble, into which grooves had been chiselled for the wheels of the above-mentioned vehicle. Recent excavations have discovered the lower part of the steps, and the entrance-gate between two towers; the gate, however, is of Roman origin.

17. After having discussed the Greek buildings supplying the ideal demands of the adoration of the gods, we now must turn to those which served the material purposes of life.

Amongst these the walls ought to be mentioned first. We have noticed the habit of the Greeks of enclosing the precincts of their temples with walls, and the same feature we find repeated in the oldest specimens of their settlements. This is proved by the numerous remnants of old cities, both in Hellas and the Peloponnesos, which tend to show that wall-enclosures were amongst the very earliest productions of Greek architecture. The Greeks themselves ascribed these colossal structures to the Cyclops, a mythical race of giants, who are said to have come from Lykia, and to have taken a prominent part in building the walls of Tiryns. Nowadays these structures are generally called Pelasgic, owing to the opinion of their being built by the tribe of that name. This opinion seems to be confirmed by the fact that these monuments are generally found in places originally possessed by the Pelasgi. At Athens, the oldest parts of the fortifications of the Akropolis were called Pelasgic walls, and their erection was ascribed to the Pelasgi, who once had a settlement there (Paus. I., 28, 3). A third name applied to these walls refers to the mode of their construction. In the more ancient walls of this kind it consists in the piling on each other of rough, many-edged stones, and is therefore called polygonal building. Amongst the remaining monuments, the walls of Tiryns are most remarkable, which consist of large blocks of stone heaped on each other, the intervals being filled up by smaller stones. "Of the town," Pausanias says (II., 25, 8), "no remnants exist but the walls, which are the work of the Cyclops. They consist of rough stones, each one of which is so large that the smallest of them could not have been carried by a yoke of mules. At an early period

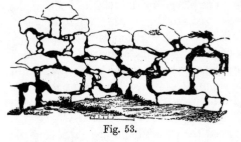

Fig. 53.

smaller stones have been placed between, so as to join the large ones together." In another place (IX., 36, 5) he calls them quite as admirable as the pyramids of Egypt, both by the grandeur of their dimensions and the difficulty of the work required in erecting them.

The walls of Tiryns seem to be, at the present time, in the same state as when Pausanias saw them. They have been examined by Gell, after whose drawing a fragment is reproduced in Fig. 53 (scale = 10 feet English measure). A second kind of these very old monuments show the stones still in their irregular polygonal form, but with some traces of workmanship upon them. The stones have been worked into the polygonal form nearest to their natural shape, and afterwards carefully joined together, so that the wall presents a firm uninterrupted surface. The finest specimens are found in the walls of the very ancient town of Mykenæ, in Argolis (Fig. 54). They are of considerable thick-

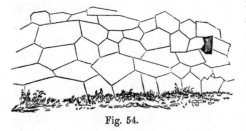

Fig. 54.

ness; the two outer surfaces consist of hewn and carefully composed stones, while the space between is filled up with small stones and mortar. This kind of construction was called by the Greeks ἔμπλεκτον; it was fur-

ther strengthened by the addition of solid inner cross-walls. The use of polygonal stones, as applied in the walls of Argos, Platææ, Ithaka, Koronea, Same, and other places, may result in great firmness, by means of the stones being put together as in a vaulted structure. In consequence it was retained occasionally by the Greeks, even after the freestone construction has been introduced (see Fig. 13); in our own time it has been applied, for instance, in the terraces which form the base of the Walhalla, at Regensburg, and in the protective walls on the shores of the German Ocean, which Forchhammer has appropriately compared to Cyclopic-Pelasgic walls.

Notwithstanding the advantages of polygonal structures, the desire for regularity led, at an early period, to the use of horizontal and regular layers of stones, as is shown by several old walls. The walls' of Argos consist partly of horizontal arrangements of totally irregular stones. In some places, as, for instance, in the remnants found in Ætolia, the layers, although horizontal, are totally irregular with regard to the cross-joints; while in other places, the transition to the regular freestone style is shown more distinctly by the application of vertical cross-joints. An instance of this are the walls of Psophis, in Arkadia (Fig. 55). A similar arrangement appears in a tower on the wall of Panopeus (Fig. 56), and still more distinctly the regular freestone style is shown in the wall of Chæronea, in Bœotia, which, moreover, has the peculiarity of not being perpendicular, but of showing a decided talus. (Compare the walls of Œniadæ, Figs. 64 and 69.)

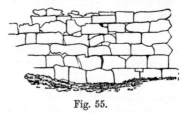

Fig. 55.

The use of regular freestone afterwards became general amongst the Greeks. Not only the walls of temples, but also those of later cities were erected in this way, as is shown, for instance, by the well-preserved walls of Messene (built 371 B.C.), of which we shall give illustrations. As the most solid and, at the same time, most artistic walls, those are mentioned by means of which the Athenians had joined the Piræus harbour to their city. Unfortunately only few remnants, consisting of single large blocks of stone, are preserved.

Fig. 56.

Fig. 57 (scale = 100 yards) shows the plan of the castle of Tiryns, which may serve as a specimen of these ancient fortifications. A signifies a gate, C a tower, and B a road ascending from

the lower plain; D is the present entrance.   Near E and H are the
galleries, to which we shall have to return; near F is another

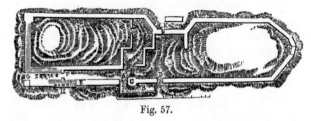

Fig. 57.

gate, up to which leads the road G.   Near I a cistern has been
found, and near K is another smaller gate.

18. Concerning gates we have to add that, where the top of a
mountain was transformed into a castle by means of walls, there
was generally but one gate.   There are, however, examples of
such castles having several gates; as, for instance, the above-
mentioned Akropolis of Mykenæ.   A town, on the other hand, as
the centre of commerce, required numerous entrances; and it was
considered a particular honour to a city to have many gates, the
fortified safeness of which symbolised, in a manner, its importance.
The importance and size of the gates naturally depended on the
importance of the roads which led to the city.   In consequence
we have to distinguish between gates and posterns (πύλαι and
πυλίδες, *Pforten*), the most important amongst the former being
called the large gate (μεγάλαι πύλαι).   Such was the dipylon
at Athens, where met the roads from Eleusis and Megara, the
large harbour road, and the roads from the Academy and the
Kolonos; while, inside, these were joined by the High and Market
Street of the city; in this way an enormous amount of traffic was
concentrated in this one point.

Originally the gates were of the simplest construction.   Where
the stones of the walls were left in a rough state, the gates were
constructed in a similar manner.   The single blocks were pushed
gradually towards each other till, at last, they touched, and in
this way formed a simple arch.   This primitive mode of construction is shown in a postern at Tiryns (Fig. 58), where, as we have
seen, the walls were of an equally simple kind.   In the same
manner the arched openings of a gallery have been constructed,
which is built into the wall of the same castle.   The gallery itself

likewise consists of layers of stone pushed towards each other, as is shown by the view of the interior (Fig. 59, compare Fig. 57,

Fig. 58.

Fig. 59.

Fig. 60.

H). The same construction also appears in the passages within the wall, of which Fig. 60 represents a section.

The construction of the gates improves in proportion to that of the walls. They may be constructed by over-laying the stones, or by the placing of a long straight block across the two side-posts. A simple specimen of the former method we see in some small posterns at Phigalia (Fig. 61) and Messene (Fig. 62); the latter is specified by a small door in the Akropolis of Mykenæ (Fig. 63), and a gate at Œniadæ, in Akarnania (Fig.

Fig. 61.

64). One of the oldest and most curious examples of such gates

Fig. 62.   Fig. 63.   Fig. 64.

is the so-called lions' gate at Mykenæ (Fig. 65). It stands

between a natural prominence of the rock and an artificial projection of the wall, and is formed by two strong and well-smoothed blocks of stone, which serve as side posts, and incline towards each other, so as to diminish the space to be covered.   On them rests, horizontally, an enormous block of stone, 15 feet long, which forms the lintel, and in this way

Fig. 65.

finishes the gate.   The wall itself is much higher than the gate; in order to weaken the pressure of the upper stones on the lintel, and to prevent it from breaking, a triangular opening has been left above it, in which, afterwards, a thinner slab of stone, about 11 feet wide by 10 high, has been placed.   On this slab we see two lions in alto-relievo, standing with their fore-paws on a broad base, which supports a column growing thinner at the lower end.   Göttling recognises in these lions, with the Phallic symbol between them, the protecting image of the castle of Mykenæ.   In any case the group is interesting as the oldest specimen of Greek sculpture in existence.

Both the larger gates and the smaller sally-ports were, as much

Fig. 66.

as possible, protected by projecting parts of the wall.   We have already mentioned this fact in speaking of the gate of Mykenæ; we add a gate at Orchomenos (Fig. 66), in which the projection of the wall on the right-hand side of the entrance may still be distinctly recognised.

A gate at Messene, showing both firmness of structure and artistic proportions, is still in existence.   This city, founded and raised to the capital of Messenia by Epaminondas, was, next to Korinth, considered as the safest stronghold of the whole Peloponnesos, owing to the solidity of its walls; the above-mentioned gate quite tallies with this statement, found repeatedly in ancient authors. The design (Fig. 67) and the section (Fig. 68, scale = 100 feet English measure) show that it was a double gate with an outer (*a*)

and inner (*b*) door. It is situated in a kind of tower, destined to
increase the strength of the wall, inside of which there is a circular
space like a courtyard.
The two gates lie oppo-
site each other in this
courtyard, the one marked
a on the outward side,
that marked *b* being
turned towards the town.

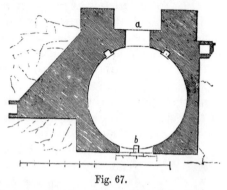

Fig. 67.

As remarkable we
have still to mention the
occurrence of vaulted
gates in Akarnania, quite
lately discovered at Heu-
zey. Generally speaking, the use of arches does not occur in Greece

Fig. 68.

Fig. 69.

before the time of the Makedonians; but in Akarnania there are
found, in old polygonal fortifications, gates, the outer walls of

F

which show a vault, while the inside part is still covered by horizontal pieces of stone (see Fig. 69).

19. The description of the gates leads us to that of the towers, which were almost universally used to increase the firmness and defensive conveniences of the walls. The gates naturally required a great deal of protection, and by this means, as Curtius has pointed out, the art of fortification itself was considerably developed. It seems, indeed, that the tower itself was only a development of the projection of the wall which is usually found to the right of the gate, as a favourable point of attack on the storming forces.

The simplest form seems to have consisted of a mere jutting out of the wall, repeated at certain intervals, by means of which the besieged could direct their defence to different points easier than would have been possible from a straight wall. Such tower-like projections we find in the old Pelasgic walls of Phigalia, in Arkadia (Fig. 70); they are partly quadrangular, partly semicircular.

Fig. 70.

We also find towers on single rocks, or prominences, the natural strength of which had to be increased by fortifications; they were used to reconnoitre the surrounding country, which, for instance, was the purpose of a tower in the Akropolis of Orchomenos in Bœotia (Fig. 71).

At Aktor a tower of two stories has been preserved. It stands on a point where the walls of the town meet at an obtuse angle. It has been preserved so well that the two stories are distinctly recognisable; but no traces of a staircase have been found. Most likely it consisted of wood, like the ceiling of the first story, so as to be easily removable, if necessary, in case of an attack. The entrances to the tower were two small gates, approachable from the top of the wall; on the three sides turned outward there were windows, which, like the embrasures of mediæval castles, are very small towards the outer side, but increase considerably in size towards the inside.

Fig. 71.

Of similar construction are the towers found on the walls of
Messene, both as a protection and an ornament.   A round tower,
amongst others, stands where the walls
meet at an obtuse angle (see the plan,
Fig. 72, scale = 10 metres, and the
view, Fig. 73); another tower, in good
preservation, illustrates the kind of entrance from the top of the wall; Fig.
74 (scale = 9 metres) gives a side-

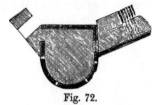

Fig. 72.

view of it.   The stones are placed on each other in layers, but the
cross-joints are mostly oblique and irregular; the former are hewn

Fig. 73.

Fig. 74.

so that the front side projects slightly from the surface of the wall
(a style called by the Italians, Rustico); the tower, as well as the
walls, are crowned by battlements, which are still distinctly recognisable; the small windows converge in an acute angle towards
the outside, the inside part widen-
ing in the form of a pointed arch.
The door, approachable from the
top of the wall (see Fig. 74), closes
in a straight line.

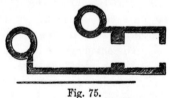

Fig. 75.

Two round towers, standing
almost separate, protect the gate of
Mantinea (see plan, Fig. 75, scale = 30 metres).

Single towers were often built on the sea-shore, particularly on
islands, both as watch-towers against pirates and as places of
refuge for the inhabitants.   (Similar strongholds built by the
Venetians, against the landing of the infidels, are found on many

points of the Greek coast.)   The most important structure of this
kind has been preserved in the isle of Keos.   It rises, in four
stories, straight from the ground, and is crowned with battlements,
and surrounded on its four sides by projecting blocks of stone,
which carried an open gallery, perhaps " the only well-preserved
example of the peridromos, so important in antique fortification."
(Ross, " *Inselreise*," I. p. 132.)

Of similar construction, but round in shape, is a tower in
Andros (Fig. 76), built most likely for the protection of the
neighbouring iron mines.   It is remarkable by winding stairs in

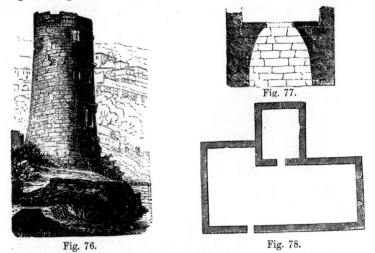

Fig. 76.

Fig. 77.

Fig. 78.

the interior and by a circular chamber in the lower story, which,
like the treasure-houses (see § 21), grows smaller towards the
top by the overlaying of the stones; the ceiling is formed by
radiating slabs of stone (Fig. 77).

To detached towers, courts surrounded by masonry were
sometimes added, as places of refuge for the inhabitants of the
neighbouring country and their goods.   Fig. 78 shows the plan
of such a combination, situated in the island of Tenos, where
the court, connected with the tower and enclosed by a strong
wall, is nearly 84 feet long.

20. After the buildings of protection follow those of utility.
Amongst these we must consider particularly aqueducts, harbours,
roads, and bridges ; of all of which considerable remains have been

preserved. Curtius (" On the Waterworks in Greek Cities " in
Archœologische Zeitung, 1847, p. 19, ss.) has laid down, as the
leading principle of Greek aqueducts, their accommodation to the
natural conditions of the soil, widely different in this respect from
the waterworks of the Romans, " who, in their imperial manner,
made the fountains follow one straight line from their origin
to the capital ; and in this way accomplished marvellous
edifices entirely independent of the conditions of the soil."
The oldest epoch of town waterworks is undoubtedly marked by
the cistern, which became necessary where the dryness of the soil
required the collection of rain-water, or where the wells became
insufficient for the increasing population. They are mostly perpendicular, gradually widening shafts, hewn into the living rock,
and covered with slabs ; one descended into them on steps. Such
cisterns are frequently found in Delos, at Iulis in Keos, at Old-
Thuria in Messenia, and at Athens in the southern parts of the
city, and on the stony backs of the hills which slope towards the
sea ; while in the eastern and northern parts of the city we find
numerous remains of wells, often connected by subterraneous
channels. To a later epoch, mostly to the time of the Tyrannis,
belong the waterworks, by means of which the fountains rising
on the neighbouring mountains are led (in communications hewn
in the rock, or enclosed by walls) into reservoirs, and distributed
thence over the town by a system of canals. By a system of this
kind the springs of the Hymettos, Pentelikon, and Parnes were
conducted into Athens ; and, in a similar manner, several villages
in the dry plains of Attika were supplied with water by subterraneous aqueducts, partly still in use. Of other waterworks we
mention an aqueduct seven stadia long, dug through a mountain
by Eupalinos ; a system of works supplying the castle of Thebes
with water ; and the underground aqueducts of Syrakusæ, the
latter of which are still in use. The remains of these, as well as of
other aqueducts near Argos, Mykenæ, Demetrias, and Pharsalos,
prove sufficiently the care taken by the Greeks in this important
branch of architecture.

Although natural harbours were frequent on the Greek coast,
many of them required additional arrangements for the safety of
the ships at anchor. We possess, for instance, the remains of a
stone jetty, built for the protection of the excellent harbour of

Pylos, on the west coast of Messenia.   It is built, like the walls of the town, in the Pelasgic manner, horizontal layers being the rule,

and extends considerably into the sea, so as to protect the harbour against storms and currents.   Fig. 79 illustrates a bird's-eye view of the remnants of the breakwater.

Fig. 79.

More extensive were the works in the harbour of Methone, or Mothone (the modern Modon), to the south of Pylos.   To the line of cliffs, which naturally protects the harbour, a wall has been added, extending into the sea in the shape of a repeatedly broken bow, and surrounds the harbour proper on three sides in connection with the equally secured shore; Fig. 80 shows the plan of the har-

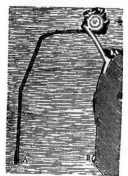

bour, which is still in frequent use.   A and B mark the points where remnants of the old masonry are still in existence.   Other harbours were on a still larger scale, and supplied with arsenals, lighthouses, temples, and works of art; of these, the Korinthian harbour at Kenchreæ and the Piræus are the most remarkable.

The harbour proper consisted in the latter also in natural bays, turned to account and further protected by walls built into the sea on both sides of the entrance, so as to defend the inner space against both waves and enemies.   No less complicated was the harbour of Rhodes ; according to Ross, it retains at the present day the original constructions; which, by turning to account the natural bays, made it one of the most important stations for commercial and war purposes.   Fig. 81 shows the design ; *a, b, c,* signify respectively the harbours for boats, commercial and war vessels ; *d* is the exterior harbour, *e* the site of the town.

Fig. 80.

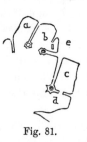

Fig. 81.

Concerning the roads of the Greeks we certainly have written evidence of carefully paved roads and streets, particularly in con-

nection with the festive processions to the great national places of
worship ; but little is said about the method of the Greeks in these
structures, and only few remnants remain to enlighten us as to the
way in which they were made even, or paved.   In low, boggy places
the want of level and secure roads was naturally felt first ; their
earliest form seems to have been that of dams ($\chi\acute{\omega}\mu\alpha\tau\alpha$, $\gamma\acute{\epsilon}\phi\upsilon\rho\alpha\iota$).
According to Curtius, a dam led from Kopai, in Bœotia, to the
opposite shore of the Kopaic bog.   It is 22 feet wide, propped by
stone walls, and supplied with a bridge, so as to give an outlet to
the water of the Kephissos.   Like the choma, which led through
the marshes of the Alphæos, and formed the border-line between
the dominions of the Tegeatai and Pallantioi, it served at the
same time both as a protection of the arable land against the
waves and as a means of communication.   Sometimes canals were
connected with such dams, an example of which is offered by
Phenea.

Roads led up to the old lordly castles " as they are found at
Orchomenos and other places."   (Curtius's " History of the Building
of Roads amongst the Greeks," 1855, p. 9.)   In later historic times,
however, the chief purposes of road-building were commercial
traffic and festive processions.   " It is the worship of the gods
which here again has given rise to art, and the holy ways were the
first artistically constructed roads amongst the Greeks " (p. 11),
connecting tribes and countries for the purpose of common celebration.   Still, at the present time Greece is crossed by roads on
which the grooves for wheels are hewn into the rocky ground.
On these the holy vehicles, with the statues of the gods and the
implements of worship, could be moved conveniently.   Between
these tracks the road was levelled by means of sand or pebbles.
Where there were no two pair of grooves, arrangements were made
to avoid collisions.

We know a little more about the construction of bridges
amongst the Greeks.   In most cases bridges across rivers and
ravines were made of wood ; as an example of a very firm, long
bridge made of wood we mention that across the Euripus,
between Aulis and Chalkis, in the island of Eubœa, built during
the Peloponnesian war, and, perhaps, afterwards superseded by a
dam-structure, remnants of which are still in existence.   There
are, however, found in Greece bridges wholly made of stone ; but

their dimensions can have been but small before the arch-vaulting
principle came into use.   Gell mentions a bridge of this kind
near Mykenæ, and another similar one near Phlius the coverings
of which consisted of blocks of stone.

Wider rivers were crossed by a mode of structure which we
have mentioned in connection with the openings of gates and
walls.   The layers of stones were pushed gradually towards each
other from both sides, and when the space between was thus
sufficiently diminished it was covered by slabs of stone, or rafters,
laid across.   This system is used in a bridge between Pylos and

Methone, near the village
of Metaxidi, in Messenia
(Fig. 82).   Only the lower
layers are antique; the
arch is of later date.

A complicated and
well-calculated structure
is the bridge across the
river Pamisos in Messenia.
It is placed where a
smaller river falls into

Fig. 82.

the river Pamisos, and consists of three parts, one of which lies
towards Messene, the second towards Megalopolis, and the third
towards Franco Eclissia (Andania).   (See plan, Fig. 83, and view,
Fig. 84).   The front parts of the pillars of the two branches

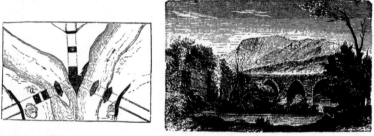

Fig. 83.   Fig. 84.

crossing the two rivers are pointed, so as to break the force of the
waves.   The piece *a* in Fig. 83 is illustrated by Fig. 85; it shows
one smaller opening which is covered with straight pieces of stone
while the larger opening shows the gradual approach of the layers

This is shown by the remaining old layers, to which, later, an arch has been added.

The same form of covering is found in a bridge across the Eurotas, near Sparta (see design, Fig. 86).   In looking at Fig.

Fig. 85.

Fig. 86.   Fig. 87.

87 it ought to be remembered that the pointed arch of the vault is a later addition.   (About a peculiar kind of waterworks, viz., the fountain-houses, see § 21, Figs. 90 and 91.)

21. After the buildings destined to protect man against man, we have to consider those which shelter him against the influences of nature, viz., the human habitation.   The first human habitations, not to mention caves, were amongst the Greeks, as amongst other primitive nations, huts, constructed differently according to the nature of the country.   They were said to have been invented by Pelasgos, the progenitor of the Pelasgic tribe in Arkadia.   Of such huts and similar more or less primitive dwellings we possess neither descriptions nor actual specimens.   The stages of development from the hut to the regular dwelling-house, as described in the Homeric poems, are likewise conjectural; the arrangements, however, of the dwellings of the old Greek royal families, which evidently are described as actually seen by that poet, can be understood, at least, in their chief features.   This applies particularly to the description of the palace of Odysseus, which, together with partial descriptions of those of Alkinoos, Priamos, and of the house-like tent of Achilles, conveys a sufficiently clear notion of the royal mansion of the time.

According to these descriptions the royal palace was divided into three parts, the distinction of which is recognisable in Homer. The same division, with such modifications as were necessitated by the more limited space, applied, undoubtedly, also to the more important private houses. The first division was intended for every-day life and intercourse; it consisted of the courtyard (called αὐλή by Homer), into which one entered from the street, through a door of two leaves (τὰ πρόθυρα, θύραι δίκλιδες). In the middle of this courtyard stood the statue of Zeus, the protector of dwellings (Ζεὺς ἑρκεῖος). It was surrounded by outhouses destined for the keeping of stores, for handmills, bedrooms of the male servants, and stables for horses and cattle, unless the latter were kept in separate farms. Opposite the gate of the yard was the frontage of the dwelling-house (δῶμα or δόμος) of the family of the Anax; in front of the entrance-gate was a covered portico (αἴθουσα δώματος), corresponding to a similar one on both sides of the yard (αἴθουσα αὐλῆς). This portico in front of the house must have been of considerable size as, according to Homer, it was occasionally used by the princes as the place of their assemblies. Through it one entered the forehouse, or πρόδομος, which is to be considered either as a kind of entrance-hall to the house proper, running along its frontage, or as the innermost part of the αἴθουσα δώματος, in which case it was, perhaps, closed by a wall. In this place the couches of the guests were prepared for the night.

The dwelling-house (δῶμα) of the Anax and his family, which follows after the πρόδομος, comprises the hall of the men, the women's rooms, the connubial chamber, the armoury, and the treasury. The hall of the men (τὸ μέγαρον) was the chief room of the palace; according to Homer it was a large room resting on columns. Perhaps, in contrast to the light and airy prodomos, it is described as shady (σκιόεις), the light entering only through windows at the sides, or through an opening in the smoky ceiling, which served also to let out the smoke. Near the back wall of the megaron, and opposite the door which led to the women's chambers, stood the hearth (ἐσχάρη), on which the meal of the revellers in the hall was prepared. The floor was of stone, perhaps varied in colour, and the walls were covered with large pieces of polished metal. It is true that the megaron of Odysseus, the ruler of a poor, rocky island, was bare of these ornaments; but the palaces of richer kings, like, for instance, that of Menelaos, undoubtedly showed this favourite old wall-decoration, not to speak of the perhaps fictitious description of the splendid hall of Alkinoos. The question about the nature of the μεσόδμαι, mentioned by Homer, we do not wish to decide definitely; some modern archæologists, like Rumpf and Winckler,[1] the one following the other's investigations, consider them to be two galleries, placed at the end of the megaron, on both sides of the entrance to the women's chambers : older commentators believe the mesodmai to be niches between the pilasters, or these pilasters themselves. We ourselves incline to the latter opinion, because such a gallery would be quite adapted to the hall of a hostelry, used as a women's room in the daytime and a sleeping-room for the men at night, but in the megaron of a palace it seems strangely out of place.

The third division was devoted to the smaller family circle ; its collective name was originally θάλαμοι, afterwards changed into γυναικωνῖτις. A small corridor (πρόθυρον) led to these rooms, the largest of which was a hall on the ground-floor, belonging to the female members of the family and their handmaidens. Smaller chambers, being the bedrooms of the maidservants, fifty in number, in the house of Odysseus, might be found by the side of this hall, while the upper story (ὑπερῷον) contained separate sleeping and sitting rooms for the members of the king's family. The connubial chamber, or thalamos proper, of the king and queen was, perhaps, in the lower story, at the end of the large hall of the women ; it seems, at least, that Odysseus placed his bedroom there, from the fact of his cutting the top off an olive-tree in his yard, and using the stem as a post of his connubial couch. Near it, most likely, was the armoury, although certain archæologists have placed it, like the connubial chamber, in the upper story.

Thus much about the house of the Anax in Homer's time. Many conjectures as to the situation of the staircases to the upper story, the place and destination of the tholos, of the corridors of the spear-stand, etc., we have purposely omitted. In Homer's time such palaces, varying according to the locality and the owner's wealth, were scattered all over Greece. Many theories as to details, mostly founded on vague conjectures, have, for the

---

[1] A. Winckler, "The Dwelling-houses of the Greeks." Berlin, 1868, p. 31-55.

greater part, been exploded by Hercher (in his meritorious paper "Homer and Ithaka, as it was in reality," in "Hermes," vol. i., p. 263, ss.)

As an important part of the fortified palace we have still to mention the treasury (θησαυρός), the firm construction of which guaranteed the safety of its valuable contents, as is proved by several vaults still in existence. Amongst these we mention particularly the treasure-house of Atreus, remains of which are found amongst the above-mentioned Cyclopic remnants at Mykenæ. This thesauros, which is expressly mentioned by Pausanias, has been re-discovered and repeatedly described by modern scholars. It consists of a round chamber lying on the slope of a hill. (See plan, Fig. 88, and section, Fig. 89.) The entrance is through a space enclosed by walls (A); the gate (B) is formed by horizontal layers of stone, and covered with an

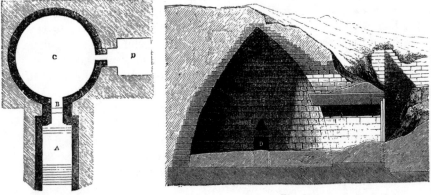

Fig. 88.   Fig. 89.

enormous slab of stone, over which, as in the lion's gate (see Fig. 65), a triangular opening has been left so as to protect it from the weight of the upper stones. Through this door, on which the traces of nails are still observable (destined evidently to fix a metal coating), one enters the chief apartment (C), which is joined at the side by another chamber (D). The latter is cut into the rock, while the walls of the chief apartment consists of horizontal layers of stones arranged in a circular form. These layers approach each other towards the top, which produces the appearance of a cupola, closed at the top by a larger stone (Fig. 89).

Pausanias mentions several thesauroi, the convenient arrange-ment of which is exemplified by the one described above. At Mykenæ he mentions, besides the treasure-house of Atreus, those of his sons, of which also remnants are still in existence. At Orchomenos, in Bœotia, he mentions the thesauros of Minyas as a wonderful work, unsurpassed by any monument in Greece or elsewhere (Pausanias, 9, 38, 1). His description tallies perfectly with the construction of the treasure-house at Mykenæ, but for the size, the latter being only 48 feet in diameter, against 70 of the Orchomenos thesauros.

The same principle of forming the vaults by overlaying has been applied to other buildings, as tombs of heroes, fountain-houses, and religious treasure-houses, at an early period. Ross has discovered a fountain-house in the island of Kos, in which the tholos principle has been applied in a similar manner. About one and a half hour's walk from the city of Kos on the slope of Mount Oromedon, lies the well Burinna, which supplies the town

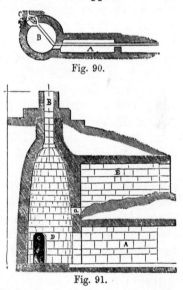

Fig. 90.

Fig. 91.

with water. In order to keep it quite cold and pure a circular chamber (2,85 metres in diameter and 7 metres in height, up to the round opening in the vault) has been erected, into which the water runs, and from which it issues through a subterraneous canal 35 metres in length, and of an aver-age height of 2 metres. Fig. 90 shows the mouth of the canal (A), the chamber (B), and the cleft in the rock (C) whence the water is-sues ; between this and the cham-ber there is a door. The chamber (see Fig. 91, D) is built like the treasure-house at Mykenæ, and opens at the top by means of a shaft (B) 3 metres high, which leads through the mountain in order to connect the water with the open air. Above the roof of the canal (A) (which consists partly of large horizontal blocks of stone, partly of long, narrow pieces of freestone) a small chamber (E) has been discovered, the entrance to which lies on the slope of the mountain, between the mouth of the canal and the opening of the shaft.   It is connected by a small window (A) with the principal chamber, and may have been the sanctuary of the nymphs of the fountain, or the watchman's dwelling, besides letting in fresh air to the fountain in addition to the shaft (B).

22. About the historic dwelling-house of the Greeks our information is almost as scanty as about the Homeric palace. Remaining specimens are totally wanting, perhaps with *one* exception ; and a systematic description of the Greek house by Vitruvius seems to relate more to the splendid mansions of post-Alexandrine times than to the houses of the common citizens. His account, moreover, is not easily understood ; so that about this most important feature of Greek domestic life little is to be ascertained.

In comparing the historic Greek house with that of the Homeric poems, we find, as an important deviation, that in the latter the women's chamber was always in the upper story ; while in the former, men's and women's apartments, although separated, lay generally on the same flat.   This rule, however, is not without exceptions with regard to both cases.

Both the Homeric and the historic houses have, in common, the important feature of a courtyard.   In both it is surrounded by columns, and forms, as it were, the centre round which the other parts of the house are grouped equally, and into which the single rooms open.   The historic house, however, was much inferior in size and splendour to that described by Homer, as was natural, seeing that it was inhabited by simple citizens instead of kings and rulers of the people.   Homer never even mentions private dwellings.   Moreover, it was a peculiarity of the Greeks, in their best times, to concentrate all their splendour and luxury in the adornment of temples and other public edifices, while their private dwellings were small and modest, not to say mean.   The homes of the Greeks were their public places, their Stoas and Agoras ; on these they looked with pride and joy ; only in the Makedonian period, when Greek freedom and greatness had vanished, luxurious private houses became the fashion ; while at the same time begin the complaints of both religious and civic buildings being more and more neglected.   But even then buildings of large size and

great splendour were more common in the country seats of the
rich than in the towns, where the limits of space and the regular
lines of the streets precluded a too great extension.

Hence one yard only was the rule for town-houses. The
descriptions by Vitruvius of numerous splendid rooms, etc.,
evidently refer to the palace-like buildings of the time after
Alexander; still these descriptions are of great importance to us.
For in that part of the house first described by him, which he
calls gynaikonitis, the original nucleus of an old Greek dwelling
seems preserved; while the second part, called andronitis, contains the additions of increased and more refined luxury. We
must try first to recognise the old simple house in his description.

" On entering[1] the door," Vitruvius says, " one comes into a
rather narrow passage, called by the Greeks θυρωρεῖον." It
corresponds to our modern passage. To right and left of it are
rooms for domestic purposes. Vitruvius mentions on the one
side tables, and on the other, the porters' rooms. Through the
passage, which is also called θυρών or πυλών, one enters the
περιστύλιον. The peristylion is an open yard surrounded by
colonnades, also described as αὐλή τόπος περικίων. " This
peristylion," Vetruvius continues, "has colonnades on three sides.
But on the southern side are two antæ (*i.e.* front and wall pillars),
which stand at a considerable distance from each other, and carry
a beam. They form the entrance to a room, the depth of which
is equal to two-thirds of the interval between the antæ. This
place is called by some προστάς, by others παραστάς;" it is,
therefore, a room which, on its broad side, opens into the yard;
an open hall, in fact, to which, most likely, the not uncommon
expression παστάς may also be applied.

" Further towards the interior," Vitruvius concludes, " are
large rooms, where the lady of the house sits with the maids at
their wheels. To the right and left of the prostas are bedrooms
(cubicula), one of which is called thalamus, the other amphitha-
lamus. All round the yard, under the colonnades, are rooms for
domestic purposes, such as eating-rooms, bedrooms, and small
rooms for the servants. This part of the house is called gynaikonitis." In this gynaikonitis, as we said before, we recognise the

---

[1] We omit the references to the Roman house contained in his description, as to
this we shall have to return hereafter.

old Greek house.   The husband, whose life passed in public, possessed only the smaller outer part of it; while in the interior

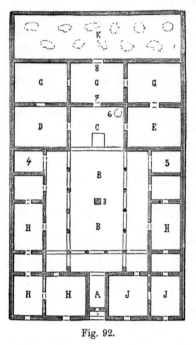

Fig. 92.

the housewife, with her maids, was in command.   Fig. 92 is meant to illustrate the plan of an old Greek dwelling on this basis.

The above-mentioned chief parts are easily recognisable. A is the small passage, B the open courtyard surrounded by colonnades, C the open hall ($\pi\rho o\sigma\tau\acute{a}\varsigma$, $\pi a\rho a\sigma\tau\acute{a}\varsigma$, $\pi a\sigma\tau\acute{a}\varsigma$), to which are joined the bedroom of the master of the house (D) (the thalamos); and on the other side the amphithalamos, perhaps the bedroom of the daughters.   At the back of these are good-sized rooms for the maids (G), working under the supervision of their mistress. Round the yard, and opening into the colonnades, lie other rooms for domestic purposes, such as storerooms, bedrooms (H), etc., some of which, on both sides of the street-door and looking towards the street, were frequently used as shops or workshops (J).   Behind the house, and more or less shut in by the neighbouring houses, might be a garden (K), frequently mentioned by ancient writers.

The street-door leading into the passage was mostly in a line with the façade.[1]   The expressions $\pi\rho\acute{o}\theta\upsilon\rho o\nu$ and $\pi\rho o\pi\acute{\upsilon}\lambda a\iota o\nu$, however, seem to indicate that in some houses there must have been a small space in front of the door, which might be adorned with antæ, or, as is proved by the still-existing remains of a private house, with columns (see Fig. 92).   By the propylaion stood frequently, if not generally, the image of Apollo Aggieus (2); perhaps at some distance from the house was placed the symbol of

[1] A street-door is illustrated in Gerhard's "Goblets of the Royal Museum of Berlin."   Table XXVII.

Hermes as the protecting god of roads and traffic. It consisted merely of a column or pillar.

In the yard usually stood an altar, separate and visible from every side, and dedicated to Zeus Herkeios, as the supreme protector of the family. This circumstance is already mentioned in Homer. According to Petersen's opinion, the sanctuaries of the θεοὶ κτήσιοι (the gods giving possession) and of the θεοὶ πατρῷοι (the gods of families or generations) were placed in the *alæ* (4 and 5), a less accessible part of the house, but connected with the colonnade. From the courtyard one entered the open hall which, as it were, formed the boundary between the public and the private life of the family, and therefore was most adapted for the gatherings of the family at religious offerings and common meals. It is therefore here that the hearth, the holy place of the house, devoted to Hestia, the all-preserving goddess, must most likely be placed. Originally it was no doubt used for cooking, but even later, when a separate kitchen had become necessary, the hearth remained the centre of the house, and on this altar all the events of domestic life were celebrated by religious acts.[1] " A particular occasion," says Petersen, " for worshipping Hestia was offered by all important changes in the family, such as a departure, a return from a journey, or a reception into the family, even of slaves, who always took part in the domestic worship of Hestia. Birth, giving of a name, wedding, or death, were celebrated in like manner. This altar was also holy as an asylum ; to it flew the slave to escape punishment, on it the stranger, nay, even the enemy of the house, found protection ; for the worship of Hestia united all the inhabitants of the house, free-born or slaves, nay, even strangers." For this important function of the altar, the place assigned to it by us seems the most appropriate.

To the right and left of the prostas were the thalamos and amphithalamos, in the former of which were placed the sanctuaries of the connubial deities ; in the back wall of the prostas was a door, which is frequently mentioned by ancient authors as particularly important for the arrangement of the Greek house. It is called μέταυλος, to distinguish it from the door leading into the

---

[1] See Petersen, "The Domestic Worship of the Greeks," in *Zeitschrift für Alterthumswissenschaft.* 1851. P. 199. Petersen places the altar in the large hall of the men, which, according to him, separates the two yards.

yard from the outside, the θύρα αὔλειος, " because it lies opposite
the αὔλειος, *beyond* or *behind* the αὐλή." [1]   In case it was closed,
the maid-servants, who seem to have been employed in the workrooms, and slept on the floor above (πύργοι), were secluded from the
other parts of the house,—a circumstance repeatedly mentioned
by Greek authors.   Where there was a garden, it was connected
with the house by a door (8), called θύρα κηπαία (garden-door).

So much about the older Greek house with one court.   The
numerous descriptions of the enlarged house differ in so many points
that a new attempt at an analysis may seem desirable ; it will be
based entirely on the practical con-
siderations which must have led
to the addition of a second yard.
In the towns, at least, this change
must at first have been applied
to buildings already in existence.
The increase of luxury made a
more commodious enlargement of
the houses of the wealthy desirable.   This extension had to be
directed towards the back, the
frontage being fixed by the line
of the street ; while, on the other
hand, the frequently occurring
gardens might be conveniently
used for the introduction of a
second yard.   In consequence,
the whole first part of the house
has remained unchanged (see
Fig. 93) ; the only innovation
being that from the metaulos
(Fig. 92, 7) one gets immediately
into the second yard (K), instead of into one of the large
workrooms.   These workrooms

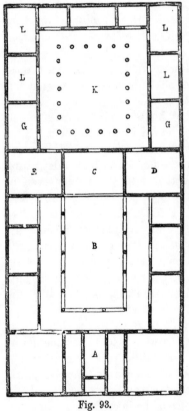

Fig. 93.

(G), together with other apart-
ments (L), were arranged in a manner which, with regard to size
and position, must have varied greatly, according to circumstances.

_____

[1] See Becker, "Charikles."   2d edition.   II., p. 88.

The additional space so gained was appropriated by the narrower family circle, while the first part became the scene of the more public intercourse. The metaulos remains the boundary between the two parts, from which circumstance alone its hitherto unexplained second name μέσαυλος can be derived. The metaulos (door *behind* the first yard) becomes in this way a mesaulos (door *between* two yards). The prostas, in the back wall of which this door lies, retains its importance, derived from the sacred hearth. This arrangement becomes still more likely from its analogy with the *tablinum* in the Roman house, which, as we shall show, was most likely an imitation of the prostas.[1]

It need not be added that the above description is intended only to convey a very general notion of the Greek dwelling-house.

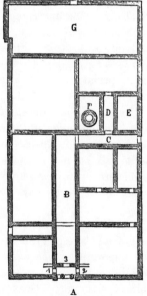

A

Fig. 94.

Fig. 95.

The rule was naturally modified by the nature of the locality, the requirements of individual families, etc., in the same way as this may be observed in the houses of Pompeii, which illustrate the construction of the Roman house in manifold varieties, or in modern dwelling-houses. The only preserved specimen, indeed, of a Greek private house shows many deviations even from the important features

---

[1] We call the reader's attention to Winckler's comprehensive researches ("The Dwelling-houses of the Greeks," Berlin, 1868, p. 133, *ss.*), from whom, however, we differ in several points.

of our plan. We are speaking of a building which has been
discovered in the isle of Delos (Fig. 94).   It shows a very
beautiful vestibule (προπύλαιον), which lies on the narrow
side towards the street, and consists of two Ionic columns
between two graceful antæ (Fig. 95).   To right and left small
doors (Fig. 94, 1 and 2) lead into side-rooms, while the large
door (3) leads into a narrow passage (B).   The aula (C) to
which this passage leads is very short and narrow, and seems
to have been without columns.   Unfortunately, the rooms adjoining the passage and the yard have not been described by
the archæologists who investigated the building; they only tell
us of the existence of a cistern (F).   The room D, open on both
sides, may perhaps be considered as a very small prostas, in which
case the room to the right of it (E) would be the thalamos; G
would then be the second yard, but here also no columns seem to
have been found.   The editors believe the building to have been
a public bath—which, however, seems unlikely from its moderate
dimensions.   The cistern, which seems to have given rise to this
idea, may just as well have belonged to a private house.   The
Greeks were just as anxious to have a water-reservoir in their
houses as we are at the present day.   Parts of the important
building in Delos have, as Ross complains, been destroyed to gain
stones and mortar for new buildings.   But for this barbarous
custom, whole quarters of the town might still be in existence.
Under many, perhaps most, of the houses cisterns were dug, partly
(according to their width) spanned by small arches, partly covered
with long pieces of granite.

    23. From the dwelling of living individuals we now turn to the
abode of the dead, from the house to the grave.   The piety of the
Hellenic people made the latter of great importance; hence the
astonishing variety of their forms.   We will divide them into groups,
according to the different modes of their construction.   Graves,
therefore, may be heaps of earth, they may be hewn into the rock,
or they may be detached buildings, according to the conditions
of the locality or the mode of burying.   Within these divisions
there are, again, many varieties of size, form, and construction.

    In places where stone was scarce, mounds were made of earth;
where stones were found in the ground, these were heaped on each
other; where the soil was rocky, natural caves were used, or arti-

ficial ones dug. Such are the oldest forms of graves; only later, when civilisation was more advanced, separate monuments were more commonly erected.

a. Tombs consisting of earth-mounds, as the oldest and simplest form of graves, were common to the Caucasian race, as is shown by numerous remains from east to west. Greece also is rich in such primitive structures, which in a small chamber contain the remains of the dead, and, by their imposing forms, serve at the same time as monuments. Owing to the primitive mode of their structure their appearance resembles more the works of nature than that of human hands; they were called by the Greeks κολωνοί (hills), another expression χώματα (heaps), being derived from their kind of construction. Of this kind are the enormous mounds of earth which are still to be seen on the shores of the Hellespont, and which, according to old Greek traditions, contain the remains of Homeric heroes, like Achilles, Patroklos, Aias, and Protesilaos. Tombs of the same kind were erected by the Athenians in the Marathonian plain to those fallen in the great battle; the largest

Fig. 96.   Fig. 97.

of these was originally 30 feet high (see Fig. 96). Smaller tumuli are numerous in the Attic plain; of a similar kind are also the large burial hills of the Bosphoranian kings which are found at Pantikapaion, on the Kimmeric Bosphorus (see Fig. 97).

In order to add to the firmness of these mounds, and to avoid the sliding down of the earth, they were frequently surrounded by a stone enclosure, as for instance was the case with the tombs of Æpytos at Pheneos, in Arkadia, and of Œnomaos at Olympia. There still exists in the island of Syme a tumulus which exactly answers to the description of Pausanias. Its diameter is 19 metres; it is quite surrounded by a stone wall

(κρηπίς or θριγκός) 1·25-2·19 metres in height, which consists of
polygonal stones (λίθοι ἀγροί, λογάδες) (see Figs. 98 and 99).　The
conical mound has been destroyed almost entirely.

Fig. 98.　　　　　　　　　　　　　　　　　　Fig. 99.

Mounds of this kind were also made of stone, as for instance
the tomb of Laïos, near Daulis, mentioned by Pausanias, to which
kind we shall have to return.

Fig. 100.

b. Another kind
of primitive tombs
were caves in rocks,
either natural or arti-
ficial, and decorated
by art.　Of these
also we have to
distinguish various
kinds.　A natural ca-
vern may have been
extended and used as
a tomb; or the rocky
soil may have been
hollowed into a sub-
terraneous chamber;
or, lastly, a more or
less separate piece of
rock may have been
excavated and deco-
rated externally.　The
caves and galleries of
quarries must have
led to the idea of

Fig. 101.

subterraneous graves in rocks at a very early period.　Structures
of this kind (the name of which, Kyklopeia, denotes their great
age) are found near Nauplia.　Similar caverns of irregular formation may be seen near Gortyna, in the isle of Crete; more

regularity is shown in the Nekropolis of Syrakuse, which also
seems to have been occasioned by quarries. Simple shafts of
great depth, ending in a burial chamber, are found amongst
the above-mentioned royal tombs of Pantikapaion (see Figs. 97

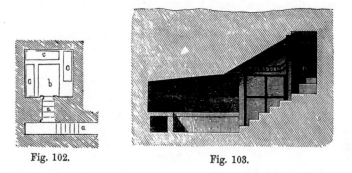

Fig. 102.   Fig. 103.

and 100), where a tunnel, erected of blocks of stone, has also been
discovered (see Fig. 101).

The burial caverns of both old and more modern dates found in
the islands are still more numerous and important than those of the
Greek peninsula. Some of them are cut into the rock in such a
manner that the ceiling requires no additional props, as is the
case, for instance, in a tomb in the island of Ægina, of which
Figs. 102 and 103 show the plan and section. A narrow staircase
(*a*) leads to the entrance, which has the form of an arch (*b*), and
through it into the burial-chamber. The latter contains three

Fig. 104.

sarcophagi, which are constructed of simple slabs of stone, with
a cover of the same material. They occupy three sides of the
chamber.

A grave in the isle of Melos contains three sarcophagi on each

side, which stand in semicircular niches, as is shown by the plan
(Fig. 104) and the section (Fig. 105, scale = 10 metres).

In other tombs the ceiling has been propped by pillars and
cross-walls, by means of which the interior is at the same time
divided into several separate chambers. A burial-chamber in

Fig. 105.

Delos shows two pillars (a) on each of the two side-walls, between
which lie small niches (b) (see plan, Fig. 106). In each of these
niches are two sarcophagi, placed one on the top of the other.
The height of the grave is 2·30 metres. The ceiling consists of
stone slabs joined closely together (see Fig. 107).

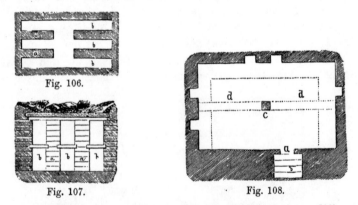

Fig. 106.

Fig. 107.   Fig. 108.

A subterraneous grave in the isle of Chalke shows a different
arrangement (Fig. 108). A narrow staircase (b) leads to the
entrance-door (a). Inside the chamber ($14\frac{1}{2}$ feet long) is a pillar
(c), from which two strong stone beams (d d) extend towards the
two smaller walls of the chamber. They carry the ceiling, consisting of slabs of stone, and lying only a few feet under the

surface. All round the room by the wall are the couches of the dead, resembling stone benches. Ross, on discovering them, found them empty. In the walls are square niches, for the reception of jugs and other objects, which it was the custom to leave with the dead. This custom (see § 35) is exemplified by the numerous graves in the small island of Chilidromia. These are

not cut into the rock, but built of chalk-stone in a simple manner, not very much below the surface. Fig. 109 shows one of them, opened by Fiedler, in which the skeletons and the offerings to the dead were found in their original position. The grave itself consists of a square hollow sufficiently large to receive the body, and surrounded by stones, the two longer walls being built of carefully fitted chalk-stones without mortar, while the two shorter sides are formed by large slabs. The body was placed with its head towards the south. Two small drinking-vessels and two copper coins were found in the same chamber, which was covered with three large stone slabs. At the foot-end of the body was

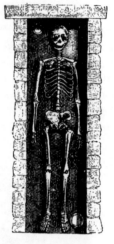

another smaller room, enclosed and covered in a similar manner, and, like a store-room, containing a number of objects, all destined for the dead. Amongst these were one large and several smaller cans, an oil-pitcher, several vases for offerings, and various drink-

Fig. 109.

ing-cups, all made of burnt clay; there was also a bronze mirror An earthen lamp showed distinct traces of having been used.

The same custom was observed when the dead were buried in coffins (σοροί). Several coffins of burnt clay have been found at Athens. Fig. 110 shows a coffin covered with three slabs; Fig. 111 is an open dead-box, filled with vessels of various kinds. Another kind of graves in rocks consisted in chambers cut into the slope of a rock, the surface near the entrance being arranged architecturally. Grave-façades of this kind are very frequent in

Phrygia and Lykia; they indicate a civilisation originally foreign
to the Greeks, but imitated
by them even during their
historic times, from which
many of these monuments
date.

Fig. 110.

The Lykian graves display
a most curious imitation of
wood-architecture, carried into the minutest details.   Usually the
façade is divided into several parts by means of beams protruding
from the surface (see Fig. 112).   Our illustration shows a grave
in a steep slope of a rock at Xanthos; the imitation of wood is
carried even to the copying of nails and pegs to join the different beams; it resembles the frontage of a house solidly built of
timber, with a ceiling of unhewn trunks of trees, such as the huts

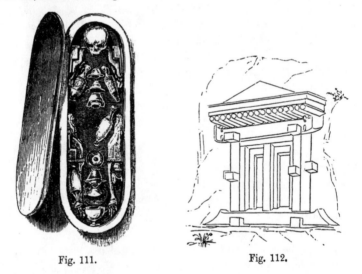

Fig. 111.   Fig. 112.

of Lykian peasants have at the present day.   A perpendicular
beam in the middle divides the façade into two deepened partitions.
Sometimes the cross-beams quite protrude from the surface, in
which case a kind of porch is formed in front of the façade.   This
arrangement is found, for instance, in a grave at Myra (see
Fig. 113), which, moreover, is decorated with excellent paintings
both by the side of the façade and inside the entrance-hall.   A

grave at Telmessos (Fig. 114) shows a complete façade in the Ionic style. Two Ionic columns between two antæ carry a pediment adorned with acroteria, and forming in this way the portico; in the back wall is the entrance to the burial-chamber.

Graves with façades of this kind are also frequently found on the Greek continent—more frequently, indeed, it seems than in the islands; sometimes artificial constructions have been added to increase the natural firmness of the rock. In a grave in the island of Thera, discovered by Ross, the chamber is formed by

Fig. 113.

a natural cleft in the rock; but the walls have been propped by masonry, and the ceiling consists of slabs of stone. Another grave in the slope of a hill, discovered by the same scholar in the island of Kos, consists of a small forecourt, which leads to the entrance-door, decorated in the best Ionic style, remnants of which have been preserved in a chapel close by. The grave itself (see plan, Fig. 115, and section, Fig. 116) consists of a vaulted chamber, 6 metres in

Fig. 114.

length (*a*), on both sides of which are the couches of the dead (*b b*), 2·50 metres long by 66 centimetres wide. Fragments in the best Ionic style found near it most likely belonged to the separate porch of this grave-chamber, which, according to an inscription, was the heroon of Charmylos and his family.

A grave at Lindos, in the isle of Rhodes, is entirely worked into the rock. It is one of the most perfect specimens of this style,

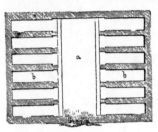

Fig. 115.

Fig. 116.

imitated most likely from the monuments of the opposite Lykian coast. Instead of the above-mentioned Lykian wood-imitations we here, however, find the forms of Greek architecture in the decoration of the façade. Fig. 117 gives an illustration of the grave, which unfortunately is in a very decayed condition. The façade resembles a Greek portico, with Doric columns, an architrave, frieze, and cornice. Of these columns, originally twelve in number, four are said to have been detached, while the others protruded from the surface of the wall

Fig. 117.

by halves or a little more. Larger structures of the kind have been discovered in Cyprus. The one discovered by Ross shows the form of a court surrounded by columns (see view, Fig. 118, and the plan, Fig. 119). Finally, we mention

the beautiful graves at Kyrene, on the north coast of Africa.

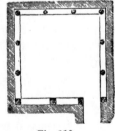

Fig. 118.

Fig. 119.

The rocky ground near the city has been worked into terraces,

in which the graves are situated. The graves themselves mostly
consist of small chambers cut into the rock, and are for the

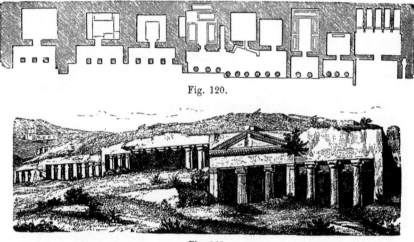

Fig. 120.

Fig. 121.

greater part adorned with porticoes, which give them a most
picturesque appearance. Fig. 120 shows the plan, Fig. 121 the
perspective view, of a terrace adorned with a long row of grave-
façades; Fig. 122 shows the dwellings of the living in the close
vicinity of the city of the dead at Kyrene.

Fig. 122.

c. In and on graves of this kind are found many objects, either
for the purpose of adorning them or for that of indicating the

identity of the body.   Of vessels and other utensils intended for
the use of the dead, we have spoken before.   When the buried
person began to be considered as a hero, the grave required an
altar.   (Graves were commonly called heroa, even if not in the
form of temples.)   Such altars, in the shape of dice, with the
name of the dead inscribed on them, are numerous in Bœotia
round the Helicon.   Others, round in shape, and either smooth,
with only an inscription (like one at Delos, Fig. 123), or adorned
with sculptures, mostly of garlands and skulls of bulls, belong
principally to the Greek islands (see Figs. 44 and 45); on others

Fig. 123.   Fig. 124.

figures are represented.   An altar found in a grave at Delos
(Fig. 124) shows the representation of an offering in bas-relief,
besides the inscription—

ΠΑΥΣΑΝΙΑΣ ΜΕΙΔΟΝΟΣ ΧΑΙΡΕ

The gravestones discovered by Ross in the isle of Kasos are of
very extraordinary appearance.   They consist of semi-globes of
blue marble, about 8-10 inches in diameter, in the smooth
front side of which the name of the deceased has been chiselled
in several lines of letters, belonging to the third or fourth century B.C.

   The most common kind of above-ground monuments for the
dead all over Greece till far into Asia, are the old Attic stelai
(στήλη).   They are narrow, slender slabs of stone, gently taper-
ing towards the top ; they stand erect, fastened in the ground, or
on a bema, and have the name of the deceased inscribed on them.

They are crowned with anthemia, *i.e.* ornaments of flowers and leaves, either in relief or painted, sometimes also with pediments adorned with rosettes; sometimes the stele shows representations, relating to the life of the deceased, in bas-relief. In the times of the Makedonians and Romans the stele becomes shorter and broader, with a pediment at the top. Fig. 125 shows a stele, found at Athens, with a palmetto-ornament.

Peculiar to Attica are the grave columns of blue Hymettic marble, with inscriptions on them, round which were wound ribbons and wreaths in memory of the dead. Figs. 126 and 127, both taken from Athenian earthen vessels, illustrate these columns, one of them being flat at the top, the other adorned with a capital of acanthus-leaves. Other stelai show the form of small chapel-like buildings (heroa), between the surrounding columns of Fig. 125. which the forms of the dead are represented in relief. Fig. 128 shows a monument of this kind, found in a grave in the isle of Delos;

Fig. 126. Fig. 127. Fig. 128.

Fig. 129, a similar one dug out at Athens, the bas-relief of which shows the taking leave of the deceased, called "Phrasykleia," from the surrounding friends, a favourite subject during the best period of Greek art. Portrait-statues, in full or half figure, were, during the Makedonian and Roman times, frequently placed on the graves, or, if space permitted it, inside the heroa; this was the custom particularly in the islands. Fragments of such statues

from the graves of the Telesikratides, the ruling noble family of
Anaphe, have been found in that island ; Ross
conjectures that the roof-like covers of sarcophagi
found in the isle of Rhenæa also used to carry
statues of this kind.

Fig. 129.

Frequently detached coffins, or sarcophagi,
wrought of stone, are found in the grave-
chambers, in which the bodies were deposited.
These are numerous in Lykia, but in Greece
they have been found only in a few cases at
Platææ, and in the islands of Thera, Karpathos,
and Anaphe.

24. In the constructions of Greek tombs above the earth, two
technical divisions must be made.

a. The first consists of graves cut from the rock, but
transformed into real buildings by means of outside and inside

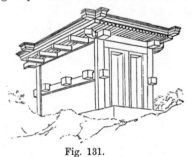

Fig. 131.

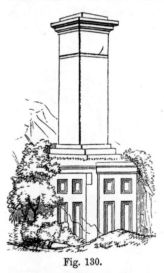

Fig. 130.

arrangements and decorations. Of
this kind the most numerous and
varied examples are naturally found
in the rocky Lykia, dating not only
from the old Lykian, but also from
the Greek times. The simplest form
consists of a square stout pillar
resting on steps, and crowned with a simple cornice. A specimen
of this form, found at Tlos, is seen Fig. 130. A second form is
that of the imitation of a complete wooden house, of which the
above-mentioned graves only gave the façade (Fig. 131).
Trunks of trees joined together seemed to form the roof, which
protrudes considerably on all sides, and is both finished and

crowned by a horizontal cornice, formed by the crossing each other of beams. In a third kind of grave the roof, instead of being flat, shows a pointed arch, somewhat like our pointed roofs (*Walmdächer*) (Fig. 132);

sometimes skulls of bulls, also wrought in stone, adorn their fronts. Fig. 133 shows a roof of this kind cut from the rock in the manner of a relief; it is found at Pinara. In Greece, also, graves of this kind were in use, as is shown by several specimens in the isle of Rhodes; the monuments of the coast of Lykia, lying opposite, may have been the models. Ross found near the village of Liana a rock rolled from the height, the interior of which contained a complete grave-chamber, with three couches for the dead; the exterior showed two niches, one on each side of the entrance (Fig. 134).

Fig. 132.

Grander than, and very different from, the Lykian graves, is another monument found by Ross in the isle of Rhodes. It consists of a large block of sandstone, the lower part of which has been hewn into a square form with vertical walls. Each of the long sides measures 27·81 metres, and contains twenty-one semi-

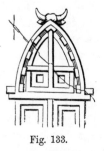

Fig. 133.

Fig. 134.

columns about 5 metres in height, which, standing on three steps, were evidently destined to carry a cornice; this, however, has been destroyed by the upper parts falling on it. Whether the top consisted of a stone pyramid, or of a hill planted with shrubs and

trees, cannot now be distinguished.   On the northern side, which
is the best preserved (see Fig. 135), between the fifth and sixth
columns of the western corner (see plan, Fig. 136; scale = 15
metres), lies a door (*a*), through which one enters the grave-
chambers.   The first compartment is an entrance-hall (*b*), 9·20
metres wide by 3 metres
deep, in the small sides of
which there are niches.   A
second door (*c*) leads into a
larger chamber (*d*), (6·70 by
4·40 metres), in the walls of
which are unequal niches,
with five couches for the
dead; these, however, were
found empty when the tomb
was opened.   On the walls of
all these chambers (which
extend only over a fourth
part of the whole basis, and
probably were joined by
others) a fine coating of
stucco has been preserved,
with some traces of painting
on it.   Tombs of this kind,
cut into the rock, were not
usual in Greece.   Detached
grave - buildings were evidently the rule, and of the
numerous varieties of these we propose to give some specimens.

Fig. 135.

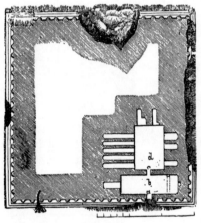

Fig. 136.

   b. The oldest and simplest buildings of this kind are the
developed forms of the above-mentioned earth-mounds.   From
surrounding these with stone walls one proceeded to building the
whole tomb of stone, and in changing the round form
for the square a quadrangular pointed stone pyramid
was arrived at.   Pausanias saw a monument of this
kind near Argos, on the road to Epidauros; it was
explained to him as the common memorial of those
slain in the fight between Proitos and Akrisios.   A
number of similar monuments have more recently
been discovered in Argolis, the most important of which, near

Fig. 137.

Kenchreai, is a pyramid built of square stones (see Figs. 137-139).
The basis is 48 feet long by 39 feet wide.   According to Ross, the
southern corner is rectangular, and here a door, covered by protruding stones in the manner of the Tirynthian galleries, leads
into a narrow passage, at the end of which one enters, by a second
door on the right-hand side, the inner chamber, measuring 10 feet
square.   It remains doubt-
ful whether this building
was a tomb or a watch-
tower.   Where the round
shape of the earth-mounds
was retained (see, for example, the grave in the isle
of Syme, Fig. 98), with
an additional architectural
arrangement of the sur-
rounding stones, the result
was a handsome round
building resting on a quad-

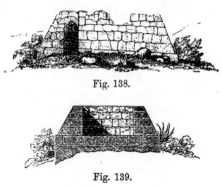

Fig. 138.

Fig. 139.

rangular base, and frequently used for tombs.   Fig. 140 shows a
beautiful specimen of this style found in the nekropolis of Kyrene.

Some of the graves at Mykenæ are old and simple.   Like the
megalithic tombs of Western Europe, they consist of roughly hewn
stones, and contain small, low
chambers, covered with large
slabs of stone.   Fig. 141 shows
the largest amongst them.

We now come to graves
of a more monumental cha-
racter.   Near Adelphi one has
been discovered which has

Fig. 140.

exactly the form of a house.   It lies amongst graves of various
kinds, and is surrounded by remnants of sarcophagi and other
ruins which indicate the site of the old nekropolis of Delphi.
Thiersch describes it as an "edifice of freestone, which shows the
antiquity of its style by the fact that the sides, the door, and a
window above it, grow narrower towards the top;" he adds that
its destination as a grave cannot be doubted (see Fig. 142).

Some tombs found at Carpuseli, in Asia Minor, are more

elegant in design. They are square and stand on some steps; the walls consist of equal blocks of freestone, showing a base at the bottom and a cornice at the top. One of the largest amongst

Fig. 141.   Fig. 142.

them (see Figs. 143 and 144) contains in the interior of the chamber, the entrance to which is not visible, a strong pillar, which carries the ceiling, consisting of large beams and slabs of stone; on it stood, perhaps, the statue of the deceased.

In the Greek islands tombs are frequently found which, like the subterraneous chambers, contain several couches for the dead. They consist of strong masonry, and their ceilings are vaulted, whence the name tholaria now commonly applied to them. The only specimen we quote (Fig. 145) has been found in the island of Amorgos. It comprises three graves, separated from each other

Fig. 143.   Fig. 144.   Fig. 145.

by slabs of stone. Over each of these is a niche in the wall, containing glass vessels, lamps, etc. The door is very low; its threshold consists of a rounded slab of stone. The tomb itself is at present covered by alluvial earth, but stood originally above ground like others of the same kind in the islands of Ikaros, Kalymnos, Leros, and others; some of these tombs contain from five to six burial compartments.

Graves of this kind were considered chiefly as safe receptacles of the remnants of the dead; others were destined at the same time to preserve the memory of the deceased by means of artistic beauty. In this manner the grave developed into the monument.

The dead, according to Greek notions, were considered as heroes, their graves were frequently called heroa, and naturally took the form of holy edifices. The façades of the above-mentioned graves in rocks remind us of those of temples, and, on the same principle, detached tombs (for instance, those in Thera and other islands) were built like temples. A tomb discovered by Fellows at Sidyma in Lykia seems to resemble a temple, with separate standing columns in the façade (see Fig. 146). The same similarity to a temple is shown by a tomb at Kyrene, the façade of which, contrary to rule, contains two doors adjoining each other (see Fig. 147).

Fig. 146.

The most perfect specimen of this style has been made known by the researches of Fellows near Xanthos in Lykia. It is in a state of almost complete destruction, but from the well-preserved base and from a number of ruins and rediscovered sculptures the plan of the whole may be con-

Fig. 147.

jectured with tolerable certainty. A model, as well as the remains of it, is in the British Museum, in which to each of the single fragments its supposed original position has been assigned. Another reconstruction, differing from the above, has been attempted by Falkener, from which we have borrowed the plan (Fig. 148) and the perspective view (Fig. 149). According to Falkener's conjectures, the monument consisted of a base 10·25 metres in length, 6·90 metres in width, and of almost the same height, adorned with two surrounding stripes of battle-scenes in relief, besides an elegant cornice. On this base rose

an Ionic peripteros, the peristylos of which had four columns
on each of the smaller, and six columns on each of the
longer, sides; the cella shows on each side two columns *in antis*.
A richly decorated door leads from the pronaos (*a*) (to which
corresponds the posticum (*b*) on the other side) into the roomy
cella (*c*). The frieze and the pediment were adorned with reliefs;
on the points of the gables stood statues, as also in the interstices

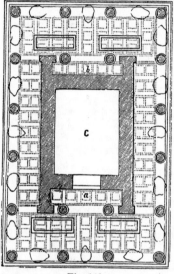

between the rich Ionic columns.
The widely-spread use of such
monuments is shown by a beautiful structure found at Cirta,
on the north coast of Africa (the
Constantine of the present day),
and said to be the grave of
King Micipsa, who founded a
Greek colony in this place. A
square structure rises on a base
of steps (as in the grave of
Theron, at Agrigentum); there
is a door on each side, worked in
relief. On the top of this structure stands a small Doric temple,
also square in shape, and showing
gables on all sides. The roof
thus formed is carried by eight
columns, again forming a square,

Fig. 148.

which stand perfectly free, and do not enclose a cella (see Fig. 150).

To conclude, we mention one of the most splendid monumental
graves that ever existed, viz., the tomb of Maussollos, King of
Karia, at Halikarnassos. Unfortunately only ruins remain, which,
by order of the British Government, have been freed from the
surrounding rubbish by Mr. C. T. Newton (1856-59), and carefully measured by the architect of the expedition, Mr. R. P.
Pullan. Pliny ("Hist. Nat.," XXXVI. 5, § 4, ed. Sillig) in his
description of this monument (considered by the ancients as one
of the seven wonders of the world) says, that Artemisia erected it
for her husband Maussollos (ob. Olympiad 167, 352 B.C.) It
is an oblong, measuring from north to south 63 feet, the front
and back being a little shorter. The circumference of the monu-

ment (*i.e.* of the peribolis) amounts to 411 feet; it rises to a height of 25 cubits ($37\frac{1}{2}$ feet), and is surrounded by thirty-six columns. The colonnade round the tomb was called the pteron. The sculptures on the east side were by Skopas, those on the north side by Bryaxis, those on the south side by Timotheos, and those on the west side by Leochares. Above the pteron rises a pyramid corresponding in size to the bottom part, which on twenty-four steps narrows itself into a pointed column. On the top is a quadriga

Fig. 149.

of marble, the work of Pythis, including which the height of the whole monument is 140 feet. From marble steps, pieces of columns, capitals, and some fragments of sculptures, together with Pliny's remarks, the mentioned English scholars have cleverly conjectured the original form of the building. The chief view of the western front is shown in Fig. 151, according to their designs. We prefer Pullan's attempt at a reconstruction to that of Falkener, inserted in our former editions. From fragments of

Fig. 150.

the horses and chariot of the quadriga, its own dimensions, as
well as the circumference of the pyramid on which it stood, can
be calculated, the height of the latter being definable by the
discovered steps, and that of the pteron by the columns, etc.   In
many places the traces of painting in red and blue have been
discovered.   Of the above-mentioned reliefs fourteen tablets
were found let into the walls of the Turkish citadel of Budrun,

Fig. 151.

built from the ruins of Halikarnassos.   In 1846 they were purchased by the English Government for the British Museum.   By
the Romans the word mausoleum was used as a general term
for tombs, reminding by their splendour or design of our monument.

   c. In some of the artistic grave-monuments the keeping of
the body was quite dispensed with.   We are speaking of the
so-called kenotaphia, erected to deceased persons whose remains
were not in the possession of their friends, or their paternal city,
which wished to honour their memory.   This leads us to monu-

ments erected in honour of living persons, for instance of
victors in public games, or wrestling competitions. The most
beautiful amongst them, and, at the same time, one of the
loveliest remnants of Greek antiquity, is the one erected at Athens
to commemorate the victory gained by the choragos Lysikrates
(334 B.C.) It is called either the choragic
monument of Lysikrates, or the lantern
of Diogenes (Fig. 152). It is altogether
34 feet high. The base is slender and
square in shape; on it rises an elegant
little round temple; six Corinthian semi-
columns protrude from the circular wall
(see Fig. 11) carrying beams, the frieze
of which represents an episode from the
history of Dionysos, the god of festive
games. Above the beams is the roof,
wrought in the shape of a flat cupola from
a large block of marble; from the middle
of it a stone-flower of acanthus-leaves
seems to grow. It served to support a
tripod, for the legs of which artistically
decorated resting-points have been preserved on the cupola.

Fig. 152.

25. Amongst public buildings we
mentioned first the gymnasia, which,
originating in the requirements of single
persons, soon became centre-points of
Greek life. Corporeal exercise was of
great importance amongst the Greeks,
and the games and competitions in the
various kinds of bodily skill (to which we
shall return) formed a chief feature of their religious feasts.
This circumstance reacted on both sculpture and architecture, in
supplying the former with models of ideal beauty, and in setting
the task to the latter of providing suitable places for these games
to be celebrated. For purposes of this kind (as far as public
exhibition was not concerned) the palæstrai and gymnasia served.
In earlier times these two must be distinguished. In the palæstra
(παλαίστρα from πάλη, wrestling) young men practised wrestling

and boxing. As these arts were gradually developed, larger
establishments with separate compartments became necessary.
Originally such places were, like the schools of the grammarians,
kept by private persons; sometimes they consisted only of open
spaces, if possible near a brook and surrounded by trees. Soon,
however, regular buildings—gymnasia—became necessary. At first
they consisted of an uncovered court surrounded by colonnades, adjoining which lay covered spaces, the former being used for running
and jumping, the latter for wrestling. In the same degree as these
exercises became more developed, and as grown-up men began to
take an interest in these youthful sports, and spent a great part of
their day at the gymnasia, these grew in size and splendour.
They soon became a necessary of life, and no town could be without them, larger cities often containing several. Minute descriptions of these establishments by Greek authors we do not
possess, but the important parts are known to us from occasional
remarks, particularly in the Platonic dialogues. There we find
mentioned the ἐφηβεῖον, where the youths used to practise;
further, the bath (βαλανεῖον), to which belonged a dry sweating
bath (πυριατήριον), for the use of both wrestlers and visitors.
The ἀποδυτήριον was the room for undressing. In another room,
the ἐλαιοθήσιον, the oil was kept for rubbing the wrestlers, and
there possibly this rubbing itself took place; in the κονιστήριον
the wrestlers were sprinkled with sand, so as to give them a firm
hold on each other. The σφαιριστήριον was destined for games
at balls, while other passages, open or covered (collectively called
δρόμος), were used for practice in running or simply for walking.
A particular kind of covered passage were the ξυστοί, which had
raised platforms on both sides for the walkers, the lower space
between being used by the wrestlers—an arrangement similar to
that of the stadia, whence the name of *porticus stadiatæ* applied
to them by the Romans.

About the connection of these different parts we receive information by Vitruvius, who, in his fifth book about architecture
(chapter xi.), gives a full description of a Greek gymnasion. He
begins his architectural rules (derived from the gymnasia of
late Greek times) with the court, which, as in the dwelling-
house, is called περιστύλιον, and may be either a perfect square or
an oblong; its whole circumference ought to be 2 stadia = 1200

feet. It is surrounded by colonnades on all four sides, that towards the south being double, in order to shelter the rooms lying on that side against the weather. Adjoining the single colonnades lay spacious halls (*exedræ*), with seats for philosophers, rhetoricians, and others ; behind the double colonnade lay various rooms, the centre one (*ephebeum*) being a large hall with seats, for the young men to practise in. Like the prostas of the older dwelling-house, it seems to have been the centre of the whole building. To the right of it were the *coryceum* (for games at balls, κώρυκος), the *conisterium* (see p. 108), and next to it, where the colonnade made an angle, the *frigida lavatio* (cold bath), called by the Greeks λουτρόν. On the other side, in the same order, lay the *elæothesium*, the *frigidarium*, or rather, which is more likely, the *tepidarium* (tepid bath), and the entrance to the *propnigeum* (heating-room), with a sweating-bath near it, to which, on the other side, were joined a *laconicum* and the *calda lavatio*.

In most cases this was the whole of the gymnasion. At a later, more splendour-loving period, these establishments were considerably enlarged, and in some cases a stadion was added to the gymnasion. Vitruvius mentions this extension in his additions to the above description. He says, that beyond this peristylos three porticoes may be added (with remarkable analogy to the addition of a second court to the older dwelling-house) : one on the side forming the peristylos (his name for the whole of the buildings just described), and two others to right and left of it. The first-mentioned one, towards the north, ought to be very broad, with a double colonnade ; the others, simple, with raised platforms (*margines*), at least 10 feet wide, going round at the side nearest to the wall and columns ; the deeper-lying centre, with steps leading to it, being destined for the wrestlers to practise in during the winter, so as not to disturb those walking on the platforms. These, he says, were the ξυστοί of the Greeks. Between these two ξυστοί are to be plantations, gardens, and public walks, called by the Greeks περιδρομίδες, by the Romans *xysti ;* on the third side of these grounds lies the stadion, a large space for the accommodation of both spectators and wrestlers.

These precepts, of course, were not carried out in every Greek gymnasion ; they only may serve to give a general notion of

such establishments.   Instead of adding a new one to the many
conjectural designs attempted by archæologists, we will give a
description of a really existing Greek gymnasion, which, although
very simple in design, tallies in the most essential points with the
description of Vitruvius.   Leake has discovered its remains at
Hierapolis in Asia Minor (see plan, Fig. 153, scale = 90 metres).
A A are covered passages, B the open colonnade, behind which
the chief building is situated.   In the latter the ephebeum (D)
forms the centre, joined on one side by the coryceum (E), the

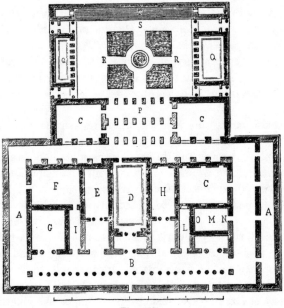

Fig. 153.

conisterium (F) and the cold bath (G), to the latter of which
belonged perhaps the room I.   In the two rooms opening towards
the portico we must recognise the apodyteria, which Vitruvius
does not mention at all.   Room H would, according to Vitruvius,
be the elæothesium, L the tepidarium, and N the entrance to the
heating-room and to the warm baths (M O), of which Vitruvius
mentions the various divisions.   Turning to the back part of the
establishment, we notice several rooms (C C), either *exedræ* or
rooms for the keepers, between which lies the double portico

(P), turned towards the north, and forming the entrance from
the first into the second division. Q Q are the covered passages
with single porticoes, the plantation (R R) lies between them, the
third side of the quadrangle being occupied by the course (S),
with steps (T) for the spectators.

Quite different is the arrangement of the Gymnasion of
Ephesos, which was built probably by the Emperor Hadrianus,
and is amongst the best-preserved ones in existence (see plan,
Fig. 154, scale = 100 feet, English measure). The frequent use
of the vault proves its Roman origin, while in the arrangement
of the chief parts the essential features of Greek construction

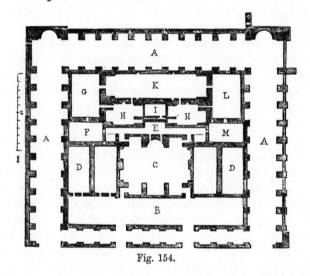

Fig. 154.

remain the same. We find no peristylos, the chief building
being, instead of it, surrounded by a portico (*crypto-porticus*, A)
joined by numerous exedræ, which, however, are not, as Vitruvius
prescribes, *spatiosæ*, but resemble small niches of both round and
quadrangular shapes. From the portico one enters an open
space, thought to be the palæstra (B), and evidently intended to
supply the peristylos. After it follows the ephebeum (C), which
here also is the real centre of the building. The rooms D D
seem to have had no communication with the ephebeum; they
open into the palæstra B, and may be considered as elæothesium
and conisterium, unless we take them for the apodyteria. Behind

the ephebeum lies a passage (E) leading to the baths, F and G being most likely the situations of the cold, L and M those of the warmer baths. H H are explained by the editors of the " Ionian Antiquities," as the hot or sudatory bath. Near I a staircase leads into a vaulted chamber, still blackened by smoke, which the editors take to be a laconicum. Perhaps it may have been a propnigeum, the room above being in that case the laconicum proper. K, which corresponds to the palæstra B, was most likely the sphæristerium or coryceum.

26. The centre of political and commercial intercourse was the agora. Like the gymnasion, and even earlier than this, it grew into architectural splendour with the increasing culture of the Greeks. In maritime cities it generally lay near the sea; in inland places at the foot of the hill which carried the old feudal castle. Being the oldest part of the city, it naturally became the focus not only of commercial, but also of religious and political life. Here, even in Homer's time, the citizens assembled in consultation, for which purpose it was supplied with seats ; here were the oldest sanctuaries ; here were celebrated the first festive games ; here centred the roads on which the intercommunication, both religious and commercial, with neighbouring cities and states was carried on ; from here started the processions which continually passed between holy places of kindred origin, though locally separated. Although originally all public transactions were carried on in these market-places, special local arrangements for contracting public business soon became necessary in large cities. At Athens, for instance, the gently rising ground of the Philopappos hill, called Pnyx, touching the Agora, was used for political consultations, while most likely, about the time of the Pisistratides, the market of Kerameikos, the oldest seat of Attic industry (lying between the foot of the Akropolis, the Areopagos, and the hill of Theseus), became the agora proper, *i.e.* the centre of Athenian commerce. The described circumstances naturally led to an ornamentation of the market-place. Nevertheless, in old towns the agora was not an artistic whole with a distinct architectural design. Its confines were originally irregular, and the site of temples, and the direction of the streets leading into it, made an alteration of its boundary-line difficult. This was different in cities founded at a later period ; the regular

construction of the agora seems indeed to have been initiated
by the colonies of Asia Minor. Pausanias says of the market-
place of Elis, that it was not built according to the Ionian custom,
but in a more ancient style.

Concerning these Ionic market-buildings, we again meet with
the form of a quadrangular court surrounded by colonnades.
This form, eminently suited to the climate, was frequently used
by the Greeks, both in private and public buildings. The description by Vitruvius ("Arch.," V. 1) of an agora evidently refers to
the splendid structures of post-Alexandrine times. According to
him it was quadrangular in size, and surrounded by wide double
colonnades. The numerous
columns carried archi-
traves of common stone
or of marble, and on the
roofs of the porticoes were
galleries for walking purposes. This, of course, does
not apply to all market-
places, even of later date ;
but, upon the whole, the
remaining specimens agree
with the description of
Vitruvius. Figs. 155 and
156 illustrate the beautiful
market-place of Delos. It
lies on a terrace near the
small harbour of the town,
and consists of a quad-

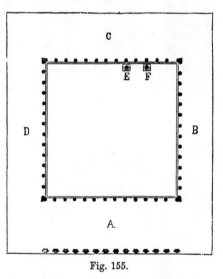

Fig. 155.

rangular court surrounded by a Doric colonnade. The length of
the whole is 170 feet (English measure). The western colonnade
(A) is the largest, being 40 feet wide ; it has a number of doors
through which the entrance from the terrace and the sea into
the agora was effected. E and F mark the sites where, most
likely, stood altars ; in the centre of the open area was a
fountain.

Richer and larger was the agora of Aphrodisias in Karia.
It occupied an area of 525 by 213 feet, and the inside of it was
adorned with an elegant Ionic colonnade containing marble

benches.　Outside of the enclosing wall was also a colonnade. Altogether 460 columns stood in this place.

To complete the picture of a Greek agora we mention a monument which once adorned the market-place of Athens.　It is

the so-called "Tower of the Winds," erected about 50 B.C. by Andronikus of Kyrrhos, and supplying two important requirements of commercial gatherings.　The interior contained a water-clock, and on the floor (see plan, Fig. 157) the grooves are still recognisable, the gradual filling of which with water from a reservoir marked the passing time. On the top of the roof is a capital, and on it stands a movable bronze figure of a Triton (no more in existence), which, moved round by the wind, pointed with its staff to the different directions of the winds, the figures of which, in bas-relief, adorned the eight sides of the building.　Underneath this frieze the lines of a sundial are chiselled into the wall.　Two small

Fig. 156.

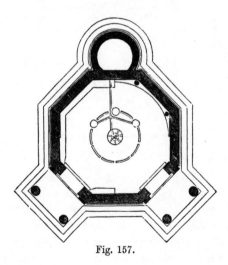

Fig. 157.

porticoes contain each two fluted columns without bases, the capitals of which remind us of the Corinthian style.　A semi-circular building is affixed to the chief edifice, the whole impression of which is extremely graceful (Fig. 158).

27. We have repeatedly mentioned the stoa or colonnade in connection with other buildings; we now have to consider it as a separate artistic erection. Something of the kind we have already seen in the xysti, where wide colonnades were terminated on one side by a wall, on the other by a row of columns. In the same manner the stoa, as an independent building, occurs both as an ornament of streets and squares, and as a convenient locality for

Fig. 158.

walks and public meetings. Its simplest form is that of a colonnade bounded by a wall. This back wall offers a splendid surface for decorations, and is frequently adorned with pictures. A stoa in the market-place of Athens contained illustrations of the battle of Œnoë, of the fight of the Athenians against the

Amazons, of the destruction of Troy, and of the battle of Marathon; hence the name στοὰ ποικίλη.

The progress from this simple form to a further extension is on a principle somewhat analogous to what we have observed in the temple; that is, a row of columns was added on the other side of the wall. The result was a double colonnade, στοὰ διπλῆ, as a specimen of which, Pausanias mentions the Korkyraic stoa near the market-place of Elis. As important we notice Pausanias's remark that this stoa " contained in the middle *not* columns,

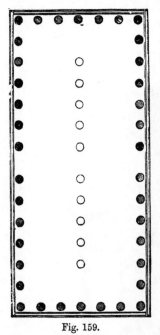

but a wall;" which shows that most of the double colonnades contained columns in the centre, as props of the roof. Indeed, such remains as are preserved indicate this arrangement more or less distinctly. This is the case particularly with the so-called basilika of Pæstum. This building, lying to the south of the small temple, looks itself at first sight like a temple, from which, however, it differs considerably on closer investigation. First of all, it has on its smaller sides an uneven number of columns (*viz.* 9), while in the temple the situation of the entrance in the middle necessitated an even number of columns. Inside the colonnade we here find instead of the walls of the cella, rows of columns, and in the middle between these another row

Fig. 159.

of slightly larger columns, which divide the building into two equal parts, and, like the wall in the Korkyraic monument at Elis, carry the roof.

The design of the colonnade at Thorikos in Attica seems to have been of a similar character (see Fig. 159). It has seven columns in each of the two smaller façades (a little over 48 English feet wide) and fourteen on each of the long sides; a row of columns in the middle (no more in existence) seems to have carried the roof.

In stoas destined for public consultations a further division

of the centre space became desirable, and, indeed, we are told that
in some of them the interior was divided by rows of columns into
three naves.   Touching the agora of Elis, towards the south lay a
stoa in which the Hellanodikai assembled for common consultations.   It was of the Doric order, and divided into three parts by
two rows of columns.   If we assume that it was surrounded by a
wall instead of a simple row of columns, Fig. 160 will show us
the design (scale = 50 feet).   A is the centre nave, B B the two
side naves, C a semicircular termination to the centre nave analogous to the *exedræ* in the gymnasia; D is the portico by means of
which the building opens towards the agora.   In this way we
gain the form of a building somewhat similar both to the cella of
a temple and to the Roman basilica.   Perhaps the στοὰ βασίλειος
in the agora of Athens, where the
Archon Basileus sat in judgment,
was arranged in a similar manner.

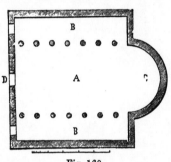

Fig. 160.

28. The arts practised in the
gymnasia were publicly displayed
at the festivals.   The buildings in
which these displays took place
were modified according to their
varieties.   The races, both on horseback and in chariots, took place in
the hippodrome (ἱππόδρομος), for
the gymnastic games of the pentathlon served the stadion (στάδιον),
while for the acme of the festivals, the musical and dramatic performances, theatres were erected.

Hippodromes were originally of very simple design.   The
heroes before Troy raced in a plain near the sea, the boundaries of
which were marked in the most primitive manner; a dry tree one
fathom (*Klafter*) in height, with two white shining stones leaning
against it, served as the goal (σῆμα).   The spectators took their
seats where they could find them on the hills, near which a
course was generally chosen with this view.

This regard to the locality, so characteristic of Greek architecture, was even observed when the recurrence of festive games had
made more complicated arrangements necessary.   This was particularly the case with the hippodrome of Olympia, of which we
possess minute descriptions, and which therefore may serve as an

example of Greek race-courses in general. Pausanias says in his description of this building (if so it may be called), that one side of it was formed by a low range of hills, where the seats of the spectators were situated. Perhaps this one side was sufficient for that purpose during the first time after the introduction of races (Olympiad 25). But when the multitudes at the Olympian festivals began to increase more and more, a wall of earth ($\chi\hat{\omega}\mu a$) was erected opposite the hillside with more seats. These two platforms bounded the course proper on its two long sides, the wall being a little longer than the hill, owing perhaps to the oblique direction of the line of starting. It lay to the left of the hill, and, being extended as far as the wall, finished the course on this side; the architectural boundary of the whole was formed on the same side by a portico built by Agnaptos. On the opposite side the wall joined the hill in a semicircle, with an outlet in the centre, which on this side finished the course. Here also was placed the goal round which

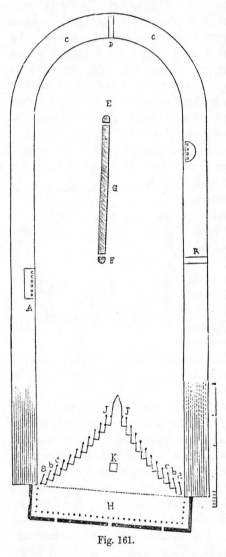

Fig. 161.

the charioteer had to turn, the most difficult operation of the whole race. "Here was," says Pausanias, after mentioning the outlet, " the horror of horses, the taraxippos (ταράξιππος). It has the form of a round altar, and when the horses pass it, they are struck, without a visible cause, with great fear, which produces restiveness and confusion; the reason why often the chariots break, and the charioteers are wounded." A second goal was at the other end of the course; on it stood the statue of Hippodameia, and it marked the spot which the chariots, after rounding the taraxippos, had to reach in order to gain the victory. The plan of the course is shown by Fig. 161 (scale = 300 feet), according to Hirt's investigations. A is the slope of the hill, R the rows of seats on the wall, C C the semicircle joining the hill, D the above-mentioned passage. Opposite this stands the taraxippos E F, being the second goal with the statue of Hippodameia. Whether between these two goals the ground was raised, in analogy to the *spina* of the Roman circus, or whether the line of separation between the up and down courses was marked by columns, Pausanias does not say. Some arrangement of this kind must certainly have been desirable, and has therefore been conjectured by several archæologists (G). The side of the Hippodrome lying opposite the curve is closed by the portico of Agnaptos (H). In front of it was a contrivance which, although Pausanias describes it with evident gusto, can hardly be recognised with certainty. It is the ἄφεσις, the start (J J) or barrier, from which, on a given sign (a bronze eagle thrown into the air by some mechanical appliance), the horses dragging the chariots set out on their run. The ἄφεσις protruded into the space of the course like the prow of a vessel, each of its two sides being about 400 feet long. Inside it were the places for horses and chariots (οἰκήματα). They were placed with a view to showing perfect impartiality to all competitors, and were assigned to them by lot. Each compartment was closed by a rope; on a sign being given the rope was first withdrawn from the compartment nearest the portico (*a a*); when the horses thus released had reached the compartment (*b b*) the rope was withdrawn there, and two other chariots (or racing horses) entered the course, and so forth up to the furthest point of the ἄφεσις.[1] Between the lists

---

[1] On this ἱππάφεσις the inventor of it, Klecœtas, the Athenian sculptor, prided himself much. The whole arrangement, however, has been doubted as too complicated for the practically-minded Greeks. Still the words of Pausanias distinctly

and the portico of Agnaptos lay an open court (K), in which the preparations for the race were made, and where stood the statues of Poseidon Hippios and Here Hippia. Altars and statues were, moreover, placed in various points of the building. Two of the former were respectively dedicated to Ares Hippios and Athene Hippia, as the protecting deities of warlike and chivalrous exercises; others were devoted to the ἀγαθὴ τύχη, to Pan, Aphrodite, and the Nymphs, not to mention several other divinities. Demeter Chamyne had a temple on the top of the hill, most likely above the spectators' seats.

29. Analogous to the design of the hippodrome was that of the stadion (στάδιον). This being originally designed for the running of foot-races, its length-wise shape was also determined.

Fig. 162.

The runners here, however, being men, both the length and width of the course were of smaller dimensions. The usual length of the stadion was 600 feet, a measure which, first decided upon by Herakles for the Stadion of Olympia, afterwards became the unit of the Greek road-measure. Some of the stadia are, however, much longer; the one at Laodikeia being, for instance, 1000 feet long by only 90 wide (see Fig. 162). Here a natural declivity of the soil had been made available. The games took place in the valley, the spectators being seated on the slope of the hill, which for that purpose had been formed into terraces. Such favourable situations, however, being scarce, generally the sides of the stadion

indicate the gradual releasing of the horses, and also the *two* sides of the starting line.

had to be artificially raised, which was done by surrounding it with a wall of earth.[1] This arrangement seems to have been the common one amongst the Greeks, and Pausanias mentions several stadia (for instance, at Corinth, Thebes, Athens, Olympia, and Epidauros) consisting of a χῶμα; moreover, he mentions expressly that this was the usual way of their construction. In later times artistic decorations were added, and the seats built of solid stone. The Stadion of Messene is a beautiful example of natural fitness and additional artistic arrangement. Lying in the lower parts of the town, its form was determined by the nature of the soil (see Fig. 163, scale = 100 metres). The area, the scene of the competitions (*a a*), lies in a natural hollow through which flows a brook. The hills on both sides were used for seats (*b b*) without any attempts being made at making the two long sides of the stadion parallel. Colonnades were erected on the top of the rising ground, and the semicircular termination of the course was fitted

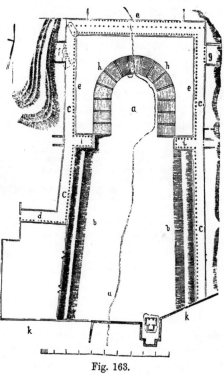

Fig. 163.

with stone seats all round. The colonnade (C) extended on one side to the end of the course, which is there finished by the

---

[1] Sometimes this was done only on *one* side of the stadion, as was, for instance, the case in that lying, according to Pausanias, behind the theatre of Ægina. Ross says of the Stadion of Delos, that its western side is bounded by a hill, the eastern one being left entirely without seats, with the exception of a kind of *tribune* about forty-five paces in length lying right in the centre, and having contained, as it seems, three or four rows of seats.

town wall (*k*); on the other it ends in an obtuse angle (*d*), owing
to the slight decline of the ground at that point.   The colonnades
also extend toward the end of the course, where they enclose a
square court, and are joined together by a double portico (*e e*).
This double portico seems to have been the chief entrance, the
wall enclosing this whole part being besides interrupted by two
minor entrances (*f* and *g*).   In the centre of this raised peristyle
lies the semicircular termination of the stadion (*h h*), called by the
Greeks σφενδόνη, or occasionally θέατρον, owing to its similitude to
the place for the spectators of a theatre.   It was reserved for
wrestling-matches, the pankration, and the like.   Here, at Olympia,
the umpires were seated ; at Messene also this space was evidently
reserved for a better class of people : hence the sixteen rows of
benches surrounding the area all made of stone.   Two protrusions
of the surrounding colonnade (*i i*) give this space a beautiful
architectural conclusion (see the section of the stadion, Fig. 164,

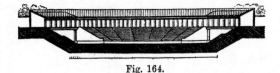

Fig. 164.

scale = 70 metres).   Right opposite, in a curve of the town wall,
lies a building evidently used for religious purposes.   The Stadion
of Ephesos was entirely a product of art ; it seems to date from the
later time of the city's splendour under the successors of Alexander
the Great, or even under the Roman emperors.

The barrier from which the runners started was on the same
side as in the hippodrome, the goal, which was not wanting in
the stadion, being placed in or near the curve of the sphendone.
Both starting-point and goal were marked by columns ; a third
column, according to one account, stood between them in the centre
of the stadion.   These three formed the line (perhaps otherwise
marked) dividing the stadion into two halves, an arrangement
necessary for the "double run" and the run against time, for in
these the runner had to turn round at the goal (νύσσα, τέρμα, etc.)
and run back.   This seems indicated by the inscription written on
the last column, according to the account of the Scholiast (Sophokles, El. 691), of κάμψον (turn !), the words on the two other

columns being ἀρίστευε (be brave !) and σπεῦδε (make haste !)   The
stadia with semicircles at both ends
required a different arrangement.
These seem to belong to a later
epoch, and may in many cases have
been imitated from Roman amphi-
theatres.   A beautiful specimen of
this later style is the Stadion of
Aphrodisias in Karia, which is about
895 English feet in length (see
Fig. 165).   Here also a natural
declivity of the soil has been turned
to account, and, in order to have
room for rows of seats the hollow
has been artificially increased.   The
whole space is surrounded by a wall
with ornamental arcades (see cross-
section, Fig. 166), through which
fifteen public entrances led into the
interior; several subterraneous passages opened into the area without
touching the seats of the spectators
(see longitudinal section, Fig. 167).
Such passages seem to have been
common.   Pausanias (VI. 20, 8)
mentions one in the Stadion of
Olympia through which the competitors and the Hellanodikai used
to enter; the Olympian stadion at
Athens still shows on its left long-
side the traces of a subterraneous
entrance cut through the rock.

30. The theatres formed the
climax of festive architecture in
Greece, in accordance with the important position of the drama in
Greek poetry.   Their beginnings
were, however, simple, the more

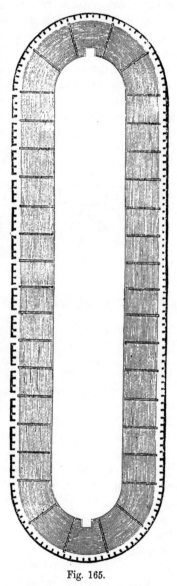

Fig. 165.

so as they were in use before the drama had attained its artistic

development.   Originally they were destined for the performance
of the choric dances and songs appertaining to the worship of
Dionysos, but soon they obtained public importance, and became
both a means of artistic culture for youths and maidens and a
source of public enjoyment.   Theatres were even used for quite
different purposes.   Pageants of all kinds could take place in
them, and at the same time they offered a convenient point for the
communications made to the people on the part of the government.
Regular public meetings were held in theatres, as was, for
instance, commonly the case at Athens in the great theatre of
Dionysos, even after the dramatic performances had reached a high
perfection.

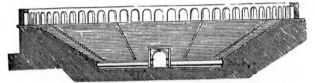

Fig. 166.

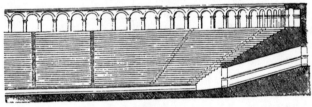

Fig. 167.

The form and construction of the buildings were here again
adapted to local circumstances, natural risings of the ground being
generally chosen for the purpose.   Differently from the hippodrome
or stadion, the action here had to be fixed to a certain point,
round which the spectators' seats had to be arranged, so as to
enable them to direct their eyes to this centre of action.   Hence
the form of a greater or smaller segment of the circle was chosen
as most convenient.

The oldest theatres consisted of two chief divisions : the stage
for the dancers (χορός, ὀρχήστρα) and the place for the spectators.
The former was levelled in the simplest manner ; in the centre

stood the altar of the god to be celebrated, most frequently Dionysos, whose worship was connected with dancing. Round the orchestra rose on the one side the seats of the spectators, in the form of a semicircle or of a large segment, mostly on the slope of a hill. Originally the people sat on the hill itself, afterwards seats (first of wood, later of stone) were put up, where the soil was soft; where it was rocky, concentric rows of seats were cut into it. This custom was not relinquished by the Greeks even after the demands of artistic beauty and perfection were pitched very high, which explains the fact that in Greece proper only one theatre (at Mantinea) has been discovered where the natural height has been supplied by an artificial one, which simply consists of an earth wall propped by surrounding walls of polygonal stones, and covered with rows of seats.

Only in very few cases, however, was the locality naturally quite adapted to the purpose. Generally alterations and enlargements were required, which ultimately, in the splendour-loving cities of Asia Minor, at a post-Alexandrine period, led to the theatre being wholly built of stone.

Other alterations of the original theatres date from a much earlier period. From the original Bacchic chorus the drama had developed into tragedy and comedy; and although these are said to have been performed at first by Thespis on a movable scaffold, they soon were transferred into the standing theatres, the more easily as the drama itself was considered as part of the Dionysos-worship. This circumstance made the erection of a stage necessary. Even in the older theatres a wall had been erected at the back of the orchestra, partly for architectural, partly for acoustic reasons, and this wall now was gradually extended into a separate stage-building. The first theatre erected of stone with a regular stage was that of Athens, which became the model of all others, both in Greece and the colonies. It was dedicated to Dionysos. After the wooden scaffolds, originally used, had broken down during a theatrical performance, in which Æschylos and Pratinas appeared as competitors, this theatre was built on the southern slope of the Akropolis (see Fig. 51, J). The hill itself was partly turned to account architecturally. The theatre was begun in Olympiad 70, and finished between 340-30 B.C., under Lykurgos. It had almost entirely disappeared under the rubbish of centuries, when it was restored to light in its whole extent by the celebrated German architect Strack in 1862 (see Fig. 181).

In the theatre of Athens a common type had been gained, which, with many local modifications, was reproduced ever after.

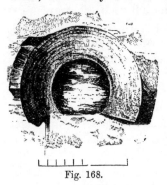

Fig. 168.

The theatre was divided into three parts—the orchestra, forming almost a complete circle, the place for the spectators, and the stage-building. The place for the spectators (τὸ κοῖλον, the hollow pit) consisted of several steps rising round the orchestra in a semicircle or larger segment, and serving the audience as seats (ἐδώλιον). Towards the stage the seats were closed by a wall, which served both as a prop and a boundary, and, following the rising line of the seats, did not obstruct the view on to the stage. The position of these walls, standing either in an obtuse angle towards each other,

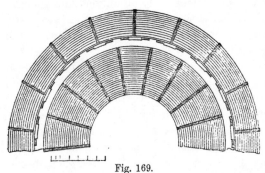

Fig. 169.

or in a straight line, was the cause of two different arrangements, according to which we may divide all the Greek theatres known

Fig. 170.

to us into two classes. As an example of the first class, we may mention the theatre of Delos (see Fig. 168, scale = 50 metres). It consists of a natural rising of the ground, being artificially brought into a more regular shape, and completed by a solid wall 19 feet thick by 30 long.

Another example is the theatre of Stratonikeia (see Fig. 169

scale = 60 feet, English measure), built most likely at the time of
the Seleukides, and enlarged under the Roman emperors.

Of theatres with a rectangular termination of their seats we
mention that of Megalopolis in Arcadia, originally one of the
largest and most beau-
tiful in Greece (see Fig.
170). It consists of a
hill considerably en-
larged, in consequence
of which Pausanias
calls it *the* largest
theatre. The accounts
of its diameter differ
from 480 to 600 feet.

Fig. 171.

In its present ruined condition neither the stage nor the seats are
distinctly recognisable.

The same form is shown by the theatre of Segesta, in Sicily,
the koilon of which dates from early Greek times; other rows of
seats on artificial bases, in addition to the original twenty, have

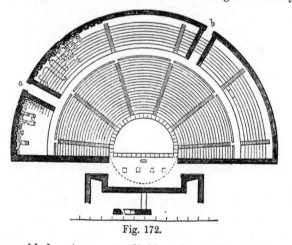

Fig. 172.

later been added. A passage divides the earlier and later parts
of the seats. The remnants of the stage belong to later Roman
times. Fig. 171 shows the perspective view, Fig. 172 the plan
(scale = 140 Sicilian palms).

The interruption of the rows of seats by wider intervals is

frequently found in theatres, particularly in the larger ones. In
order to facilitate the ascent to the rows and single seats, these
passages (διαζώματα) used to divide the seats into several concentric stripes. *One* diazoma only occurs both in the theatres of
Segesta and Stratonikeia (Fig. 169). Others have two, as, for
instance, the small theatre of Knidos, which has also been considered
as an odeum (see Fig. 173; width of the orchestra = about 65
English feet). Its koilon is enclosed by rectangular walls, most likely
owing to the direction of the streets between which the theatre lies.

The theatre at Dramyssos in Epeiros has three diazomata,

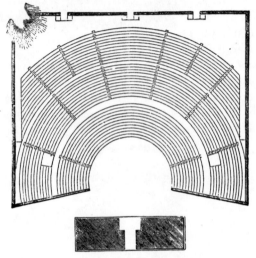

Fig. 173.

two dividing the seats, and one enclosing the whole koilon; it
may at the same time serve as an example of the above-mentioned
rectangularly closed theatre. The koilon (see Fig. 174; scale =
100 English feet) is well preserved; in the place of the upper
third diazoma Donaldson conjectures a colonnade, of which,
however, no remnants are now in existence. The diameter of the
orchestra is very small compared with that of the spectators' place;
d and *e* mark steps leading up to the second diazoma. The style of
the building is very simple, and it therefore is considered by many
as very early and of Greek origin; according to others it belongs to
Roman times. Of the stage building no recognisable parts remain.

On the outside the koilon was generally enclosed by a wall, as is shown by the theatre of Dramyssos and others; Vitruvius in his description of the Greek theatre speaks of a colonnade, but of this no authentic traces remain in ruins of the Greek period.

The entrances to the seats were generally between the propping walls and the stage-building; the spectators ascended from the orchestra. In larger theatres other entrances became desirable. In the theatre of Dramyssos stairs on the outside of the propping wall led to the first diazoma. In other theatres, where the locality permitted, entrances to the upper parts of the koilon had been arranged, as, for instance, in the theatre of Segesta, and also in that of Sikyon (see Fig. 175; scale = 60 metres). In the latter, two passages (*a* and *b*) led through the mountain itself into

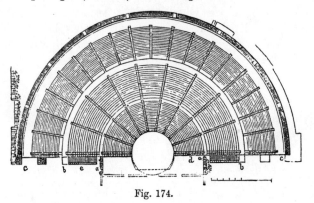

Fig. 174.

the centre of the koilon (see a view of passage *a*, Fig. 176). Moreover, the single rows of seats intercommunicated in all theatres by means of narrow stairs, which, verging like radii towards the centre of the orchestra, divided the koilon into several wedge-like partitions (κερκίδες). In Greek theatres these are generally found in even numbers, varying, according to size and other local conditions, from two to ten. Where several diazomata are found, the mutual position of the stairs has been changed (as at Knidos, Segesta, Stratonikeia), or their number has been doubled (as at Dramyssos). Two of the stair-steps are equal in size to one of the sitting-steps, the latter being so arranged that the spectators had room to sit at ease without being inconvenienced by the feet of those occupying the upper rows. Their height was,

according to Vitruvius, no less than 1 foot, and not more than
1 foot 6 inches, which small measure is accounted for by the
custom of raising the seats by means of bolsters and cushions ; the

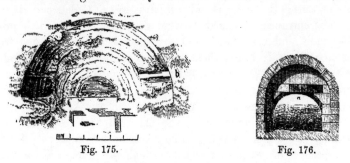

Fig. 175.   Fig. 176.

width of the seats was equal to about twice their height.   The
steps are generally simple in design, with a view, however, to convenience and comfort.   Frequently they are slightly raised in
front, the lower part at the back being destined for the feet of

Fig. 177.   Fig. 178.

those sitting in the row behind.   This is illustrated in the simplest
manner by the sitting-steps of the theatres of Catana (Fig. 177)
and of Akrai (Fig. 178), in Sicily, *a* being the sitting-steps, *b*
those of the stairs.

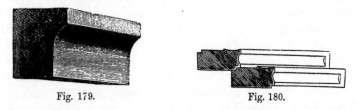

Fig. 179.   Fig. 180.

In other theatres the front side of the steps has been slightly
pushed back or hollowed out, so as to gain room for the feet.
Such is the case in the theatres at Megalopolis (Fig. 179), at

Tauromenium, and at Side in Asia Minor.   Particularly comfortable are the steps of the theatre at Sparta, with their seats slightly
hollowed out (Fig. 180); those at Iasos, in Asia Minor, are formed
in the manner of arm-chairs, the seats in front of the diazoma
being real arm-chairs with backs to them, as was also the case
in the theatre of Epidauros, celebrated amongst the ancients.
Particularly interesting with regard to these arm-chairs is the
above-mentioned theatre of Dionysos at Athens, rediscovered in

Fig. 181.

1862.   The place for the spectators consists of about one hundred
rows of seats, divided into thirteen kerkides by means of fourteen
stairs, the two last of which lie near the entrances, close by the
side-wall.   The height of each step is 0·345 metre, the horizontal depth 0·782 metre; the latter is divided into two parts,
the front one (0·332 metre deep) being used as the seat; the
back one (0·45 metre deep) slightly hollowed, being destined for
the feet of those sitting higher.   The width of the stair-steps is

K

0·70 metre, their height corresponding with that of the sitting
steps in this manner, that the stair-step at first is 0·22 metre high,
but gradually rises towards the back.   In this sloping part grooves
have been cut into the step, so as to prevent people from slipping.
The lowest row of steps immediately surrounding the orchestra
(Fig. 181) is occupied by sixty-seven arm-chairs, by ones, twos,
or threes, hewn from blocks of Pentelic marble.   These, as is
proved by their inscriptions, were destined for the priests, archontes,
and thesmothetai, the centre one, richly decorated with bas-reliefs,
being reserved for the priest of Dionysos Eleuthereus.   The wall
of the proskenion, also decorated with bas-reliefs, was erected by
the Archon Phaidros, perhaps in the third century after Christ,
while the older wall and the oldest proskenion were placed, the
former by six, the latter by eight, metres farther back, owing to
the orchestra required for the chorus of the old tragedy and
comedy being much larger than that wanted for the mimic performances of late Roman times.

The orchestra, as we said before, was the scene of the choric
dances in which the drama had its origin.   Even in later theatres
a large space was reserved for this purpose between the place for
the spectators and the stage.   This space was larger in the Greek
than in the Roman theatres, in which latter no dances of this
kind took place.   Vitruvius describes the Greek orchestra as a
circle into which a square had been designed, so that the four
corners touched the periphery.   The side of the square turned
towards the stage terminates the orchestra, the space between this
line and the tangent parallel to it being occupied by the stage.
On the other side the orchestra is enclosed by the seats of the
spectators.   In the centre of it stands the thymele, the altar of
Dionysos, which at the same time forms the central point of the
choric dances.   The soil was simply levelled; at meetings it was
perhaps strewn with sand (hence κονίστρα); only in case dances
were performed the thymele was surrounded with a floor of boards,
resting most likely on several steps.   In case of dramatic performances different arrangements became necessary.   For the
chorus had not only to sing and dance, but also to speak to the
actors on the stage, and its place of action had to be raised accordingly.   This was done by erecting a scaffolding over one half of the
konistra as far as the thymele, and placing boards thereon.   This

raised part was called the orchestra proper, or the scenic orchestra, to distinguish it from the choreutic one. The latter, by some feet lower than the stage, was entered by the choreutai by the same passages (παρόδος), between the walls and the koilon, through which the spectators reached the konistra, and thence their seats. Steps led up to the orchestra, which again was connected with the stage by means of low movable stairs (κλίμακες) of three or four steps each (κλιμακτῆρες), as the course of the drama required frequently the ascending by the chorus of the stage, and its returning thence to the orchestra. Of these temporary arrangements naturally nothing remains; hence the various theories regarding them started by archæologists. Upon these, however, we cannot enter.

Of the stage-building we have fewer and less well-preserved remnants than of the place for the spectators. The stage was called ἡ σκήνη (tent), an expression dating most likely from the time when at the back of the orchestra a scaffolding was erected from which the actors entered as from a kind of tent. Afterwards the same expression was transferred to the stone theatre, its meaning being now either the whole stage-building, or, in a narrower sense, the back wall of the stage. Hence the expression found in Vitruvius of *scena tragica, comica*, and *satyrica*, from the different changes of scenery applied to it. Sometimes the small space in front of the back wall on which the actors performed was called σκήνη, instead of the more common προσκήνιον. Sometimes also the name λογεῖον was used for this place, or more particularly for the centre of it, from which the actors mostly delivered their speeches. This proskenion was considerably higher than the floor of the konistra, in order to raise, as it were, the actors into a strange sphere. Probably the whole space below the wooden floor of the proskenion was called ὑποσκήνιον; its outer wall facing the orchestra was, according to Pollux, decorated with columns and sculptures. From it the " Charonic steps " (χαρώνειοι κλίμακες) led up to the proskenion, on which the ghosts of dead persons and river gods ascended the stage. The entrance was closed by a sliding slab of wood. Παρασκήνια were the two juttings of the stage-building enclosing the proskenion to right and left, ἐπισκήνια the different stories of the stage-wall.

Several stage-buildings have been preserved, particularly in

Asiatic cities, but in most of them Roman influences must be
suspected, and they hardly can serve as specimens of purely
Greek arrangements.   The theatre of Telmessos in Lykia is

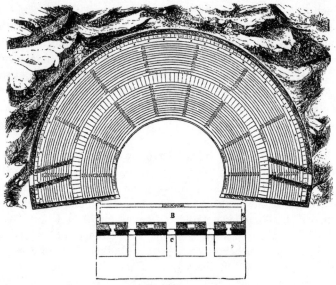

Fig. 182.

perhaps most adapted to this purpose, owing to its great simplicity (see Fig. 182).   The koilon is formed by a hill, the seats
being closed in obtuse angles ; one diazoma divides them into two

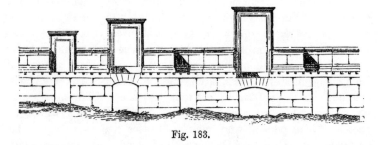

Fig. 183.

halves, another serves as an upper passage round them ; eight
stairs divide the place for the spectators into nine κερκίδες ; the
orchestra is very large, and agrees exactly with the statement of

Vitruvius ; the proskenion rested on a wooden scaffolding. The wall of the skene shows five doors, each of them originally enclosed by two columns. Beneath these one still recognises the hollows into which the beams of the floor of the proskenion were placed (see Fig. 183) ; the doors underneath led into the hyposkenion, the position of which we have described above. Other specimens of preserved stage-buildings we shall mention in speaking of the Roman theatre (§ 84); we conclude our description with a perspective view of a Greek theatre, designed by Strack according to the statements of ancient writers and the preserved remnants (Fig. 184).

Fig. 184.

31. In our description of the private dwellings of the Greeks, we mentioned that more even than the public buildings they have suffered from the influence of time. The same applies to their interior fittings ; only the utensils deposited in graves have escaped the common destruction ; in other cases pictures on vases and sculptural representations must aid us in our description.

The different kinds of seats are specified by the following expressions—δίφρος, κλισμός, κλιντήρ, κλισίη and θρόνος. Diphros is a small, backless, easily movable stool, with four legs, either crossed or perpendicular. The first-mentioned form of the diphros, called also ὀκλαδίας δίφρος, ὀκλαδίας, or θρόνος πτυκτός, δίφρος ταπεινός, could easily be folded, as the seat consisted only of interwoven straps. It was therefore the custom amongst the Athenians to have these folding-stools carried after them by

slaves.   No less frequent were the diphroi with four perpendicular legs, which could naturally not be folded.   Both forms of
the diphros are found on ancient monuments in many varieties.
Fig. 185, *a*, a diphros okladias, is taken from the marble
relief of a grave at Krissa.   The two folding-stools, Fig. 185, *b*
and *c*, are from pictures on vases; the legs appear gracefully
bent and neatly carved.   The second form of the diphros is
shown by Fig. 185, *d*, and Fig. 186, *c*.   The first is taken from the
frieze of the Parthenon, where similar stools are carried on their
heads by the wives and daughters of the metoikoi who, at the
Panathenea, had to submit to the custom of stool-carrying
(διφροφορεῖν): the second illustration is derived from a marble
relief at Athens; it is remarkable by its neatly bent legs and by
the turned knobs above the sitting-board, perhaps destined to
fasten the cushion placed thereon.   If to this solid diphros we add

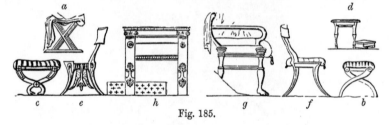

Fig. 185.

a back, we come to the second species of chairs, called κλισμός,
κλιντήρ, and κλισίη (see Fig. 185, *e*, *f*).   They are like our
ordinary drawing-room chairs, but for the upper part of the
back, which is bent semicircularly, and therefore much more
comfortable than our straight-backed chairs.   The legs bent
outward gracefully are in perfect harmony.

Under θρόνος we comprise all larger chairs with a straight
back and low arms; the former reaches either to the middle of
the back, or up to the head, of the sitting person.   The thronoi in
the temples were the seats of the gods; in private houses they
were reserved as seats of honour for the master and his guests.
The thronoi in private houses were mostly made of heavy
wood; those in the temples, the ekklesiai, dikasteria, bouleu-
teria, the stadion, and hippodrome, reserved for the judges and
leaders of the people, were generally wrought in marble.   The
thronoi were in different parts richly decorated with carved

garlands or figures; in sculptures they occur in various forms.
The low-backed thronos is shown in Figs. 185, *g*, and 186, *a*, the
former from the Harpy-monument at Xanthos, the latter from the
frieze of the Parthenon. The old wooden throne with a high
back appears in a marble relief of the best period (Fig. 186, *b*),
while several richly ornamented marble seats in the theatre of
Dionysos (Fig. 181), in the Akropolis of Athens (Stuart and
Revett, "Antiquities," iii., p. 19), illustrate the seats of honour of
the athlothetai in the market-places. The existence of thronoi
without backs is proved by the picture on a vase of a thronos
(Fig. 185, *h*) on which Aigisthos is being killed by Orestes. On
the seats of all these chairs woolly hides, blankets, or bolsters, used

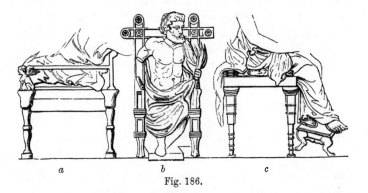

a   b   c

Fig. 186.

to be put, as is mentioned by Homer (see Fig. 185, *b*, *c*, *e*, *f*, *g*).
To the throne belonged the footstool (θρῆνυς), either attached to
its front legs, and therefore immovable, or as a separate piece of
furniture. It was considered as indispensable both to rest the
feet and to mount the high throne. It was used, however, also
with low seats, resembling very much our modern footstool (Fig.
185, *d*, and Fig. 186, *c*). Something similar may have been the
massive wooden footstool (σφέλας) which, in the house of Odysseus,
Eurymachos applies as a missile. The width of the footstool
corresponds to that of the chair, those used for couches being
naturally longer (see Fig. 188).

32. The oldest specimen of a bedstead (κλίνη) is that
mentioned by Homer as joined together by Odysseus in his own
house. He had cut off the stem of an olive-tree a few feet from

the ground, and joined to it the boards of the bed, so that the trunk supported the bed at the head. It therefore was immovable. The antique bed must be considered as the prolongation of the diphros. The cross-legged diphros prolonged became the folding bed; that with perpendicular legs, the couch. The former could easily be moved and replaced; they are perhaps identical with the δέμνια frequently mentioned in the "Odyssey," which were put into the outer hall for guests. One of them is shown as the notorious bed of Prokrustes in a picture on a vase (Fig. 187, *a*). The second diphros corresponds to the couch resting on four legs (Fig. 187, *b*), at first without head and foot-board, which were after-wards added at both ends (ἀνάκλιντρον or ἐπίκλιντρον). By the further addition of a back on one of the long sides, it became what we now call a *chaise longue* or sofa (Fig. 187, *c*, Figs. 188-190). This sleeping kline was no doubt essentially the same as that used at meals. The materials were, besides the ordinary woods, maple or box, either massive or veneered. The legs and backs, and other parts

a   c   b
Fig. 187.

not covered by the bedclothes, were carefully worked. Sometimes the legs are neatly carved or turned, sometimes the frames are inlaid with gold, silver, and ivory, as is testified in the "Odyssey" and elsewhere.

The bedding mentioned in Homer did not consist of sumptuous bolsters and cushions, as in later times. It consisted, even amongst the richer classes, first of all of the ῥήγεα, *i.e.* blankets of a long-haired woollen material, or perhaps a kind of mattress. Hides (κώεα), as spread by the poor on the hard floor, were sometimes put under the ῥήγεα and other additional blankets (τάπητες), so as to soften the couch. The whole was covered with linen sheets. The χλαῖναι served to cover the sleeper, who sometimes used his own dress for this purpose; sometimes they consisted of woollen blankets woven for the purpose. After Homer's time, when Asiatic luxury had been introduced into Greece, a mattress (κνέφαλον, τυλεῖον or τύλη) was placed

immediately on the bed-straps (κειρία). It was stuffed with
plucked wool or feathers, and covered with some linen or woollen
material. On this mattress blankets were placed, called by Pollux
περιστρώματα, ὑποστρώματα, ἐπιβλήματα, ἐφεστρίδες, χλαῖναι,
ἀμφιεστρίδες, ἐπιβόλαια, δάπιδες, ψιλοδάπιδες, ξυστίδες χρυσό-
παστοι, to which must be added the τάπητες and ἀμφιτάπητες
with the rough wood on either or both sides. Pillows, like the
mattresses stuffed with wool or feathers, were added to complete
the bedding, at least in more luxurious times. Of a similar

Fig. 188.   Fig. 189.

kind were the klinai placed in the sitting-rooms, lying on which,
in a half-reclining position, people used to read, write, and take
their meals. They were covered with soft blankets of gorgeous
colours, while one or more cushions served to support the body in
its half-sitting position, or to prop the left arm (Fig. 187, c).
Fig. 187, a shows the folding-bed, Fig. 187, b the simple kline
covered with the ῥήγεα. Fig. 187, c
shows the kline with one upright end on
which two persons are reclining, one of
them resting the left arm on a cushion
covered with a many-coloured material,
the other leaning with her back against
two cushions. Much richer is the couch
in Fig. 188, which has a head and foot-

Fig. 190.

board and is covered with mattresses and pillows; a long ornamented footstool has been added. Fig. 190, after a marble relief,
exactly resembles our sofa. Fig. 189 shows a peculiar kind of
kline, on which a sick person is lying, to whom Asklepios is giving
advice. Sometimes the drapery is evidently intended to hide the
roughly carved woodwork, as is shown by the picture of a symposion (Fig. 304), to which we shall have to return.

33. Tables were used by the ancients chiefly at meals, not for reading and writing. The antique tables, either square with four legs, or circular or oval with three connected legs, afterwards with one leg (τράπεζαι τετράποδες, τρίποδες, μονόποδες), resemble our modern ones but for their being lower. Mostly their slabs did not reach higher than the kline; higher tables would have been inconvenient for the reclining person (see Fig. 187, *c*). In Homeric and even in later times, a small table stood before each thronos. The use of separate dishes for each guest is comparatively new. Originally the meat was brought in on large platters, divided by the steward, and each portion put on the bare table. In want of knives and forks the fingers were used. The pastry was put in baskets by the tables. Whether the Homeric tables were as low as the later ones, when lying instead of sitting had become the custom, we must leave undecided in want of sculptural evidence. The legs of the tables were carefully finished, particularly those of the tripods, which frequently imitated the legs of

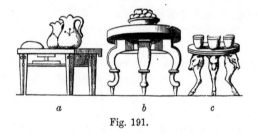

a   b   c

Fig. 191.

animals, or at least had claws at their ends (Fig. 191, *a*, *b*, *c*). The four-legged tables were more simple in design. The material was wood, particularly maple; later on, bronze, precious metals, and ivory were introduced.

34. For the keeping of articles of dress, valuable utensils, ornaments, bottles of ointment, and documents, larger or smaller drawers and boxes were used. Chests of drawers and upright cupboards with doors seem to have been unknown in earlier times; only in few monuments of later date (for instance, in the wall-painting of a shoemaker's workshop at Herculaneum) we see something resembling our wardrobe. The wardrobes mentioned by Homer (φωριαμός, χηλός) doubtlessly resemble our old-fashioned trunks (*Truhe*). The surfaces showed ornaments of

various kinds, either cut from the wood in relief or inlaid with
precious metals and ivory. Some smaller boxes with inlaid figures
or painted arabesques are shown in Fig. 192, *b, c, f, g, h*, all taken
from pictures on vases. The ornamentation with polished nails
seems to have been very much in favour (Fig. 192, *c, f, h*)—a
fashion reintroduced in modern times. The most celebrated
example of such ornamentation was the box of Kypselos, in
the opisthodomos of the temple of Hera at Olympia. It dates
probably from the time when the counting by Olympiads was
introduced, and served, according to Bötticher, for the keeping of
votive tapestry and the like. According to Pausanias, it was
made of cedar-wood, and elliptic in shape. It was adorned with
mythological representations, partly carved in wood, partly inlaid
with gold and ivory, encircling the whole box in five stripes, one
over the other. Boxes for articles of dress are seldom found in
old pictures on vases (Fig. 192, *a*) ;[1] very frequent are, on the

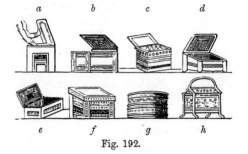

Fig. 192.

other hand, portable cases for ornaments, spices, etc. (Fig. 192, *b,
d, e, f, g, h*). Fig. 192, *c* contains evidently bottles of ointment.
Another box, standing before a reading ephebos, and showing the
inscription " **XEIPONEIΣ KAΛE** " evidently contained documents (see Micali, " L'Italia avanti il dominio dei Romani," Tav.
CIII.) The cover was fastened to the box by a ribbon tied in a
knot. The custom of securing the ends of this ribbon by the impression of a signet-ring on wet sealing-earth or wax is of later date.
Locks, keys, and bolts, known at an early period for the closing of

[1] The inner surface of a drinking-goblet at the Royal Museum of Berlin
(Gerhard, "Trinkschalen und Gefässe," I. Taf. IX.) shows the large box in which
Hypsipyle, the princess of Lemnos, has hidden her father Thoas. See also our
Fig. 231.

doors, were later applied to boxes, as is sufficiently proved by the still-existing small keys fastened to finger-rings (see § 93), which, although all of Roman make, were most likely not unknown to the Greeks. For doors these would have been too small.

35. The furniture of Greek houses was simple, but full of artistic beauty. This was particularly displayed in vessels for the keeping of both dry and fluid stores, as were found in temples, dwellings, and even graves. Only the last mentioned have been preserved to us. Earthen vessels are the most numerous. The invention of the potter's wheel is of great antiquity, and was ascribed by the Greeks in different places to different mythical persons. The Corinthians named Hyperbion as its inventor. In the Kerameikos, the potters' quarter of Athens, Keramos, the son of Dionysos and Ariadne, was worshipped as such. The name of the locality itself was derived from this "heros eponymos." Next to Corinth and Athens (which latter became celebrated for earthen manufactures, owing to the excellent clay of the promontory of Kolias), Ægina, Lakedæmon, Aulis, Tenedos, Samos, and Knidos were famous for their earthenware. In these places the manufacture of painted earthenware was concentrated; thence they were exported to the ports of the Mediterranean and the Black Sea for the markets of the adjoining countries. Owing to the beautiful custom of the ancients of leaving in the graves of the dead the utensils of their daily life, a great many beautiful vessels have been preserved which otherwise would have shared the destruction of the dwellings with other much less fragile implements. From the pictures on these vases we derive, moreover, valuable information as to the public and private habits of the Greeks. The greatest number of graves in their original condition, and filled with vessels, are found in Italy. The chief places where pottery has been and is still being found are—in Sicily, Gela and Girgenti (the old Akragas); in Southern Italy, the necropoles of the Apulian cities of Gnatia (Fasano), Lupatia (Altamura), Cælia (Ciglia), Barium (Bari), Rubi (Ruvo), Canusium (Canosa); in Lucania, the cities of Castelluccio, Anxia (Anzi), Pæstum, and Eboli; in the old Campania, the cities of Nola, Phlistia (Santa Agata de' Goti), Cumæ, and Capua; in Central Italy, the necropoles of the old Etruscan cities of Veii (Isola Farnese), Cære, Tarquinii, Vulci,

Clusium (Chiusi), Volterræ (Volterra), and Adria. In Greece and Asia Minor things are different. The political conditions of these countries have prevented their scientific investigation; some of the smaller vessels have been found only at Athens and Ægina, some of the larger in Thera, Melos, and Rhodes. Besides these we mention the discoveries in the grave-mounds of the old Pantikapaion, the capital of the Bosphoric empire. They consist of utensils worked in precious metals or bronze, and numerous painted vessels belonging to the later period of pottery, which must have been brought by merchants from Attika to this distant outpost of antique culture. Of Athenian origin were also the celebrated Panathenaïc prize-vases dating from the fourth century B.C. which have been found amongst the ruins of the Kyrenaic Pentapolis. They are amphoræ with two handles, and the picture of Athene painted on them in an archaic style. In Greece, principally in Attika, were un-doubtedly the manu-factures which sup-plied the enormous demands of both co-lonies and barbaric countries. In the style of their paintings the

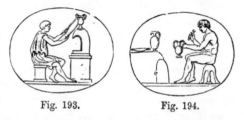

Fig. 193.   Fig. 194.

shrewd Attic men of business tried to hit the taste of their bar-baric customers, not unlike our present manufacturers. The whole trade was thus monopolised by Greece, a competition existing only in those places where local manufacturers worked after Greek patterns.

36. The *technique* of antique pottery may be learnt from two gems. The first (Fig. 193) represents an ephebos clad in the chiton, sitting in front of a handsome oven, from the top of which he takes by means of two sticks a newly glazed two-handled vessel. The second illustration also shows the interior of a potter's workshop (Fig. 194). A nude potter gives the last polish to a finished vessel (most likely with a piece of hard leather); on a kind of baking oven, closed by a door, stand a pitcher and a drinking-bowl for the purpose of drying. Two pictures on vases, published by Jahn ("Berichte der kgl. sächsischen Gesellschaft der Wissensch.," VI., 1854, hist. phil. Cl.

p. 27 *et seq.*), show, one of them, a potter similarly occupied as ours
(Fig. 194) ; the other, a little less finished in style, the whole interior
of a potter's workshop with wheel and oven.   Good (γῆ κεραμῖτις),
particularly red, clay was in demand for superior goods, and of this
the promontory of Kolias, near Athens, furnished an unlimited
supply.   The potter's wheel (κεράμειος τροχός) was in use at a
very early period.   On it were formed both large and small
vessels ; with the difference, however, that of the former the foot,
neck, and handles were formed separately, and afterwards attached,
as was also the case in small vessels with widely curved handles.
In order to intensify the red colour the vessel was frequently
glazed and afterwards dried and burnt on the oven.   The outlines
of the figures to be painted on the vase were either cut into the
red clay and filled up with a brilliant black varnish, or the
surface itself was covered with the black varnish up to the
contours, in which case these stood out in the natural red colour of
the clay.   The first-mentioned process was the older of the two,
and greater antiquity is therefore to be assigned to vessels with
black figures on a red ground.   In both kinds of paintings
draperies or the muscles of nude figures were further indicated by
the incision of additional lines of the colour of the surface into the
figures.   Other colours, like dark red, violet, or white, which on
close investigation have been recognised as dissolvable, were put on
after the second burning of the vessel.

37. About the historic development of pottery we know
nothing beyond what may be guessed from the differences of style.
As we said before, figures of a black or dark-brown colour painted
on the natural pale red or yellowish colour of the clay indicate
greater antiquity.   The black figures were occasionally painted
over in white or violet.   These vessels are mostly small and
somewhat compressed in form ; they are surrounded with parallel
stripes of pictures of animals, plants, fabulous beings, or arabesques (Fig. 195).   The drawings show an antiquated stiff type,
similar to those on the vessels recently discovered at Nineveh and
Babylon, whence the influence of Oriental on Greek art may be
inferred.   This archaic style, like the strictly hieratic style in
sculpture, was retained together with a freer treatment at a more
advanced period.   As a first step of development we notice the
combination of animals and arabesques, at first with half-human,

half-animal figures, soon followed by compositions belonging
mostly to a certain limited circle of myths.   The treatment
of figures shows rigidity in the calm, and violence in the active,
positions.   The Doric forms of letters and words on many vases of
this style, whether found in Greece or Italy, no less than the
uniformity of their *technique,* indicate *one* place of manufacture,
most likely the Doric Corinth, celebrated for her potteries ; on the
other hand, the inscriptions in Ionian characters and written in
the Ionian dialect on vessels prove their origin in the manu-
factures of the Ionian Eubœa and her colonies.[1]   The pictures on
these vases, also painted in stripes, extend the mythological
subject-matter beyond the Trojan cycle to the oldest epical myths,
each story being represented in its consecutive phases.

The latter vases form the transition to the second period.
The shapes now become more varied, graceful, and slender.   The
figures are painted in black, and covered with a brilliant varnish ;
the *technique* of the painting, however, does not differ from that of

Fig. 195.

the first period.   The outlines have been neatly incised and
covered up with black paint ; the details also of draperies and
single parts of the body are done by incision, and sometimes
painted over in white or dark red.   The principle seems to be that
of polychrome painting, also applied in sculpture.   Single parts of
the armour, embroideries, and patterns of dresses, hair, and beards
of men, the manes of animals, etc., are indicated by means of dark
red lines.   This variety of colour was required particularly for the
draperies, which are stiff and clumsily attached to the body.   The
same stiffness is shown in the treatment of faces and other nude

[1] See the excellent preface of Jahn's description of vases in the Royal Pinakothek at Munich (p. cxlviii. *et seq.*), where the different periods of pottery have been
characterised.   See also Jahn's essay, "Die griechischen bemalten Vasen," in his
"Populäre Aufsätze aus der Alterthumswissenschaft."   Bonn, 1868 (p. 307 *et seq.*)

parts of the body, as also in the rendering of movements. The faces are always in profile, the nose and chin pointed and protruding, and the lips of the compressed mouth indicated only by a line. Shoulders, hips, thighs, and calves bulge out, the body being singularly pinched (Fig. 196). The grouping is equally imperfect. The single figures of compositions are loosely connected by the general idea of the story. They have, as it were, a narrative character; an attempt at truth to nature is, however, undeniable. The subjects are taken partly from the twelve-gods cycle (like the frequently occurring birth of Athene, Dionysian processions, etc.) or from Trojan and Theban myths; partly also from daily life, such as chases, wrestlings, sacrifices, symposia, and the like. To this class belong most of those large Pana-

Fig. 196.

thenaïc prize-vases, which are of such importance for our knowledge of gymnastic competitions.

In our third class the figures appear in the natural colour of the surface, which itself has been painted black. The character of the figures in consequence appears gay and lively. Both styles seem at one time to have existed together, for we find them used severally on two sides of one and the same vessel, till at last the painting of black figures was disused entirely. The drawings now become more individual, and are freed from the fetters of conventional tradition—a proof of the free development of both political and artistic feelings, even amongst the lower classes of artificers. The specimens of the third class show the different stages of this process of liberation. At first the figures are still somewhat hard, and the drapery, although following the lines of the body more freely than previously, shows still traces of archaic severity of treatment; the details, indicated by black lines, are still carefully worked out. For smaller folds and muscles, a darker shade of the red colour is used; wreaths and flowers appear dark; red white is used only in few cases—for instance, for the hair of an old man. The composition shows greater concentration and symmetry in the grouping, according to the conditions of the space at disposal. The figures show a solemn dignity, with signs, however, of an attempted freer treatment.

Kramer justly calls this period that of the "severe style," and compares it with the well-known "Æginetic" style in sculpture. The further development of the "severe style" is what Kramer calls the "beautiful style," in which grace and beauty of motion and drapery, verging on the soft, have taken the place of severe dignity. In high art this transition might be compared to that from Perugino's school to that of Raphael, or, if we may believe the ancient writers, from the school of Polygnotos to that of Zeuxis and Parrhasios.

Fig. 197.

The form of the vessels themselves next calls for our attention. The vases, two-handled amphorai and krateres, found most frequently during this period, are slender and graceful. Together with them we meet with beautifully modelled drinking-horns (Fig. 201), and heads (Fig. 197, *d*) or whole figures, used to put vessels upon. The variety of forms, and the largeness of some vessels, overloaded as they were with figures, soon led to want of care in the composition. The moderation characteristic of the "beautiful style" was soon relinquished for exagger-

ated ornamentation, combined with a preference for representing
sumptuous dresses and the immoderate use of white, yellow, and
other colours. This led gradually to the decadence of pottery.
Lucania and Apulia are the places where sumptuous vessels of the
degenerating style are most frequently found (see Fig. 197, *a, b, c*).
The handles of the splendid amphora (Fig. 197, *a*) are attached to
the brim, adorned with an ovolo, the handles being in the form of
volutes, the centres of which contain heads of the Gorgon; their
lower parts end in heads of swans. The neck of the vessel is
adorned with three stripes of garlands, in the centre of which are
female heads—a common feature of this style (see the vase, Fig.
197, *c*). The body of the vessel is occupied by pictures from the
myth of Triptolemos, who himself is discovered in the centre on a
chariot drawn by dragons. The pictures are in two rows, one above
the other, a peculiarity frequently found in larger vases of this style.
Above them we see a double ovolo; beneath them a " meandering "
ornamentation. The arrangement of the figures in Fig. 197, *c*, is
similar. In the centre of the picture is an open building (frequently met with on vases of this style), round which the figures
are grouped in two rows, one over the other. The vessel itself
is an amphora resembling a candelabrum, the excessively slender
body of which, resting on a weak foot, shows its merely ornamental purpose (compare the picture on a vase in § 60, representing the burial of Archemoros). Fig. 197, *b*, shows Kadmos
fighting with the dragon: the busts of gods being painted above
the chief action, as if looking down upon it from heights, are also
peculiar to this style.

The subject-matter of these pictures has undergone similar
changes as the old mythical stories themselves, when looked at
through the medium of poetry, both lyrical and dramatic. Attic
myths were treated in preference. The infinitely varied treatment
proves the popularity of those lyrical and dramatic versions. In
the decaying style, not only battles of Amazons and Kentaurs,
and scenes from the Hades, but also the subjects of tragedies, are
depicted, the situations of the latter being evidently imitated
from the stage, including even the variegated colours of the
costumes. The whole impression becomes theatrical in consequence. Sometimes mythological scenes and characters have been
caricatured as on the comic stage (see pictures of this kind in § 58).

The vases of Lucania and Apulia, moreover, show frequently representations of Greek burial-rites as modified by the South Italian populations. Jahn from this fact concludes the existence of local manufactures (*l. c.* p. ccxxxi.), which is confirmed by the inscriptions on the vessels. They belonged to a post-Alexandrine period, those of the "beautiful style" dating from the time between Perikles and Alexander.

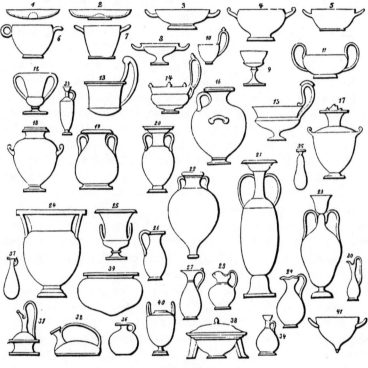

Fig. 198.

In some Etruscan cities earthenware was manufactured by local artists working after Greek patterns. The figures are distinguished from genuine Greek work by the contours being incised very deeply and filled up with red colour. The clay also is coarser. The compositions show an admixture of local myths and usages, not to mention Etruscan inscriptions.

38. Hitherto we have considered the various artistic styles of

vessels.   Now we must try to distinguish their names and forms by
the varieties of their uses.   Ancient writers have transmitted to us
a variety of names for them, which in some cases may be verified
by inscriptions on individual vessels.   The naming, however, of
many of them is very difficult, and the attempts of Panofka in
this direction have met with much contradiction amongst archæologists.   Their nomenclature amongst the ancients seems to have
been much more diversified than is the case at the present day.
We have collected forty-one of the most striking forms (Fig. 198),
by means of which the innumerable varieties in our museums may
be to some extent classified.

Vessels may be divided, according to their uses, into those
for storing, mixing, and drawing liquids.   Amongst the vessels
for keeping wine, oil, honey, water, etc., the pithos ($\pi i\theta o\varsigma$)
is the largest.   It is made of strong clay, without a foot,
either pointed or flattened at the bottom.   If pointed, the
pithos, in that case generally a small one, was dug into the
earth to keep it upright ; if flat-bottomed, it was larger, and had
a wide mouth.   The cubic measure of the large pithos was equal,
at least, to our large wine-vats, as is shown by the fact of those
kept in the rocky cellars of Gallias at Agrigentum holding
one hundred amphorai of wine each.   During the Peloponnesian
war, the poorer people seeking shelter in Athens lived in pithoi,
also called $\pi\iota\theta\acute{a}\kappa\nu\alpha\iota$.   Of mythological celebrity is the pithos of
the Daniades in which Eurystheus hid himself ; the tub of
Diogenes is generally known.   Similar to the pithos, but smaller
and more easily movable, must have been the $\sigma\tau\acute{a}\mu\nu o\varsigma$ (Fig. 198,
18, called stamnos by both Panofka and Gerhard, and Fig. 198,
40, described by Panofka as a lekane, by Gerhard as an Apulian
stamnos) and the $\beta\hat{\iota}\kappa o\varsigma$.   Wine, oil, figs, and salt meat were
preserved in them.   About the forms of the wine-vessels called
$\H{\upsilon}\rho\chi\eta$ and $\pi\upsilon\tau\acute{\iota}\nu\eta$ we are quite uncertain.   Equally uncertain is
the form of the $\kappa\acute{a}\delta o\varsigma$, a larger vessel, also for wine, unless we
consider it as belonging to the class of amphorai.   The form of
the amphora ($\grave{a}\mu\phi o\rho\epsilon\acute{\upsilon}\varsigma$), a two-handled vessel ($\acute{o}$ $\grave{\epsilon}\kappa\alpha\tau\acute{\epsilon}\rho\omega\theta\epsilon\nu$ $\kappa\alpha\tau\grave{a}$
$\tau\grave{a}$ $\mathring{\omega}\tau\alpha$ $\delta\upsilon\nu\acute{a}\mu\epsilon\nu o\varsigma$ $\phi\acute{\epsilon}\rho\epsilon\sigma\theta\alpha\iota$), mentioned by Homer, is sufficiently
known from many representations on vases, bas-reliefs, coins, and
gems.   They are more or less bulky vessels, with necks shorter
or longer in proportion, but with mouths always of moderate

size compared to the bulk (Fig. 198, 20-23); frequently resting on feet, but sometimes (Fig. 198, 22) ending in a flattened point, in which case the amphora was either put against a wall or fitted into a frame. The variety consists in the form of the handles, essentially modified by the size of the vessel, and in the larger or smaller opening of the mouth. Amongst the amphorai we count the Panathenaïc prize-vases, in which the victor received the oil from the sacred olive-tree, and which even during the period of the "beautiful style" preserved the archaic manner of black figures on a red background. Hydria (ὑδρία) and kalpis (κάλπις) (Fig. 198, 16 and 17) seem to be different names of one and the same kind of bulky, short-necked vessel, the use of which is shown by its being carried on their heads, in the pictures on vases, by maidens fetching water. Its characteristic is a third handle in the centre of the vessel, which prevented its sinking in the water, and, at the same time, made the lifting of the filled pitcher on the head easier. The diminutive ὑδρίσκη signifies a smaller vessel for the keeping of ointment, formed, most likely, in imitation of the hydria. The krossos (κρωσσός, κρωσός, κρωσσίον) was used for keeping water and oil, but also ashes. It most likely resembled the hydria, but cannot with certainty be recognised in any of the existing vessels. A smaller wine-vessel, most likely bulky and long necked, was the λάγυνος. Gerhard compares it to the modern Orvieto-bottle. The lagynos, surrounded with wicker-work, called φλασκίον by Suidas, may have been the model of our bottles or flasks. Travellers and soldiers in the field used the κώθων, a bulky flask with a narrow neck and a handle, which had the advantage of clearing the water from muddy substances, most likely by means of a par-ticular clay of which it was made. A similar drinking flask was the bombylios (βομβυλιός, βομβύλη), the narrow neck of which emitted the fluid by single drops only, and in this way produced a kind of gurgling sound, like the βησίον or βήσσα used by the Alexandrians. Whether the little flask with handles (Fig. 198, 37), called bombylios, by Gerhard and Panofka, answers to the Greek term we will not venture to decide. The λήκυθοι, mentioned by Homer, served for the keeping of ointment; their form is sufficiently defined both by pictures on vases and numerous still-existing specimens

(Fig. 198, 33). In these the oil was preserved for the rubbing of the limbs of wrestlers, or of bathers after their baths; out of them also was poured the sacred oil over the graves of the dead. All these vessels show very much the same type. The neck was narrow in order to let the oil pass only in single drops, by means of which the above-mentioned gurgling sound (λακεῖν, λακάζειν) was produced. The numerous vessels of this kind were chiefly manufactured in Attika; they were necessary both to men and women. About the form of the olpe (ὄλπη, ὄλπα, ὄλπις), also used for oil, and peculiar to the Doric tribe, we know nothing. According to Athenæus, olpe seems to have been an old name of the oinochoë; hence the notion of the vessels, Fig. 198, 26 and 27, being of the oinochoë kind. The former is called by Panofka, olpe, by Gerhard, oinochoë; the latter Gerhard calls an olpe approaching the Egyptian style. About the form of the alabastron (ἀλάβαστρον, ἀλάβαστον) we are better informed. It is a small cylindrical vessel, narrowing a little in the neck so as to produce the gradual dripping of the perfumed ointment preserved in it. All the specimens preserved to us, although varying in size and form, agree in the essential points, but for the style of the pictures and the material of which the vessels are made. The use of the alabastron is shown in the wall-picture of the so-called Aldobrandini wedding (see Fig. 232).

The generic term for mixing-vessels used at meals and libations is krater (κρατήρ, κρητήρ, from κεράννυμι). Its form, greatly modified by different ages and tastes, is sufficiently known from pictures and existing specimens (Fig. 198, 25; compare Fig. 197, *b*). It had to hold larger quantities of wine and water (unless these were mixed afterwards in the drinking-glasses), and was accordingly bulky and broad necked. A handle on each side made the krater easily portable when empty. It rested on a foot divided into several parts, and on a broad base. Of the several divisions of the krater, as the Argolian, Lesbian, Korinthian, Lakonian, we have, no doubt, specimens in our collections, without, however, being able to distinguish them. Hypokreteria, *i.e.* large flat dishes, were placed under the krateres, to receive the overflowing liquid. Similar to the krater was the ψυκτήρ, a cooling-vessel for wine before it was mixed. Its dimensions varied greatly; in some cases topers emptied a whole ψυκτήρ of moderate dimensions. According to Pollux, this vessel was also called δῖνος, and rested on a base consisting of dice or knobs, instead of a foot. Its shape was somewhat like a pail, and resembled the kalathos, the working-basket of Greek women ; this name was, indeed, also applied to it. We have in our collections several vases resembling this shape, to which, therefore, the names of ψυκτήρ and δῖνος may be applied.

Amongst vessels for drawing liquids we first mention those called ἀρύταινα, ἀρύστιχος, and ἀρύβαλλος, all derived from ἀρύω, to scoop. Of the aryballos Athenæus says, that it expanded towards the bottom, and that its neck narrowed like a purse with its string tightened, which latter was called by the same name. Specimens of it are numerous in our museums (Fig. 198, 34 and 36). It was also used for the keeping of ointment, and as such belonged, like the arytaina or arysane, to the bathing utensils. The οἰνοχόη, χοῦς, πρόχους, and ἐπίχυσις served, as their names indicate, for the drawing and pouring out of liquids, especially of wine. They had one handle and resembled a jug. Their size varied considerably (Fig. 198, 26-31). Their use is sufficiently illustrated by pictures. Fig. 199 shows a picture on a vase in which the ephebos kneeling to the right is taking wine from the krater with the oinochoë, in order to fill the drinking-vessel of the other ephebos. The prochous seems to have been used chiefly as a water-jug. Accurate accounts of its different forms we do not possess. Moreover, according to Athenæus, the terms had been changed. What originally was called pelike, afterwards received the name of choë. The pelike resembled the Panathenaïc vases ; and is said

Fig. 199.

to have taken afterwards the form of the oinochoë, as used at those festivities. At the time of Athenæus the pelike was only a piece of ornament used at festive processions, the vessel in common use being called chous, and resembling the arytaina. The kotyle (κοτύλη, κότυλος) was used as a measure of both liquid and dry substances, but also for drinking purposes. The captive Athenians in the Syrakusian quarries, for instance, received one kotyle of water and two kotylai of food a day (see

Fig. 198, 4 and 7; the former called by Panofka, kotyle, by Gerhard, skyphos; the latter, by Panofka, kotylos, by Gerhard, kotyle). Its form was that of a deep, pot-like, two-handled dish, with a short foot. Several small kotylai with covers to them were sometimes combined and carried by one handle, similar to what we find amongst peasants in Central Germany at the present day. Athenæus calls this combination a κέρνος (Fig. 200). Its elegant form makes its use at table as a kind of cruet-stand appear probable. The κύαθος was used both for drinking and drawing liquids. It resembles our drinking-cups but for the handle, which is considerably higher than the brim of the vessel (Fig. 198, 10, 13, 14), in order to prevent the dipping of the finger into the liquid on drawing it. It was used as a measure at the symposia, before inebriation became the rule, when larger vessels were used.

Fig. 200.

Amongst drinking-vessels we mention the phiale, the kymbion, and the kylix. The φιάλη was a flat saucer without a foot (Fig. 198, 1 and 2), the centre of which was raised like the boss of a buckler, and called like it ὀμφαλός. Smaller phialai were used for drinking; larger ones served at libations and lustrations and as anathemata in the temples, particularly those wrought in precious metals. The kymbion (κυμβίον, κύμβη) is said to have been a deep, long dish like a boat, without a handle, used for drinking or libations; a specimen we do not possess, as far as we know. The κύλιξ is a drinking-cup with two handles, resting on an elegantly formed foot (Fig. 198, 8). We meet with it frequently in pictures and in museums. The kylix of Argos differed from that of Attika by having its brim bent inward a little. Whether the so-called Therikleic kylikes had their name from the animals painted on them, or from the potter Therikles, who was celebrated at Korinth at the time of Aristophanes, we must leave undecided. Athenæus describes these as deep goblets with two small handles, and adorned at the upper brim with ivy-branches. Fig. 199 shows an ephebos holding in his right hand the skyphos (σκύφος), while a kylix stands on his extended left. The former resembles a cup, sometimes with a flat bottom, at others resting on a small Doric base (Fig. 198, 6), at others,

again, ending in a point (Fig. 198, 41). It generally had two
small horizontal handles just underneath the brim. Originally
used by peasants (Eumaios, for instance, offers one to Odysseus),
it afterwards became part of the dinner-service. According to
different forms, peculiar to different localities, we distinguish
Bœotian, Rhodian, Syrakusian, and Attic skyphoi. The skyphos
was generally designated as the drinking-cup of Herakles. The
κάνθαρος was a goblet resting on a high foot, and having widely
curved thin handles; it was peculiar to Dionysos and to the
actors in the Dionysian thiasos (Fig. 198, 12, compare Fig. 199), and
appears frequently in their hands in pictures on vases and other
representations. The old kantharos was larger than that later in
use, as appears from a passage in Athenæus which says, that the
modern kantharoi are so small, as if they were meant to be
swallowed themselves, instead of having the wine drunk out of
them. As the oldest drinking-vessel the καρχήσιον is mentioned.
According to Athenæus, it was lengthy in form, with the centre
of the body slightly bent inward, and two handles reaching to
the bottom. Whether it had a foot or a flat base (Fig. 198, 11)
cannot be decided. Homer mentions a δέπας ἀμφικύπελλον, *i.e.*
double goblet, which, as appears from Aristotle ("Hist. Anim.,"
IX. 40), was also known at a later period. A specimen of it has not

been preserved, as far as
is known to us. Being
mostly wrought in precious
metals, they were prob-
ably, at a later period,
frequently remodelled into
more fashionable shapes.

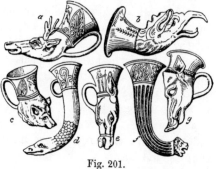

To conclude, we men-
tion the beautifully
modelled drinking-horns,
wrought partly in clay,
partly in metal, and used

Fig. 201.

at feasts (κέρας and ῥυτόν) (see Fig. 201). The horn has been used
as a drinking-utensil since the oldest times, particularly amongst
barbarous nations. Both Æschylos and Xenophon quote examples
of this custom. In pictures on vases the Kentauroi and Dionysos
frequently appear with drinking-horns. The rhyton is an artistic

development of this primitive form. Its end has been modelled
into the head of an animal, according to the nature of which the
rhyton has received the surnames of γρύψ (Fig. 201, *b*), λύκος
(Fig. 201, *c*), ὄνος, ἡμίονος (Fig. 201, *e*), κάπρος (Fig. 201, *g*),
ἔλεφας, ἵππος, ταῦρος, etc. (compare the picture on a vase in § 56
in which one of the topers pours the wine from a panther-rhyton
(πάρδαλις) into a goblet). The rhyton had to be emptied at one
draught, and was afterwards placed (probably to be filled again)
on a stand (ὑπόθημα, ὑποπυθμήν, περισκελίς). As appears from
the cited picture, the rhyton had an opening (which most likely
could be stopped) inside the mouth of the animal, from which the
wine was poured out, and had to be caught by the drinker in his
glass.

As another means of keeping wine and oil we now mention
the ἀσκός, the wine-skin, still in use in the East and in Southern
Europe, consisting of the hide of an animal sewed and tied
together. In pictures we often see it on the backs of fauns and
Sileni, and its form has even been imitated in clay in small vessels
for wine and oil. Our museums contain several vases of this kind
(see Levezow, "Gallerie der Vasen," etc., Table IX., No. 189).
Even that common form of handled vessels called by Gerhard
askos (Fig. 198, 32) may originally have been suggested by the
wine-skin.

Of Greek crockery nothing remains, with the exception of a
few dishes. It was destroyed with the dwelling-houses, and had
not the advantage of being deposited in the grave-chambers. On
the other hand, the kitchen utensils of the Romans are fully illustrated by the excavations at Pompeii; to these we refer the
reader. The χύτρα no doubt resembled our saucepans with one
or two handles. Porridge, meat, and vegetables were cooked in
it, and out of it the first portion was offered to the domestic gods
and to Zeus Herkaios at every meal, and at the consecration of
temples and altars. Sometimes the chytra had three feet (see
Fig. 198, 38), but usually, and particularly if it was oval in shape
and without feet, it was placed on a kind of tripod (χυτροπούς,
λάσανον). Homer already mentions large vessels (τρίποδες),
standing on tripods or having three feet, used particularly for
heating the bathing-water. Identical with the chytra was the
λέβης, mostly made of bronze. Both names occur frequently

amongst the enumerations of temple treasures. They were made
of bronze, silver, or gold. On a cameo (Panofka, " Bilder antiken
Lebens," Table XII., No. 5) we see a huge lebes, but without
the tripod, in which two boys are cooking a pig, while a third
one is poking the fire under the vessel. Besides these, we
possess some dishes in our museums, the painting of which with
fish of various kinds indicates their being used for the preparing
of these; whence the name of ἰχθύαι applied to them.

As a domestic utensil we also mention the bath. In Homer
baths are mentioned, most likely made of polished stone (ἀσάμινθοι)
and large enough to hold one person. These
asaminthoi, however, were soon replaced by
large scale-like baths (λουτῆρες, λουτήρια,
Fig. 202) resting on one or several feet, and
filled by pipes in the walls, Fig. 202. They
appear in the pictures of bathing-scenes
in all kinds of varieties. Larger baths for
several persons, which were placed in the public or private bathing-chambers (βαλανεῖα),
were called κολυμβήθρα, πύελος, and μάκτρα.

Fig. 202.

They were either dug into the earth and surrounded with masonry,
or cut into the living rock. They may have also been built of
stone.

39. We now have to add a few remarks about vessels made of
metal, of stones more or less precious, and of glass. All these
were numerous, both as ornaments and for practical use. The
names mentioned for earthenware apply in general also to them.
Instead of paintings, however, we here find plastic ornamentations.
Amongst stones the fine white alabaster was most frequently used,
for those delicate little ointment-bottles called by the name of
alabastron (see p. 150), partly because of the softness of the
colour of the stone, partly because of its great coldness, which
tended to keep the ointment fresh. Its use for drinking-cups
was less frequent. Its sides were with great skill, by means
of turning, reduced to the thinness of note-paper, as can be
seen in an alabastron at the Museum of Berlin. For the same
purposes as the alabastron were also used the onyx and the agate.
Mithridates VI. Eupator had amongst his treasures two onyx
vases, which Lucullus brought to Rome as spoil. Only few of

these precious vessels are preserved at the present day. Amongst these we mention the so-called "Mantuan goblet" in the possession of the late Duke Charles of Brunswick, formerly owned by the Gonzaga family, an ointment-vase of onyx-agate in the *Münz- und Antiken-Cabinet* at Vienna, an onyx vase in the Antiquarium of the Royal Museum at Berlin (all these decorated with sculptures), and two onyx vases at the museums of Vienna and Naples respectively. As the finest specimen of Oriental agate in existence we mention a vase in the just-mentioned collection at Vienna $28\frac{1}{2}$ inches in diameter, including the handle. It was brought to Western Europe after the conquest of Constantinople by the Crusaders, and came afterwards into the possession of Charles the Bold, Duke of Burgundy, whence it was transferred to Vienna as part of the dowry of Maria of Burgundy, wife of the Emperor Maximilian I. For larger vessels, like the krater or the urn, white or coloured marble, porphyry, and also various metals, were used, and we still possess numerous vases of this kind adorned with beautiful reliefs. Particularly the krater is, according to its destination, frequently adorned with the Dionysian attributes, such as Silenus-masks, goblets, musical instruments, etc., beautifully grouped together with flower and fruit ornamentations; the handles and the finely developed foot are in perfect harmony. Bronze vessels of this kind are frequently mentioned by the ancients. Achilles offers a silver krater wrought by Sidonian artists as a prize for runners at a race. Crœsus made a votive offering to the Delphic oracle of one golden and one silver krater, the latter holding 600 amphorai, being a work of Theodoros, the Samian bronze-founder; a bronze krater, resting on three colossal kneeling figures, was dedicated by the Samians to Hera. Amongst the votive offerings at the Parthenon were numerous goblets of this kind, made both of gold and silver. The most celebrated Greek toreutai, like Kalamis, Akragas, Mys, Stratonikos, Antipater, Pytheas (who, however, according to Pliny, worked only in silver and bronze), cultivated this branch of their art, and the vessels from their *ateliers* were sought after, up to the latest period, by the Romans. With the exception of the smaller oil and drinking vessels, these vases served only as ornaments in the houses of the rich, as votive offerings in temples and graves, as decorations of the gables of buildings, and as prizes at the games. The art of making vessels of glass seems to have been a later importation from the East, particularly from Egypt. At first vessels made of glass (λίθος χυτή) were appreciated as much as those of precious metals; afterwards glass bottles and drinking glasses become more common. Still the Greek manufacture of this article never was equal to those of Rome and Egypt (compare § 91).

Amongst domestic utensils we also count articles made of basket-work, which frequently occur in antique pictures (see Fig. 203). The kalathos (κάλαθος, καλαθίς, καλαθίσκος), the basket for keeping wool (used for weaving and embroidering), and also flowers and fruit, is frequently met with in vase-paintings illustrating the life of Greek women (Fig. 203, *a*); perhaps Fig. 203, *b*, also went by the name of kalathos. As early as Homer's time baskets (κάνεον), probably round or oval, were used, at meals, to keep bread and pastry in. They had a low rim and handles (Fig. 203, *c*). The kaneon was also used at offerings, as is proved by Fig. 203, *c*, where it is filled with pomegranates, holy boughs, and ribbons. At the Panathenaia noble Athenian maidens carried such baskets, filled with holy cakes, incense, and knives, on their heads, whence the name κανηφόροι applied to them. These graceful figures were a favourite subject of antique sculpture. Both Polyklete and Skopas had done a celebrated kanephore—the former in bronze, the latter in marble. The σπυρίς, chiefly used for carrying fish, was also a flat basket, similar to that used at the present day by fishermen in the South. Other baskets used by peasants appear frequently in antique pictures, such as Fig. 203, *d*, in the original carried by a peasant on a stick over his shoulder, together with another basket of the same pear-like shape; Fig. 203, *f* and *e*, are taken from a

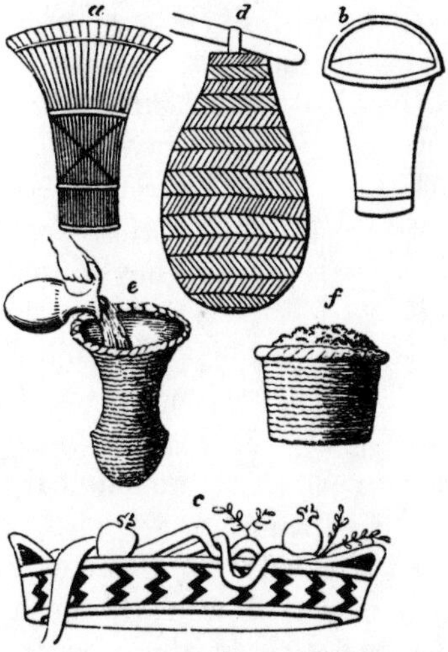

Fig. 203.

bas-relief representing a vintage, in which the former appears filled with grapes, while the latter is being filled with must by a boy. This proves, at the same time, the knowledge amongst the Greeks of the art of making the basket-work dense enough to hold fluids. The same fact is shown by a passage in Homer, in which Polyphemos lets the milk coagulate to cheese in baskets ($\tau\acute{a}\lambda\alpha\rho\sigma\varsigma$ $\pi\lambda\epsilon\kappa\tau\acute{o}\varsigma$), which cheese was afterwards placed on a hurdle ($\tau\alpha\rho\sigma\acute{o}\varsigma$), through which the whey trickled slowly. Of plaited rushes, or twigs, consisted also a peculiar kind of net ($\kappa\acute{v}\rho\tau\sigma\varsigma$), a specimen of which is seen on the reverse of a medal coined under the Emperor Macrinus, as the emblem of the maritime city of Byzantium (see Dumersan, "Descript. d. Médailles ant. du Cabinet du feu M. Allier de Hauteroche," Pl. III., No. 8). Baskets, roughly plaited, appéar also in the vase-painting of the "Weighing out of the Silphion" (Panofka, "Bilder antiken Lebens," Taf. XVI., No. 3), where the silphion is being carried in them. According to Athenæus, basket-work was imitated in precious metals.

40. To light and heat the rooms, at Homer's time, fire-baskets, or fire-basins ($\lambda\alpha\mu\pi\tau\hat{\eta}\rho\epsilon\varsigma$), were used, standing on high poles, and fed with dry logs of wood or splinters ($\delta\hat{a}\delta\epsilon\varsigma$). The cinders were, at intervals, removed by serving-maids, and the flames replenished. Such fire-baskets, on poles, are still used by night-

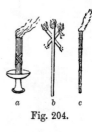

travellers in Southern Russia, and at nightly ceremonies in India. The use of pine-torches ($\delta\alpha\acute{\iota}\delta\omega\nu$ $\acute{v}\pi\grave{o}$ $\lambda\alpha\mu\pi\omega\mu\epsilon\nu\acute{a}\omega\nu$) is of equal antiquity. They consisted of long, thin sticks of pine-wood, tied together with bark, rushes, or papyrus (Fig. 204, *c*). The bark of the vine was also used for torches, called $\lambda o\phi\acute{\iota}\varsigma$. The golden statues on pedestals, in the hall of Alkinoos, undoubtedly held such torches in their hands.

a b c
Fig. 204.

In vase-paintings we also see a different form of the torch, carried chiefly by Demeter and Persephone, which consists of two pieces of wood fastened crosswise to a staff (Fig. 204, *b*). An imitation of this wooden torch was undoubtedly the torch-case, made of clay or metal, in the shape of a salpinx. Their surface was either smooth or formed in imitation of the bundles of sticks and the bark of the wooden torch, the inside being

filled with resinous substances. A different kind of torch was
the phanos (φανός, φανή), which consisted of sticks tied together,
and perforated with pitch, resin, or wax. They were put into a
case of metal, which again was let into a kind of dish,
turned either upwards or downwards (Fig. 204, *a*). This
dish (χύτρα) served to receive the cinders or the dripping
resin. The phanoi were either carried, or, when their
case was prolonged to a long stem (καυλός), and had a
foot (βάσις) added to it, might be put down (Fig. 205),
and received, in that case, the names of λαμπτήρ or
λυχνοῦχος. The further development of this form was
the candelabrum, carrying either fire-basins or oil-
lamps (see the Roman lighting-apparatus, § 92). The
date of oil-lamps in Greece cannot be stated with
accuracy: they were known at the time of Aristophanes. They were made of terra-cotta or metal, and
their construction resembles those used by the Romans.

Fig. 205.

They are mostly closed semi-globes with two openings, one
in the centre, to pour the oil in, the other, in the nose-shaped
prolongation (μυκτήρ), destined to receive the wick (θρυαλλίς,
ἐλλύχνιον, φλομός). Amongst the small numbers of Greek
lamps preserved to us, we have chosen two of the most graceful
specimens, one of them showing the ordinary form of the lamp
(Fig. 206), the other that of a kline,
on which a boy is lying (Fig. 207).
Both are made of clay, the latter being
painted in various colours. The Athenians
also used lanterns (λυχνοῦχος) made of
transparent horn, and lit up with oil-lamps.

Fig. 206.

They were carried at night in the streets like
the torches. Sparks, carefully preserved under
the ashes, served both Greeks and Romans to light
the fire. The ancients had, however, a lighting
apparatus (πυρεῖα) consisting of two pieces of
wood, of which the one was driven into the other

Fig. 207.

(στορεύς or ἐσχάρα), like a gimlet, the friction effecting a flame.
According to Theophrast, the wood of nut or chestnut trees was
generally used for the purpose.

41. We now come to the dress of the Greeks. We shall

have to consider those articles of dress used as a protection against the weather, and those prescribed by decency or fashion, also the coverings of the head and the feet, the arrangement of the hair, and the ornaments.   Unfortunately, the terminology is, in many cases, uncertain.   Many points, therefore, must remain undecided. Before entering upon details, we must remark that the dress of the Greek, compared with modern fashion, was extremely simple and natural.   Owing to the warmth of the climate and the taste of the inhabitants, both superfluous and tight articles of dress were dispensed with.   Moreover, the body was allowed to develop its natural beauty in vigorous exercise; and in this harmony and beauty of the limbs the Greeks prided themselves, which, of course, reacted favourably on the character of the dress.

The two chief divisions of garments are the ἐνδύματα, which are put on like a shirt, and the ἐπιβλήματα, or περιβλήματα, resembling a cloak, loosely thrown over the naked body, or the endymata.   Weiss ("Kostümkunde," I., p. 703 *et seq.*) remarks rightly that the original character of Greek dress, consisting of the two parts just mentioned, remained essentially the same. The later changes apply only to the mode of using these, and to their material and ornamental qualities.

The χιτών, in its various forms, was used both by men and women as their endyma—*i.e.* the under-garment touching the naked body.   A second under-garment like a shirt, worn under the chiton, seems not to have been in use.   The expressions μονοχίτων and ἀχίτων only indicate that in the first case the chiton was worn without the himation; in the second, *vice versâ*.   The chiton was an oblong piece of cloth arranged round the body so that the arm was put through a hole in the closed side, the two ends of the open side being fastened over the opposite shoulder by means of a button or clasp.   On this latter side, therefore, the chiton was completely open, at least as far as the thigh, underneath of which the two ends might be either pinned or stitched together.   Round the hips the chiton was fastened with a ribbon or girdle, and the lower part could be shortened as much as required by pulling it through this girdle.   A chiton of this kind is worn by a soldier in Fig. 208, taken from a beautiful relief on an Attic urn representing the leave-taking of an Athenian warrior from his wife and child. This sleeveless chiton, made of wool, was worn chiefly by the Dorians. The Athenians adopted it about the time of Perikles, after having worn previously the longer chiton peculiar to the Ionians of Asia Minor. Frequently sleeves, either shorter and covering only the upper arm, or continued to the wrist, were added to the chiton, which resembled, in consequence (at least, in the former case), exactly the chemises worn by women at the present day. The chiton, with sleeves coming down to the wrist ($\chi\iota\tau\grave{\omega}\nu\ \chi\epsilon\iota\rho\iota\delta\omega\tau\acute{o}\varsigma$), undoubtedly an invention of the luxurious Asiatic Greeks, is worn, for instance, by Skiron (northwest wind) and Boreas (north wind), amongst the portraitures of the eight chief winds on the octagonal tower of the winds at Athens (see Fig. 158). The so-called pedagogue amongst the group of the Niobides also wears this chiton ;

Fig. 208.

but the arms of this statue have been restored. The short-sleeved chiton is frequently worn by women and children on monuments. Of the sleeveless chiton, worn by men over both shoulders, as in Fig. 208 ($\dot{a}\mu\phi\iota\mu\acute{a}\sigma\chi\alpha\lambda o\iota$), it is stated that it was the sign of a free citizen. Slaves and artisans are said to have worn a chiton with one hole for the left arm, the right arm and half of the chest remaining quite uncovered. The $\dot{\epsilon}\xi\omega\mu\acute{\iota}\varsigma$ was another form of the chiton, worn on monuments, chiefly by Hephaistos, Daidalos, and workmen, $\kappa\alpha\tau$' $\dot{\epsilon}\xi o\chi\acute{\eta}\nu$, as also by fishermen and sailors, whose occupations required the right arm to be quite unencumbered. A bas-relief (Fig. 209) shows two ship-carpenters dressed in the exomis, representing, perhaps, master Argos and an assistant, working at the ship *Argo*, under the supervision of Athene. Two charming statuettes of fisher-boys at the British Museum and the Museo Borbonico of Naples (Clarac, " Musée," Nos. 881, 882), respectively, also illustrate this picturesque costume.

Fig. 209.

M

Identical with this in form is the chiton worn by Doric women. It was simple, short-skirted, and with a slit in the upper part at both sides. It was fastened with clasps over both shoulders, and shortened as far as the knees by means of pulling it through the girdle. In this form it is worn by two maidens in the Louvre, destined for the service of the Lakonian Artemis at Karyæ. They carry kinds of baskets (σαλία) on their heads, and are performing the festive dance in honour of the goddess (Fig. 210). The exomis, as described above, is worn by the female statue in the Vatican known as the "Springing Amazon"

Fig. 210.   Fig. 211.   Fig. 212.

(Müller's "Denkmäler," I. No. 138, *a*), and also by statues of Artemis, and representations of that goddess on gems and coins. The long chiton for women reaching down to the feet, and only a little pulled up at the girdle, we shall see in a vase-painting (§ 57, Fig. 310) representing dancing youths and maidens, the former wearing the short, the latter the long, chiton. A development of the long chiton is the double-chiton. It was a very large, oblong piece of woven cloth, left open on one side, like the Doric chiton for men. It was equal to about one and a half lengths of the body. The overhanging part of the cloth was folded round the chest and back, from the neck downwards, the upper

edge being arranged round the neck, and the two open corners
clasped together on one shoulder. On this open side, therefore,
the naked body was visible (Fig. 211). Over the other shoulder
the upper edge of the chiton was also fastened with a clasp, the
arm being put through the opening left between this clasp and
the corresponding corner of the cloth.

In the same way was arranged the half-open chiton, the open
side of which, from the girdle to the lower hem, was sewed up. A
bronze statuette (Fig. 212) illustrates this way of putting it on.
A young girl is about to join together on her left shoulder the
chiton, which is fastened over the right shoulder by means of an
agraffe. It appears clearly that the whole chiton consists of one
piece. Together with the open and half-open kinds of the chiton,
we also find the closed double-
chiton (χιτών ποδήρης) flowing
down to the feet. It was a piece
of cloth considerably longer than
the human body, and closed on both
sides, inside of which the person
putting it on stood as in a cylinder.
As in the chiton of the second form,
the overhanging part of the cloth
was turned outward, and the folded
rim pulled up as far as the
shoulders, across which (first on
the right, and after it on the left
side) the front and back parts were
fastened together by means of clasps,
the arms being put through the two
openings affected in this manner.
Round the hips the chiton was
fastened by means of a girdle
(ζώνιον στρόφιον), through which
the bottom part of the dress trailing

Fig. 213.

along the ground was pulled up just far enough to let the
toes be visible. Above the girdle the chiton was arranged in
shorter or longer picturesque folds (κόλπος). Most likely the
overhanging part of the chiton, which we shall meet with again
as an independent garment, was called by the Greeks διπλοΐς or

διπλοίδιον. We have illustrated the chiton by two representations
from the best period of Greek art. Fig. 213 shows a running
female figure, the arms and feet of which have unfortunately been
destroyed. The original is ten inches high. She seems to

Fig. 214.

implore the help of the gods against a
ferocious animal, the claws of which have
already caught her floating garment.[1]
Chiton and diploïs are arranged most
gracefully, and the violent motion of the
body has been softened by a certain quiet
treatment of the drapery. Fig. 214, on
the other hand, shows one of the sublime
female forms carrying the roof of the
southern portico of the Erechtheion (compare Fig. 38). The attitude of the kanephore is quiet and dignified. Kolpos and
diploïs are gracefully arranged in symmetrical folds. In spite of the calm attitude
required by the architectural character of
the figure, the artist has managed to convey the idea of motion by means of the
left leg being slightly bent, and the
straight folds of the chiton modified in
consequence. The chief alterations of varying fashion applied to the arrangement of
the diploïdion which reached either to the
part under the bosom or was prolonged
as far as the hips; its front and back
parts might either be clasped together
across the shoulders, or the two rims might
be pulled across the upper arm as far as
the elbow, and fastened in several places
by means of buttons or agraffes, so that
the naked arm became visible in the intervals, by means of
which the sleeveless chiton received the appearance of one

---

[1] On the back part of the garment the paw of a large animal is distinctly
visible; for which reason we have adopted the above explanation in preference
to that of her being a Bacchante, against which opinion moreover the modest dress
and the absence of orgiastic emblems seem to speak.

with sleeves (Fig. 219). Where the diploïdion was detached
from the chiton, it formed a kind of handsome cape; which,
however, in its shape, strictly resembled the diploïdion proper.
This cape was most likely called by the
Greeks ἀμπεχόνιον. Its shape was considerably modified by fashion, taking sometimes
the form of a close-fitting jacket, at others
(when the sides remained open) that of a
kind of shawl, the ends of which sometimes
equalled in length the chiton itself (Fig. 215).
In the latter case, the ampechonion was
naturally at least three times as long as it
was wide. In antique pictures women
sometimes wear a second shorter chiton over
the χιτὼν ποδήρες. A great many varieties
of dress, more distinguishable in the vase-
paintings representing realistic scenes than
in the ideal costumes of sculptural types, we

Fig. 215.

must omit, particularly as, in most cases, they may be reduced to
the described general principles.

42. From the ἐνδύματα we now pass to the ἐπιβλήματα or
περιβλήματα, *i.e.* articles of dress of the nature of cloaks. They
also show throughout an oblong
form, differing in this essentially
from the Roman toga. The
ἱμάτιον, belonging to this class,
was arranged so that the one
corner was thrown over the left
shoulder in front, so as to be
attached to the body by means of
the left arm. On the back, the
dress was pulled toward the right
side so as to cover it completely
up to the right shoulder, or, at least,

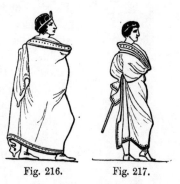

Fig. 216.   Fig. 217.

to the armpit, in which latter case the right shoulder remained
uncovered. Finally, the himation was again thrown over the left
shoulder, so that the ends fell over the back. Figs. 216 and 217,
taken from vase-paintings, show two male figures completely
enveloped in the himation according to the fashion of the time

(ἐντὸς τὴν χεῖρα ἔχειν).   Both men and women wore the himation in a similar manner (see Fig. 218, taken from a terra-cotta at

Athens).   The complete covering, even of the face, in this last figure indicates a chastely veiled Athenian lady walking in the street, or, according to Stackelberg, a bride.

A second way of arranging the himation, which left the right arm free, was more picturesque, and is therefore usually found in pictures (see, for instance, Fig. 219).   The first-mentioned himation, however, was commonly given by the artist to figures meant to express noble dignity.   The truth of these statements will be recognised in looking, for instance, at the statue of the bearded Dionysos in the Vatican, enveloped in the himation according to strictest usage. In the beautiful statues of Asklepios at Florence and in the Louvre, the left side and the lower part of the body are covered by the himation, which is also the case in

Fig. 218.

the figure of the enthroned Zeus in the Museo Pio Clementino, where one corner of the garment rests on the left shoulder and falls in beautiful

folds over the lap of the figure.   The arrangement of the himation worn by women was equally graceful, as appears from the pictures, without, however, being subjected to a strict rule, as in the case of men.   Perhaps the costume of the maidens carrying hydriai on the frieze of the Parthenon may be considered as the common type.   The picturesque arrangement of the himation would undoubtedly be acquired only by long practice.   In order to preserve the folds and prevent the dress from slipping from the shoulders, the Greeks used to sew small

Fig. 219.

weights into the corners.

Different from the himation was the much smaller and oblong

τρίβων or τριβώνιον, worn amongst the Doric tribes by epheboi and grown-up men, while boys up to the twelfth year were restricted to the use of the chiton. At Athens also, the inclination towards the severe Doric customs made this garment common. Up to the time of the Peloponnesian war the dress of the Athenian boy consisted of the chiton only. On attaining the age of the ephebos he was dressed in the χλαμύς, introduced into Attika from Thessaly or Makedonia. The chlamys also was an oblong piece of cloth thrown over the left shoulder, the open ends being fastened across the right shoulder by means of a clasp; the corners hanging down were, as in the himation, kept straight by means of weights sewed into them. The chlamys was principally used by travellers and soldiers. Fig. 220, representing the statue of Phokion in the Museo Pio Clementino, illustrates this handsome garment. Hermes, Kastor, Polydeukes, the wandering Odysseus, soldiers, and horsemen (for instance, the epheboi on horseback on the frieze of the Parthenon) generally wear the chlamys.

Fig. 220.

Concerning the materials of the described garments, we have mentioned before that linen was used principally by the Ionians, wool by the Dorians; the latter material in the course of time became the rule for male garments all over Greece. The change of seasons naturally required a corresponding modification in the thickness of these woollen garments; accordingly we notice the difference between summer and winter dresses. For women's dresses, besides sheep's wool and linen, byssos, most likely a kind of cotton, was commonly used. Something like the byssos, but much finer, was the material of which the celebrated transparent dresses were woven in the isle of Amorgos. They were called ἀμόργινα, and consisted of the fibre of a fine sort of flax, undoubtedly resembling our muslins and cambrics. The introduction of silk into Greece is of later date, while in Asia it was known at a very early period. From the interior of Asia the silk was imported into Greece, partly in its raw state, partly worked into dresses. Ready-made dresses of this kind were called σηρικά to distinguish them from the βομβύκινα, *i.e.* dresses made in Greece of the imported raw silk (μέταξα, μάταξα). The isle of Kos was the first seat of silk manufacture, where silk dresses were produced rivalling in transparency the above-mentioned ἀμόργινα. These diaphanous dresses, clinging close to the body, and allowing the colour of the skin and the veins to be seen (εἵματα διαφανῆ), have been frequently imitated with astonishing skill by Greek sculptors and painters. We only remind the reader of the beautifully modelled folds of the chiton covering the upper part of the body of Niobe's youngest daughter, in a kneeling position, who seeks shelter in the lap of her mother; in painting, several wall-pictures of Pompeii may be cited.

The antiquated notion of white having been the universal colour of Greek garments, a coloured dress being considered immodest, has been refuted by Becker ("Charikles," III. p. 194). It is, however, likely that, with the cloak-like epiblemata, white was the usual colour, as is still the case amongst Oriental nations much exposed to the sun. Brown cloaks are, however, by no means unusual; neither were they amongst Greek men. Party-coloured Oriental garments were also used, at least by the wealthy Greek classes, both for male and female dresses, while white still remained the favourite colour with modest Greek women. This is proved, not to mention written evidence, by a number of small painted statuettes of burnt clay, as also by several pictures on lekythoi from Attic graves. The original colours of the dresses, although (particularly the reds) slightly altered by the burning process, may still be distinctly recognised. In Fig. 320, from a vase-painting, the female form on the left wears a chiton of saffron-yellow hue (κροκωτά), perhaps in imitation of the colour of the byssos, and a violet peplos, the chiton of the woman on the right being golden brown. Men also appear in these pictures with the cherry-coloured chlamys and the red himation; while Charon wears the dark exomis usual amongst fishermen (see Stackelberg, "Gräber der Hellenen," Tafs. 43-45). These dresses, both with regard to shape and colour, are undoubtedly taken from models of daily life.

The dresses were frequently adorned with inwoven patterns, or attached borders and embroideries. From Babylon and Phrygia, the ancient seats of the weaving and embroidering arts, these crafts spread over the occidental world, the name "Phrygiones," used in Rome at a later period for artists of this kind, reminding of this origin. As we learn from the monuments, the simplest border either woven or sewed to the dresses, consisted of one or more dark stripes, either parallel with the seams of the chiton, himation, and ampechonion (see Figs. 215-217, 219, 221), or running down to the hem of the chiton from the girdle at the sides or from the throat in front. The vertical ornaments called

ῥάβδοι or παρυφαί correspond to the Roman *clavus*. Besides these ornaments in stripes, we also meet with others broader and more complicated; whether woven into, or sewed on, the dress seems doubtful. They cover the chiton from the hem upwards to the knee, and above the girdle up to the neck, as is seen in the chiton worn by the spring goddess Opora, in a vase-painting (" Collection des Vases gr. de M. Lamberg," Pl. 65). The whole chiton is sometimes covered with star or dice patterns, particularly on vases of the archaic style. The vase-painters of the decaying period chiefly represent Phrygian dresses with gold fringes and sumptuous embroideries of palmetto and "meandering" patterns, such as were worn by the luxurious South-Italian

Fig. 221.

Greeks. Such a sumptuous dress is worn by Medea (Fig. 221) in a picture of the death of Talos on an Apulian amphora in the Jatta collection at Ruvo. In the same picture the chitones of Kastor and Polydeukes, and those of the Argonautai, are covered with palmetto embroideries, the edges at the bottom showing mythological scenes on a dark ground. We also call to mind the rich peploi offered at high festivals to adorn the holy images, and also of the himation, fifteen yards long and richly ornamented, which was offered by the Sybarite Alkimenes to the Lakinian Hera in her temple near Kroton, and afterwards sold to the Carthaginians for 120 talents by the elder Dionysios. Plastic art in its noble simplicity has disdained to imitate these ornaments, which it introduces only in rare cases to adorn certain parts of the dress. The upper garment of a statue of Artemis in the Museo Borbonico, at Naples, shows a border imitating embroidery; and the archaic statue of Pallas in the Museum of Dresden wears a peplos, imitated from the celebrated Panathenaïc peplos, covered with scenes from the gigantomachy (see Müller, " Denkmäler der alten Kunst," I. Taf. X., Nos. 36, 38).

43. In the cities Greeks walked mostly bareheaded, owing most likely to the more plentiful hair of southern nations, which, moreover, was cultivated by the Greeks with particular care. Travellers, hunters, and such artificers as were particularly exposed to the sun, used light coverings for their heads. The different forms of these may be classified as κυνῆ and πῖλος. The κυνῆ was a cap made of the skins of dogs, weasels, or cows; its further development was the helmet, to which we shall have to return. In Homer already we read of a peasant with a cap of goat's skin (κυνέη αἰγείη), most likely of the shape of a semi-globe, and fastened under the chin with straps. In a vase-painting in the Berlin Museum, representing the interior of a foundry, the workman poking the fire wears this cap as a protection against the heat (Fig. 222, a). The shape of the πῖλος was conical, either without a shade, like the κυνῆ (see Fig. 208), or with a small brim. It was made of felt. Sailors, merchants, and several gods and demigods may be recognised by it, particularly Charon, Odysseus and his companions, and Hephaistos the artificer; also Kadmos, the Dioskuroi (for instance, on Spartan coins), and the Amazons, in several vase-paintings. Tydeus also wears the pilos in a vase-painting (Fig. 222, b), and the cap worn by a shepherd blowing the double-pipe (Fig. 222, c) may lay claim to the same appellation (compare Fig. 208). It resembles in form the cap worn by South-Italian shepherds at the present day. Nearly related to the pilos is the well-known Phrygian cap, but for the top, which is turned over in front. The latter, now worn by Greek and Italian fishermen, was, in old times, used by the barbarous nations of Asia, which may be

recognised by it.   Paris, Ganymede (Fig. 222, *d*), Anchises,
Olympos, Atys, Mithras, and the Amazons are frequently represented with it, also barbarous warriors on Roman monuments of the
imperial period.   An interesting combination of head-coverings,
with a flattened pilos amongst them, appears in a large vase-
painting (Millin, "Galérie Mythologique," Pl. CXXXV.) representing a battle between Greeks and Amazons with their Scythian
allies, perhaps an imitation of the battle of the Amazons represented by Phidias on the shield of Athene Parthenos.   Similar to
the Phrygian is another cap worn by Amazons and noble
Asiatics.   It consists of wool or leather, and resembles a helmet.
The top is only a little turned down in front, the back part being
prolonged by means of a flap (Fig. 222, *e*, compare Fig. 212).

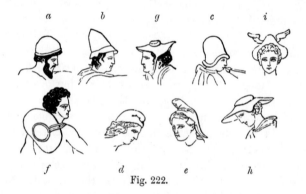

Fig. 222.

It appears in paintings on the heads of Asiatic men and women,
sometimes in the quaintest shapes (see Fig. 221).   It is generally
called μίτρα, although this word seems to imply the covering of
the head with a scarf.   Such a turban-like covering of the
forehead, cheeks, and neck, with only the point of the Asiatic cap
protruding from it, is worn, for instance, by the Persians in the
Pompeian mosaic called the Battle of Alexander.   The Oriental
turban is undoubtedly a remnant of this costume.   The third
form of the hat is the πέτασος, originally worn in Makedonia and
Thessaly, and introduced into Greece together with the chlamys
worn by epheboi.   It resembled our wideawakes, but for the very
small headpiece, and was fastened to the head by means of straps,
which, at the same time, prevented it from slipping when thrown

over the back (Fig. 222, *f*), in the same way that the medieval biretta was worn occasionally. This petasos is worn by the epheboi on horseback on the frieze of the Parthenon (Fig. 222, *h*). and also by Kastor (Fig. 222, *g*) and Hermes in vase-paintings. The latter god may be recognised by a winged petasos peculiar to him (Fig. 222, *i*). What name must be assigned to a hat resembling a plate, which appears on coins of the Thessalian city of Krannon (Mus. Hunter., Tab. 21, No. XVII.), and of the Thrakian city of Ainos (Mus. de Hauteroche, Pl. III., No. 3), remains doubtful; it may be the καυσία worn by the Makedonians.

44. The hair is considered in Homer as one of the greatest signs of male beauty amongst the long-haired (καρηκομόωντες) Achaioi; no less were the well-arranged locks of maidens and women praised by the tragic poets. Amongst the Spartans it became a sacred custom, derived from the laws of Lykurgos, to let the hair of the boy grow as soon as he reached the age of the ephebos, while up to that time it was cut short. This custom prevailed amongst the Spartans up to their being overpowered by the Achaic federation. Altogether the Dorian character did not admit of much attention being paid to the arrangement of the hair. Only on solemn occasions, for instance on the eve of the battle of Thermopylæ, the Spartans arranged their hair with particular care. At Athens, about the time of the Persian wars, men used to wear their hair long, tied on the top of the head in a knot (κρώβυλος), which was fastened by a hair-pin in the form of a cicada. Of this custom, however, the monuments offer no example. Only in the pictures of two Pankratiastai, on a monument dating most likely from Roman times (" Mus. Pio Clement." vol. iv. p. 36), we discover an analogy to this old Attic custom. After the Persian war, when the dress and manners of the Ionians had undergone a change, it became the custom to cut off the long hair of the boys on their attaining the age of epheboi, and devote it as an offering to a god, for instance, to the Delphic Apollo or some local river-god. Attic citizens, however, by no means wore their hair cropped short, like their slaves, but used to let it grow according to their own taste or the common fashion. Only dandies, as, for instance, Alkibiades, let their hair fall down to their shoulders in long locks. Philosophers also

occasionally attempted to revive old customs by wearing their hair long.

The beard was carefully attended to by the Greeks. The barber's shop (κουρεῖον), with its talkative inmate, was not only frequented by those requiring the services of the barber (κουρεύς) in cutting the hair, shaving, cutting the nails and corns, and tearing out small hairs, but it was also, as Plutarch says, a symposion without wine, where political and local news were discussed. Alkiphron depicts a Greek barber in the following words (III. 66): "You see how the d——d barber in yon street has treated me; the talker, who puts up the Brundisian looking-glass, and makes his knives to clash harmoniously. I went to him to be shaved; he received me politely, put me in a high chair, enveloped me in a clean towel, and stroked the razor gently down my cheek, so as to remove the thick hair. But this was a malicious trick of his. He did it partly, not all over the chin; some places he left rough, others he made smooth without my noticing it." After the time of Alexander the Great, a barber's business became lucrative, owing to the custom of wearing a full beard (πώγων βαθύς or δασύς) being abandoned, notwithstanding the remonstrances of several states.[1] In works of art, particularly in portrait statues, the beard is always treated as an individual characteristic. It is mostly arranged in graceful locks, and covers the chin, lips, and cheeks, without a separation being made between whiskers and moustache. Only in archaic renderings the wedge-like beard is combed in long wavy lines, and the whiskers are strictly parted from the moustache. As an example we quote the nobly-formed head of Zeus crowned with the stephane in the Talleyrand collection. The usual colour of the hair being dark, fair hair was considered a great beauty. Homer gives yellow locks to Menelaos, Achilles, and Meleagros, and Euripides describes Menelaos and Dionysos as fair-haired (ξανθοῖσι βοστρύχοισιν εὔκοσμος κόμην).

45. The head-dress of women was in simple taste. Hats were not worn, as a rule, because, at least in Athens, the appearance of women in the public street was considered improper, and therefore

---

[1] According to tradition, many Makedonians were killed by the Persians taking hold of their long beards, and pulling them to the ground. Alexander, in consequence, had his troops shaved during the battle.

happened only on exceptional occasions. On journeys women wore a light broad-brimmed petasos (see p. 171) as a protection from the sun. With a Thessalian hat ($\theta \epsilon \sigma \sigma a \lambda i s \ \kappa v v \hat{\eta}$) of this kind Ismene appears in "Œdipus in Kolonos." The head-dress of Athenian ladies at home and in the street consisted, beyond

Fig. 223.

the customary veil, chiefly of different contrivances for holding together their plentiful hair. We mentioned before, that the himation was sometimes pulled over the back of the head like a veil. But at a very early period Greek women wore real shorter

or longer veils, called κρήδεμνον, καλύπτρα, or κάλυμμα, which
covered the face up to the eyes, and fell over the neck and back
in large folds, so as to cover, if necessary, the whole upper part
of the body. The care bestowed on the hair was naturally still
greater amongst women than amongst men. Fig. 223 shows a
number of terra-cotta heads of Athenian women published by
Stackelberg. These, and the numerous heads represented in
sculptures and gems, give an idea of the exquisite taste of these
head-dresses. At the same time, it must be confessed that most
modern fashions, even the ugly ones, have their models, if not in
Greek, at least in Roman antiquity. The combing of the hair
over the back in wavy lines was undoubtedly much in favour.
A simple ribbon tied round the head, in that case, connected the
front with the back hair. This arrangement we met with in the
maidens of the Parthenon freize and in a bust of Niobe (Müller,
"Denkmäler," I., Taf. XXXIV., c). On older monuments, for
instance, in the group of the Graces on the triangular altar in the
Louvre, the front hair is arranged in small ringlets, while the
back hair partly falls smoothly over the neck, and partly is made
into long curls hanging down to the shoulders. It was also not
unusual to comb back the front hair over the temples and ears,
and tie it, together with the back hair, into a graceful knot
(κόρυμβοι, Fig. 223, e, c). Here, also, the above-mentioned
ribbon was used. It consisted of a stripe of cloth or leather,
frequently adorned, where it rested on the forehead, with a plaque
of metal formed like a frontal, and called στεφάνη (Fig. 223,
a). This stephane appears on monuments mostly in the hair of
goddesses ; the ribbon belonging to it, in that case, takes the form
of a broad metal circle destined no more to hold together, but to
decorate the hair. This is the case in a bust of Here in the Villa
Ludovisi, in the statue of the same goddess in the Vatican, and
in a statue of Aphrodite found at Capua (Müller, "Denkmäler," II.
Taf. IV., Nos. 54, 56, 268). Besides this another ornamented
tie of cloth or leather was used by the Greeks, broad in the
centre and growing narrower towards both ends. It was called
σφενδόνη, owing to its similarity to the sling. It was either put
with its broader side on the front of the head, the ends, with
ribbons tied to them, being covered by the thick black hair, or *vice
versâ ;* in which latter case the ends were tied on the forehead in

an elaborate knot. The latter form was called ὀπισθοσφενδόνη.
The στλεγγίς resembles the sphendone. The net, and after it the
kerchief, were developed from the simple ribbon, in the same
manner as straps on the feet gradually became boots. The
different kinds of nets may collectively be called κεκρύφαλοι. The
kekryphalos proper consists of a net-like combination of ribbon
and gold thread, thrown over the back hair to prevent it from
dropping. The large tetradrachmai of Syrakuse, bearing the
signature of the engraver Kimon, show a beautiful head of
Arethusa adorned with the kekryphalos. More frequent is the
coif-like kekryphalos covering the whole hair, or only the back
hair, and tied into a knot at the top (σάκκος) (see Fig. 223, *b*, *i*,
Fig. 229, and the group of women to the right in Fig. 232).
The modifications of the sakkos, and the way of its being tied,
are chiefly illustrated by vase-paintings. Related to the sakkos is
the μίτρα, at first only a ribbon, but gradually developed into the
broad frontlet and the kerchief. The front of the head might,
besides these coifs, be adorned with a stephane, as is shown by
Fig. 223, *i*, and by the statue of Elpis in the Museo Pio
Clementino (IV., Taf. 8), which shows the sphendone and stephane
on the front and back parts of the head respectively. At the
present day the Greek women of Thessaly and the isle of Chios
wear a head-dress exactly resembling the antique sakkos (see
v. Stackelberg, "Trachten und Gebräuche der Neugriechen,"
Part I., Tafs. XIII., XIX.) The acquaintance of the Greeks
with the curling-iron and cosmetic mysteries, such as oil and
pomatum, can be proved both by written evidence and pictures (see Fig. 223, *b*, *d*). It quite tallied with the æsthetical
notions of the Greeks to shorten the forehead by dropping the
hair over it, many examples of which, in pictures of both men and
women, are preserved to us.

46. Gloves (χειρίδες), worn by the enervated Persians, were
not usual among the Greeks. At home, nay even in the streets,
Greeks often walked with naked feet, and, like modern Orientals,
took off their shoes on entering their own or a stranger's house.
Homer states how a man on leaving the house ties the splendid
soles (πέδιλα) to his feet, which custom was continued for a long
time. In a bas-relief representing the visit of Dionysos to Ikarios
(Müller, "Denkmäler," II., Taf. L., No. 624), a Panisk bares

the feet of the god previous to his lying down to dinner. We know a great many varieties of shoes from the monuments, and we are, on the other hand, told of a number of terms by ancient writers. But to apply the ones to the others will be in most cases impossible. Three chief forms may, however, be recognised; which, according to our modern nomenclature, may be denominated the sole, the shoe, and the boot. Our word sole, whether fastened to the foot with one simple or with several straps intertwined, may be rendered by ὑπόδημα. The simple sole might be fastened by a strap (ζυγός) right across the instep, or by two straps issuing from its two sides, and tied or buckled together on the instep (see Fig. 224, 1, representing the foot of the statue of Elpis, in the Vatican). Whether this arrangement

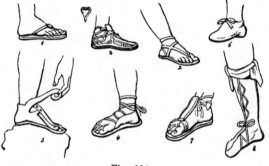

Fig. 224.

is identical with a kind of sandal called βλαύτη must remain undecided. By the addition to the sole of several intertwined straps the σάνδαλον is formed, worn originally by women, but also by men, as is sufficiently proved by the monuments. In the sandal a strap was sewed on the sole one to two inches from the tip, and pulled through the big and first toes (sometimes combined with a second strap between the third and little toes); to it were added two or four other laces, fastened by twos to the edges of the sole, and held together by a *fibula* in the form of a heart on the centre-point of the foot, where the straps crossed each other. The whole intertwined system of straps terminated above the ankles. Fig. 224, 2, shows a female foot with the simple, Fig. 224, 3, the foot of Apollo of Belvidere,

with the compound, sandal.   Above the latter the *fibula*, in the
form of a heart, is shown separately.   Instructive is also the
sandal worn by Dirke in the group called the "Farnesian Bull."
The net-like entanglement of the straps, together with the
leather laces of the compound sandal, gives it the appearance
of a broken high shoe, as it appears, for instance, on the coins
of the Thessalian city of Larissa, commemorating the one-shoed
(μονοσάνδαλος) Jason.   The sole itself, being mostly made of
several layers of cow's hide, appears very thick in sculptures,
making the otherwise graceful sandal look rather heavy.

By the addition of a closed heel, and of larger or smaller
side-pieces sewed to the sole of the shoe, our second class was
formed, perhaps identical with the ancients' κοῖλα ὑποδήματα.
The sides of the shoe were tied with straps to the foot and
ankle, leaving the toes and the upper part of the foot
uncovered.   The different forms of the shoe are illustrated by
Fig. 224, 4, 5, 7—No. 5 being taken from the statue in the
Vatican of a youth tying his shoe, formerly called Jason,
at present Hermes.   In No. 7, taken from the statue of
Demosthenes in the Vatican, the juncture of the heel and
side-pieces is covered by a dropping piece of the lace.   The
closed shoe, tied across the foot, we find in many statues of
both men and women (Fig. 224, 6).

We now have to mention the boots (ἐνδρομίδες)—our third
class.   They were made of leather or felt, closely attaching to the
foot, and reaching up to the calf.   They were open in front
and tied together with laces.   To Diana a light hunting-boot
is peculiar, resembling the mocassins of the Indians (Fig. 224, 8).
The same kind of boots are worn by the so-called pedagogue
amongst the group of the Niobides.   A fringe of cloth generally
surrounded the upper rim of the boot.   We have purposely limited
ourselves in our remarks almost entirely to monumental evidence, the explanation of many expressions in ancient writers, as,
for instance, of ἐμβάς and κρηπίς, being throughout conjectural.

47. We conclude our remarks about dress with the description of some ornaments, the specimens of which in Greek graves
and in sculptural imitations are numerous.   In Homer the
wooers try to gain the favour of Penelope with golden breast-
pins, agraffes, earrings, and chains.   Hephaistos is, in the same

work, mentioned as the artificer of beautiful rings and hair-pins.
The same ornaments we meet with again at a later period as
important articles of female dress. Many preserved specimens
show the great skill of Greek goldsmiths. Hair-pins, in our
sense, and combs for parting and holding up the hair were
unknown to the Greeks. The double or simple comb of Greek
ladies (κτείς), made of boxwood, ivory, or metal, was used only
for combing the hair. The back hair was prevented from dropping by means of long hair-pins, the heads of which frequently
consisted of a graceful piece of sculpture (see Fig. 226, *a*, a gold
pin found in a grave at Pantikapaion adorned with a hart's head).
Well known are the hair-pins adorned with a golden cicada
which, in Solon's time, were used by both Athenian men and
women for the fastening of the krobylos.

It was the custom of the Greeks to adorn their heads on
festive occasions with wreaths and garlands. Thus adorned
the bridegroom led home the bride. Flowers full of symbolic
meaning were offered on the altars of the gods, and the topers
at carousals were crowned with wreaths of myrtle, roses, and
violets, the latter being the favourite flower with the Athenians.
The flower-market (αἱ μυρρίναι) of Athens was always supplied
with garlands to twine round the head and the upper part of the
body; for the latter also was adorned with garlands (ὑποθυμίδες,
ὑποθυμιάδες). Crowns consisting of other flowers, and leaves of
the ivy and silver-poplar, are frequently mentioned. Wreaths
also found a place in the serious business of life. They were
awarded to the victors in the games; the archon wore a myrtle-
wreath as the sign of his dignity, as did also the orator while
speaking to the people from the tribune. The crowning with
flowers was a high honour to Athenian citizens—awarded, for
instance, to Perikles, but refused to Miltiades. The head and
bier of the dead were also crowned with fresh wreaths of myrtle
and ivy (see Fig. 318—a vase-painting representing the adorning
of the dead Archemoros). The luxury of later times changed the
wreaths of flowers for golden ones, with regard to the dead of the
richer classes. Wreaths made of thin gold have repeatedly been
found in graves. The barrows of the old Pantikapaion have
yielded several beautiful wreaths of ivy and ears of corn (Ouvaroff,
"Antiquités du Bosphore Cimmérien," Pl. IV.); a gold imitation

of a crown of myrtle has been found in a grave in Ithaka (Stackelberg, " Gräber der Griechen," Taf. 72). Other specimens from Greek and Roman graves are preserved in our museums. A golden crown of Greek workmanship, found at Armento, a village of the Basilicata (at present in Munich), is particularly remarkable (Fig. 225). A twig of oak forms the ground, from amongst the thin golden leaves of which spring forth asters with chalices of blue enamel, convolvulus, narcissus, ivy, roses, and myrtle, gracefully intertwined. On the upper bend of the crown

Fig. 225.

is the image of a winged goddess, from the head of which, amongst pieces of grass, rises the slender stalk of a rose. Four naked male genii and two draped female ones, floating over the flowers, point towards the goddess, who stands on a pedestal bearing this inscription :—

ΚΡΕΙΘΩΝΙΟΣ ΗΘΗΚΗ ΤΟΝ ΕΤΗΦΑΝΟΝ.

Earrings (ἐνώτια, ἐλλόβια, ἑλικτῆρες) were, in Greece, only worn by women; while amongst the Persians, Lydians, and

Babylonians they were common to both sexes.   Their form varies
from simple rings to elaborate, tasteful pendants.   Fig. 226, *b*,
shows a pendant, found in Ithaka, in the shape of a siren, holding
a double pipe in her hand.   Fig. 226, *f*, shows an earring trimmed
with garnets, found in the same place, with the head of a lion
at one end, and that of a snake at the other.   Fig. 226, *c*, is an

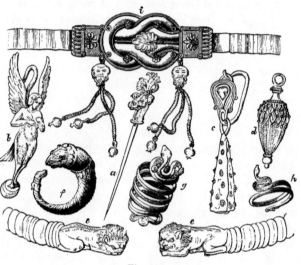

Fig. 226.

ornament, found near Pantikapaion, in the form of two clubs,
hanging on an earring of Syrian garnet.   Fig. 226, *d*, shows a
pendant, found in the same neighbourhood, resembling those now
in use.   Numerous other illustrations are supplied by vase-
paintings, coins, and gems; while works of sculpture reproduce
ornaments only in rare cases.

Necklaces (περιδέραια, ὅρμοι), bracelets for the upper and
under arm (ψέλια ὄφεις), and rings worn round the leg, above
the ankle (πάδαιχρυσαι περισκελίδες, περισφύρια), are frequently
met with on monuments.[1]   Neck-ornaments either consisted of rings
joined into a chain, or of one single massive ring, spiral in form,
and made of bronze or precious metals, the latter being worn

---

[1] A statue of Aphrodite in the Glyptothek of Munich wears a broad ring round
the upper arm.

principally by barbarous nations.[1]   Fig. 226, *e*, shows a στρεπτὸς
περιαυχένιος of this kind, undoubtedly of Greek workmanship,
with figures of couching lions at each end.   It has been found
in a grave near Pantikapaion.   Armlets and anklets are mostly
of the form of snakes, whence their name ὄφεις.

It was an old custom, and the sign of a freeman, to wear rings
on the fingers, used both as signets and as mere ornaments.   With
the signet (σφραγίς) documents or property were marked.   Solon
made the forging of a seal a capital crime.   About the age of the
use of gems amongst the Greeks little is known: they most
likely belong to a period after Homer, instruments sufficiently
hard to cut them being wanting previously.   The beginnings of
the art of engraving amongst the Assyrians, Egyptians, and
Etruscans are of much earlier date.   The common use of the signet
soon caused the artistic treatment of the gem.   The setting
(σφενδόνη), on the contrary, was most simple, at least in most of
the rings preserved to us.   On the other hand, the *technique* of the
Greeks in cutting and polishing the stone has not been equalled
even by the great skill of the celebrated engravers of the Cinque-
cento and the eighteenth century.

The stones chosen were such as did not resist the drill too
much, and allowed of a smooth line of incision.   A further requisite
consisted in the stone being either of pure colour, or in its facili-
tating the varied representation of whole figures or parts of the
body and dress by means of patches, veins, or layers (*zonæ*) of
various colours.   The stones used most frequently were the
carnelian, sardonyx, chalcedony, agate, onyx, jasper, and
heliotrope, more rarely the nephrite, turquoise, and rock-crystal,
the silvery magnet-ironstone, the amethyst, green quartz, and
precious serpentine.   Of jewels proper only few were used, like
the ruby, genuine sapphire and emerald, the green beryl, the
felspath-opal, and the bluish genuine aquamarine.   Topaz,
hyacinth, Syrian, and Indian garnets and chrysophrase (the latter
being introduced into Greece after the time of Alexander) were
used equally.   The ancients also knew how to imitate jewels in
coloured glass, particularly the emerald in coloured crystal.
These paste copies were, according to Pliny, a most lucrative
article of counterfeiting industry.   They were the result of the

[1] A torque is seen, for instance, round the neck of the dying gladiator.

desire of the middle classes for rich ornaments, and are frequently
found in our museums. The accuracy and finish of the minutest
details justify us in supposing that the ancients knew all the
utensils of the trade, *e.g.* the wheel, the diamond point, diamond
dust, and even magnifying glasses, which latter are generally
claimed as an invention of modern times. The figures were either
incised into the gem, which in that case was used as a signet,
or they were formed out of the different layers of certain stones
like onyx and sardonyx, in relief. In the former case they are
called gems (ἀνάγλυφα, *gemmæ sculptæ, exsculptæ, intaglio*), in
the latter cameos (ἔκτυπα, *gemmæ cœlatæ*). The latter, only
used as ornaments, might, when small, be set in rings; when of
larger dimensions, they were used to adorn agraffes, girdles,
necklaces, and weapons, or they were let into the surfaces of vases
and precious goblets. The finest cameos and gems were made in
Alexander's time, who was not only painted by Apelles and
sculptured by Lysippos, but also had his portrait cut in a jewel
by Pyrgoteles. The passion for gems amongst all classes of both
Greeks and Romans is proved by the great number of them of
more or less good workmanship found in graves. Fig. 226, *g, h,*
shows two elastic gold rings trimmed with garnets, found in a grave
in Ithaka. Their form resembles the above-mentioned opheis.

Fig. 226, *i,* shows an ornamented girdle, also found in a grave
in Ithaka. It is made of gold, and is held together by means of
a gold clasp richly ornamented with hyacinthine stones. On it
hang two Silenus-masks, to each of which are attached three little
gold chains adorned with garnets (compare the girdle of the
marble statue of Euterpe in the Museo Bor-
bonico, XI., Taf. 59).

Greek, particularly Athenian, women
carried a sunshade (σκιάδειον), or employed
slaves to hold it over them. In the Panathenaïc
procession even the daughters of metoikoi
had to perform this service (σκιαδηφορεῖν).
Such sunshades, which, like our own, could
be shut by means of wires, we often see

b   a   c
Fig. 227.

depicted on vases and Etruscan mirrors (Fig. 227, *a*). This form
was undoubtedly the most common one. The cap-like sunshade
painted on a skyphos, which a Silenus, instead of a servant, holds

over a dignified lady walking in front of him, is undoubtedly
intended as a parody, perhaps copied from the scene of a comedy
(Gerhard, " Trinkschalen," II. 27).   In vase-paintings we also see
frequently the leaf-like painted fan (σκέπασμα) in the hand of
women (Fig. 227, *b c*).

Of the secrets of Greek *toilette* we will only disclose the fact
that ladies knew the use of paint.   The white they used
consisted of white lead (ψιμύθιον); their reds were made either
of red minium (μίλτος) or of the root of the ἄγχουσα.   This
unwholesome fashion of painting was even extended to the eye-
brows, for which black colour was used, made either of pulverised
antimony (στίμμι, στίμμις) or of fine soot (ἀσβόλη).

The mirrors (ἔνοπτρον, κάτοπτρον) of the Greeks consisted
of circular pieces of polished bronze, either without a handle
or with one richly adorned.[1]   Frequently
a cover, for the reflecting surface, was added.
The Etruscan custom (see § 97) of engraving figures on the back of the mirror or the
cover seems to have been rare amongst the
Greeks, to judge, at least, from the numerous
specimens of mirrors found in Greek graves.
Characteristic of these are, on the other hand,
the tasteful handles, representing mostly
Aphrodite, as in a manner the ideal of a
beautifully adorned woman (see Fig. 228).
These hand-mirrors frequently occur in
vase-paintings, particularly in those containing bathing utensils (see Fig. 231).

Fig. 228.

The carrying of a stick (βακτηρία, or σκῆπτρον) seems to have
been a common custom.   It is mostly of great length, with a
crutched handle ; young Athenian dandies may have used
shorter walking-sticks (see Fig. 217).   The first-mentioned
sticks seem to have been used principally for leaning upon in
standing still, as is indicated by frequent representations in
pictures.   Different from this stick was the σκῆπτρον proper, a
staff adorned with a knob or a flower, which, as early as Homer,
was the attribute of gods, and of rulers descended from the gods.

[1] Compare the collection of ornamented Etruscan mirror-handles in Gerhard's
" Etruskische Spiegel."   Pl. XXIV. *et seq.*

In regal families the sceptre was a valued heirloom. The sceptre serving as the emblem of judicial power (ῥάβδος) was a little shorter; it was also used by ambassadors, and a herald had to present it to the orator on his rising to address the council. In sculptures we frequently see the sceptre as the attribute of divinities, for instance, on the triangular altar in the Louvre. Our modern commander's staff is a modification of it.

48. The life of married women, maidens, children while in the care of women, and of female slaves, passed in the gynaikonitis, from which they issued only on rare occasions. The family life of Greek women widely differed from our Christian idea; neither did it resemble the life in an Oriental harem, to which it was far superior. The idea of the family was held up by both law and custom, and although concubinage and the intercourse with hetairai was suffered, nay favoured, by the State, still such impure elements never intruded on domestic relations. Our following remarks refer, of course, only to the better classes, the struggle for existence by the poor being nearly the same in all ages. In the seclusion of the gynaikonitis the maiden grew up in comparative ignorance. The care bestowed on domestic duties and on her dress was the only interest of her monotonous existence. Intellectual intercourse with the other sex was wanting entirely. Even where maidens appeared in public at religious ceremonies, they acted separately from the youths. An intercourse of this kind, at any rate, could not have a lasting influence on their culture. Even marriage did not change this state of things. The maiden only passed from the gynaikonitis of her father into that of her husband. In the latter, however, she was the absolute ruler, the οἰκοδέσποινα of her limited sphere. She did not share the intellectual life of her husband—one of the fundamental conditions of our family life. It is true that the husband watched over her honour with jealousy, assisted by the gynaikonomoi, sometimes even by means of lock and key. It is also true that common custom protected a well-behaved woman against offence; still her position was only that of the mother of the family. Indeed, her duties and achievements were hardly considered, by the husband, in a much higher light than those of a faithful domestic slave. In prehistoric times the position of women seems to have been, upon the whole, a more

dignified one.   Still, even then, their duties were essentially
limited to the house, as is proved, for instance, by the words
in which Telemachos bids his mother mind her spindle and loom,
instead of interfering with the debates of men.   As the State
became more developed, it took up the whole attention of the
man, and still more separated him from his wife.   Happy
marriages, of course, were by no means impossible; still, as a
rule, the opinion prevailed of the woman being by nature inferior
to the man, and holding a position of a minor with regard to
civic rights.   This principle has, indeed, been repeatedly pro-
nounced by ancient philosophers and lawgivers.   Our remarks
hitherto referred chiefly to the Ionic-Attic tribe, renowned for
the modesty of its women and maidens.   The Doric principle,
expressed in the constitution of Sparta, gave, on the contrary,
full liberty to maidens to show themselves in public, and to steel
their strength by bodily exercise.   This liberty, however, was
not the result of a philosophic idea of the equality of the two
sexes, but was founded on the desire of producing strong children
by means of strengthening the body of the female.

The chief occupation of women, beyond the preparing of the
meals, consisted in spinning and weaving.   In Homer we see the
wives of the nobles occupied in this way; and the custom of
the women making the necessary articles of dress continued
to prevail even when the luxury of later times, together with
the degeneracy of the women themselves, had made the establishment of workshops and places of manufacture for this
purpose necessary.   Antique art has frequently treated these
domestic occupations.   The Attic divinities, Athene Ergane and
Aphrodite Urania, as well as the Argive Here, Ilithyia the
protecting goddess of child-bearing, Persephone, and Artemis,
all these plastic art represents as goddesses of fate, weaving
the thread of life, and, at the same time, protecting female
endeavours; in which twofold quality they have the emblem of
domestic activity, the distaff, as their attribute.   Only few
representations of spinning goddesses now remain; but many are
the pictures of mortal spinning-maidens painted on vases, chiefly
for female use.   Fig. 229 is one of them.   It shows a woman
winding the raw wool from a kalathos round the distaff.   For
the spinning, a spindle was used, as is still the case in places

where the northern spinning-wheel has not supplanted the antique
custom. Homer describes noble ladies handling the distaff
(ἠλακάτη, *colus*) with the spindle (ἄτρακ-
τος, *fusus*) belonging to it. Helen
received a present of a golden spindle,
with a silver basket to keep the thread
in. The distaff, with a bundle of wool
or flax fastened to its point, was held
under the left arm, while the thumb and
first finger of the right hand, slightly
wetted, spun the thread at the end of
which hung the spindle, made of metal.
The web (κλωστήρ) was, from the spindle,
wound round a reel, to be further prepared on the loom.

Fig. 229.

Akin to spinning are the arts of weaving (ὑφαντική) and
embroidering (ποικιλτική). We frequently see in vase-paintings
women with embroidering-frames in their laps.
The skill of Greek ladies in embroidery is sufficiently proved by the tasteful embroidered
patterns and borders on Greek dresses, both of
men and women. The vase-paintings supply
many examples. Fig. 230, after a vase-painting,
shows a woman occupied with embroidering at
a frame which she holds on her knees.

We know, from Homer, that, next to
spinning, weaving was one of the chief female
occupations. Even at that period the art must have been
highly developed, as we conclude from the description of
Penelope's work. In historic times the weaving of both
male and female articles of dress was the business of women;
in some places we even hear of corporations of women being
bound by law to weave the festive garments of certain holy
images. The Attic maidens were obliged to weave a peplos
for the statue of Athene Parthenos at the return (every four
years) of the Panathenaïa. Into this were woven the portraits
of men worthy of this high honour (ἄξιοι τοῦ πέπλου). These
peploi, therefore, served, as it were, as an illustrated chronicle
of Athens. Sixteen matrons were bound to weave a peplos for

Fig. 230.

the statue of Here at Olympia. The same duty devolved on the
noble maidens of Argos with regard to a statue of Artemis.
Spartan ladies had to renew the chiton of the old statue of
the Amiklaïc Apollo every year. Unfortunately, we have no
pictures illustrating the weaving process itself. Our information,
therefore, is but scanty. Originally weaving was done by means
of a frame placed perpendicularly (ὄρθιος ἱστός), over which the
long or chain threads (στήμιον, *stamen*) were pulled in parallel
lines downwards, the bottom ends being made into bunches, and
having weights (ἀγνῦθες) attached to them ; the woof (κρόκη,
ἐφυφή, *subtemen*) was drawn through them with a needle, in a
horizontal direction. The improved horizontal loom, invented
by the Egyptians, more resembled that at present in use (see
Marquardt's "Handbuch der römischen Alterthümer," V., 2,

Fig. 231.

p. 130 *et seq.*) Ovid's description (Metam. VI., 53 *et seq.*) ought
to be read in connection with it.

The pretty vase-painting, Fig. 231, refers to this branch of
female occupation. Two maidens, in richly-embroidered dresses,
are occupied in folding a garment with a star-pattern embroidered
on it, perhaps part of the dowry of a third maiden, standing to
the right of them. Other garments are either hung up on the
wall (together with the inevitable hand-mirror) or lie piled up
on a chair between the two girls. The large press on the left
most likely also contains garments. In case we wish to give
mythologic significance to the picture, we may take it as an
illustration of Nausikaa bidding two servants to prepare the
garments that are to be taken to the washing-place (compare the

picture of Nausikaa and two servants drying garments in Panofka's "Bilder antiken Lebens," Pl. XVIII., 5).

Our remarks about female duties in preparing the meal must be short. The heavy parts of the duty, like grinding the corn in hand-mills, were performed by servants. In the palace of Odysseus twelve female slaves were employed all day in grinding wheat and barley in an equal number of hand-mills, to supply the numerous guests. The hand-mill (μύλη, χειρομύλη) consisted (like those still used in some Greek islands) of two stones, each about two feet in diameter, the upper one of which was made to rotate by means of a crooked handle, so as to crush the corn poured through an opening in it (compare the Roman hand-mills found at Pompeii, § 101). Baking and roasting meat on the spit were amongst the duties of female slaves. In every house of even moderate wealth, several of these were kept as cooks, chambermaids, and companions of the ladies on their walks, it being deemed improper for them to leave the house unaccompanied by several slaves. How far ladies took immediate part in the preparing of dainty dishes we cannot say. In later times it became customary to buy or hire male slaves as cooks.

Antique representations of women bathing, adorning themselves, playing, and dancing, are numerous. The Athenian maiden, unlike her Spartan sister, did not think it proper to publicly exhibit her bodily skill and beauty in a short chiton, but taking a bath seems to have been amongst her every-day habits, as is shown by the numerous bathing scenes on vases. In one of them, a slave pours the contents of a hydria over her nude mistress. Cowering on the floor in another we see an undressed woman catching in her hand the water-spout issuing from a mask of Pan in the wall into a bath. An alabastron and comb are lying on the floor (see Panofka, "Bilder antiken Lebens," Pl. XVIII., 10, 11). A picture on an amphora in the museum of Berlin offers a most interesting view of the interior of a Greek bath-chamber. We see a bathing establishment built in the Doric style. By a row of columns the inner space is divided into two bath-chambers, each for two women. The water is most likely carried by pressure to the tops of the hollow columns, the communication amongst which is effected by means of pipes about six feet from the ground. The openings of the taps are formed into neatly modelled heads of boars, lions, and panthers, from the mouths of which a fine rain spray is thrown on the bathers. Their hair has been tightly arranged into plaits. The above-mentioned pipes were evidently used for hanging up the towels; perhaps they were even filled with hot water to warm the bathing linen. Whether our picture represents a public or private bath seems doubtful. The dressing after the bath has also been frequently depicted. We need not enter upon the subject here, having mentioned the chief utensils, as the comb, ointment-bottle, mirror, etc., on a former occasion. The scenes thus depicted are undoubtedly borrowed from daily life, although Aphrodite, with her attendance of Cupids and Graces, has taken the place of mortal women. For music, games, and dances, we refer to §§ 52 *et seq.* Here we mention only a game at ball, which was played in a dancing measure, and therefore considered as a practice of graceful movements. Homer mentions Nausikaa as a skilled player of this game. It is remarkable that wherever women playing at ball appear in pictures they are represented in a sitting posture.

The swing (αἰώρα) was essentially a female amusement. In commemoration of the fate of Erigone, daughter of Ikarios, a festival had been ordained at Athens at which the maidens indulged in the joys of the swing. Illustrations of this pastime occur frequently on vases, free from any mythological symbolism, even in cases where Eros is made to move the swing (see Panofka, "Griechinnen und Griechen nach Antiken," p. 6, and the same author's "Bilder antiken Lebens," Pl. XVIII., 2).

49. We now come to the point in the maiden's life when she is to preside over her own household as the legitimate mate of her husband (γαμετή, in Homer κουριδίη ἄλοχος). In most cases Greek marriage was a matter of convenience, a man considering it his duty to provide for the legitimate con- tinuation of his family (παιδοποιεῖσθαι γνησίως). The Doric tribe does not attempt to disguise this principle in its plain-spoken laws; the rest of Greece acknowledged it but in silence, owing to a more refined conception of the moral significance of marriage. The seclusion of female life, indeed, made the question of personal charms appear of secondary importance. Equality of birth and wealth were the chief considerations. The choice of the Athenian

citizen (ἀστός) was limited to Athenian maidens (ἀστή); only
in that case were the children entitled to full birthright
(γνήσιοι), the issue of a marriage of an Athenian man or maiden
with a stranger (ξένη or ξένος) being considered illegitimate
(νόθοι) by the law. Such a marriage was, indeed, nothing but a
form of concubinage. The laws referring to this point were, however, frequently evaded. At the solemn betrothal (ἐγγύησις), always
preceding the actual marriage, the dowry of the bride (προίξ,
φερνή) was settled; her position as a married woman greatly
depended upon its value. Frequently the daughter of poor,
deserving citizens were presented with a dowry by the State or
by a number of citizens. In Homer's time the bridegroom wooed
the bride with rich gifts; Iphidamas, for instance, offers a
hundred heifers and a thousand goats as a nuptial present. But
afterwards this was entirely reversed, the father of the bride
having to provide the dowry, consisting partly in cash, partly in
clothes, jewellery, and slaves. In case of separation the dowry
had, in most cases, to be returned to the wife's parents. The most
appropriate age for contracting a marriage, Plato in his Republic
fixes, for girls, at twenty, for men, at thirty. There was,
however, no rule to this effect. Parents were naturally anxious
to dispose of their daughters as early as possible, without taking
objection to the advanced years of the wooer, as is tersely pointed
out by Aristophanes (Lysist., 591 *et seq.*)

The actual marriage ceremony, or leading home, was preceded
by offerings to Zeus Teleios, Hera Teleia, Artemis Eukleia, and
other deities protecting marriage (θεοὶ γαμήλιοι). The bridal
bath (λουτρὸν νυμφικόν) was the second ceremony, which both
bride and bridegroom had to go through previous to their union.
In Athens the water for this bath was, since the earliest times,
taken from the well Kallirrhoë, called after its enclosure by
Peisistratos, Enneakrunos. Whether a boy or a girl acted as
water-carrier on this occasion (λουτροφόρος) is differently
stated by ancient authors. The latter supposition is supported,
amongst other things, by an archaic picture on a hydria (Gerhard,
"Auserlesene griechische Vasenbilder," III., 306). To the left of
the spectator lies, as the inscription indicates, the holy fountain
Kallirrhoë, flowing from the head of a lion under a Doric super-
structure. A girl, holding in her hand branches of laurel and

myrtle, as used at lustrations, looks musingly down on the hydria which is filling with the bridal water. Five other maidens occupy the remaining space of the picture. Some of them, with empty pitchers on their heads, seem to wait for their turn ; others are about to go home with their filled pitchers. Gerhard's opinion of their forming a sacred procession is contradicted by the evidence of ancient writers. As most weddings took place in the month of marriage (λαμήλιον), the meeting of several bridal water-carriers was, in a populous city like Athens, anything but unlikely ; and a scene of this kind is evidently the subject of our picture.

On the wedding day, towards dark, after the meal at her parental home (θοίνη γαμική) was over,[1] the bride left the festively adorned house, and was conducted by the bridegroom in a chariot (ἐφ ἁμάξης) to his dwelling. She sat between the bridegroom and the best man (παράνυμφος, πάροχος) chosen from amongst his relatives or intimate friends. Accompanied by the sounds of the hymenæos, and the festive sounds of flutes and friendly acclamations from all passers-by, the procession moved slowly towards the bride-groom's house, also adorned with wreaths of foliage. The mother of the bride walked behind the chariot, with the wedding torches, kindled at the parental hearth, according to custom immemorial. At the door of the bridegroom his mother was awaiting the young couple with burning torches in her hand. In case no wedding meal had been served at the bride's house, the company now sat down to it. To prognosticate the desired fertility of the union, cakes of sesame (πέμματα) were distributed. The same symbolic meaning attached to the quince, which, according to Solon's law, the bride had to eat. After the meal the couple retired to the thalamos, where for the first time the bride unveiled herself to her husband. Before the door of the bridal chamber epithalamia were sung, a charming specimen of which we possess in the bridal hymn of Helena by Theokritos. On the two first days after the wedding (ἐπαύλια and ἀπαύλια) wedding-presents were received by the pair. Not till after these days did the bride appear without her veil.

Antique art has frequently illustrated the various customs of the marriage feast. A series of archaic vase-paintings (Gerhard,

---

[1] At this meal, contrary to the usual custom, women were present.

"Auserlesene griechische Vasenbilder," III. Pl. 310 *et seq.*) show *bigæ* and *quadrigæ* containing the bridegroom with the veiled bride, followed by the paranymphos, and surrounded by female relatives and friends, who carry the dowry in baskets on their heads. Hermes, the divine companion and herald, precedes the procession, looking back on it. Another vase-painting (Panofka, "Bilder antiken Lebens," Pl. XI. 3) shows the crowned bridegroom on foot leading the veiled bride to his house, at the entrance of which stands the nympheutria with burning torches waiting for the procession. A youth preceding the couple accompanies the hymenaios on a kithara; the bride's mother, recognisable by her matron-like dress, with a torch in her hand, closes the procession. The most remarkable of all wedding scenes is the glorious wall-painting known as the "Aldobrandini Wedding" (Fig. 232). It is 4 feet

o

Fig. 232.

high by 8½ long. It represents three different scenes painted on one surface, without regard to perspective, as is frequently the case in antique bas-reliefs. The straight line of the wall in the background is broken by two pillars, by means of which the artist undoubtedly intended to open a view into two different parts of the gynaikonitis, while the third scene is meant to take place in front of the house. The picture illustrates three different scenes of the marriage ceremony, such as might take place inside or in front of the bride's house before the starting of the bridal procession. From this point of view we must first consider the centre picture. In a chamber of the gynaikonitis we see the bride [1] chastely veiled and reclining on a beautiful couch. Peitho, the goddess of persuasion, sits by her side, as appears from the crown on her head, and from the many-folded peplos falling over her back. She pleads the bridegroom's cause, and seems to encourage the timorous maiden. A third female figure to the left of the group, leaning on a piece of column, seems to expect the girl's surrender, for she is pouring ointment from an alabastron into a vase made of shell, so as to have it ready for use after the bridal bath. Her peplos, only held by the shoulder-clasp, leaves the upper part of her body almost uncovered. Most likely she represents the second handmaiden of Aphrodite, Charis, who, according to the myth, bathed and anointed her mistress with ambrosial oil in the holy grove at Paphos. The pillar at the back of Charis indicates the partition-wall between this chamber and the one next to it on the left, to which we now must turn. We here see a large basin filled with water, standing on a columnar base. The water is perhaps that of the well Kallirrhoë, fetched by the young girl standing close by for the λουτρὸν νυμφικόν. The girl seems to look inquiringly at the matronly figure approaching the basin on the other side, and putting her finger into the water as if to examine it. Her sublime form and priestly dress, together with the leaf-shaped instrument in her hand (probably the instrument used at lustrations), seem to betray her as Here Teleia, the protecting goddess of marriage, in the act of examining and blessing the bridal bath. The meaning of the third figure in the background holding a large tablet is difficult to explain. Bötticher (" Die

---

[1] Compare the statuette, Fig. 218.

aldobrandinische Hochzeit," p. 106) believes that on the tablet is
written the horoscope of the impending marriage.   The third scene,
to the right of the spectator, is placed at the entrance of the bride's
house.   The bridegroom, crowned with vine-branches, is sitting on
the threshold, as if listening impatiently for the close of the ceremony
inside the house.   In front of him we see a group of three girls, one
of whom seems to be offering at a portable altar, while the two
others begin the hymenæos to the accompaniment of the kithara.

Very different from the social position of chaste women was
that of the hetairai.   We are not speaking of the lowest class of
unfortunates, worshipping Aphrodite Pandemos, but of those
women who, owing to their beauty and grace of conversation,
exerted great influence even over superior men.   We only remind
the reader of Aspasia.   In the graces of society the hetairai were
naturally superior to respectable women, owing to their free
intercourse with men.   For the hetairai did not shun the light of
day, and were not restrained by the law.   Only the house of the
married man was closed to them.

50. Before passing from private to public life, we must cast
a glance at the early education of the child by the mother.   We
begin with the earliest days of infancy.   After the first bath the
new-born child was put into swaddling clothes ($\sigma\pi\acute{a}\rho\gamma\alpha\nu\alpha$), a
custom not permitted by the rougher habits of Sparta.   On the
fifth or seventh day the infant had to go through the ceremony of
purification; the midwife, holding him in her arms, walked several
times round the burning altar.   The day was called in conse-
quence $\delta\rho o\mu\iota\acute{a}\mu\phi\iota o\nu$ $\mathring{\eta}\mu\alpha\rho$, the ceremony itself, $\dot{a}\mu\phi\iota\delta\rho\acute{o}\mu\iota\alpha$ (the run
round).   A festive meal on this day was given to the family, the
doors being decorated with an olive crown for a boy, with wool for
a girl.   On the tenth day after its birth, when the child was
named, another feast ($\delta\epsilon\kappa\acute{a}\tau\eta$) took place.   This ceremony implied
the acknowledgment, on the part of the father, of the child's
legitimacy.   The name of the child was chosen by both parents,
generally after the name of either of the grandparents, sometimes,
also, after the name or attributes of a deity, under whose particular
protection the child was thus placed.   A sacrifice, offered chiefly
to the goddess of child-bearing, Here Ilithyia, and a meal,
concluded the ceremony.   At the latter friends and relatives
presented the infant with toys of metal or clay, while the mother

received painted vases.   The antique cradle consisted of a flat
swing of basket-work (λίκνον), such as appears in a terra-cotta
relief in the British Museum, of the infant Bacchus being carried
by a satyr brandishing a thyrsus, and a torch-bearing bacchante.
Another kind of cradle, in the form of a shoe, is shown (Fig. 233)
containing the infant Hermes, recognisable by his petasos.   It
also is made of basket-work.   The advantage of this cradle consists in its having handles, and, therefore, being easily portable.

It also might be suspended on ropes, and
rocked without difficulty.   Other cradles,
similar to our modern ones, belong to a later
period.   The singing of lullabies (βαυκα-
λήματα, καταβαυκαλήσεις), and the rocking
of children to sleep, were common amongst

Fig. 233.

the ancients.   Wet-nurses (τίτθη) were com-
monly employed amongst Ionian tribes ; wealthy Athenians chose
Spartan nurses in preference, as being generally strong and
healthy.   After the child had been weaned it was fed by the dry
nurse (ἡ τροφός) and the mother with pap, made chiefly of honey.

The rattle (πλαταγή), said to be invented by Archytas, was
the first toy of the infant.   Other toys of various kinds were
partly bought, partly made by the children themselves   on
growing older.   We   mention   painted clay puppets (κόραι,
κοροπλόθοι, κοροπλάσται), representing human beings or animals,
such as tortoises, hares, ducks, and mother apes with their
offspring.   Small stones were put inside, so as to produce a
rattling noise ; which circumstance, together with the fact of
small figures of this kind being frequently found on children's
graves, proves their being toys.   Small wooden carts (see Panofka,
" Bilder antiken Lebens," Pl. I., 3), houses and ships made of
leather, and many other toys, made by the children themselves,
might be instanced.   Up to their sixth year boys and girls were
brought up together under their mother's care ; from that point
their education became separate.   The education proper of the
boy (παιδεια) became a more public one, while the girl was
brought up by the mother at home, in a most simple way,
according to our notions.   From amongst the domestic slaves a
trustworthy companion (παιδαγωγός) was chosen for the boy.   He
was, however, not a tutor in our sense, but rather a faithful

servant, who had to take care of the boy in his walks, particularly
on his way to and from school.   He also had to instruct his pupil
in certain rules of good behaviour (εὐκοσμία).   The boy had, for
instance, to walk in the street with his head bent, as a sign of
modesty, and to make room for his elders meeting him.   In the
presence of the latter he had to preserve a respectful silence.
Proper behaviour at table, a graceful way of wearing his
garments, etc., might be mentioned as kindred subjects of
education.   Boys were accompanied by pedagogues up to their
sixteenth year.   The latter appear frequently in vase-paintings,
and are easily recognisable by their dress, consisting of chiton and
cloak, with high-laced boots ; they also carry sticks with crooked
handles, and their hair and beards give them a venerable aspect ;
while their pupils, according to Athenian custom, are clad more
lightly and gracefully.   The pedagogue of the group of the
Niobides is well known.

Education was, at Athens, a matter of private enterprise.
Schools were kept by private teachers, the government supervision extending only to the moral not to the scientific quali-
fication of the schoolmaster.   Grammar (γράμματα), music
(μουσική), and gymnastics (γυμναστική), to which Aristotle adds
drawing (γραφική), as a means of æsthetic cultivation, were the
common subjects of education at schools and gymnasia.   The
expression γράμματα comprised reading, writing, and arithmetic.
The method of teaching how to write consisted in the master's
forming the letters, which the pupils had to imitate on their
tablets, sometimes with the master's assistance.   The writing
materials were small tablets covered with wax (πίνακες, πινάκια,
δέλτοι), into which the letters were scratched by means of a
pencil (στύλος, γραφεῖον) made of metal or ivory.   It was pointed
at one end and flattened or bent at the other (Fig. 234, *a*) so as
to extinguish the writing, if required, and, at the same time,
to smooth the surface again for other letters.   The burnisher,
Fig. 234, *b*, the broad side of which is about equal in width
to a tablet, most likely served to smooth the wax cover of a
whole tablet at once.   By means of joining several tablets
together, in the manner of a book, the so-called πολύπτυχοι δέλτοι
were formed (Fig. 234, *c*).   Waxed tablets were used also for
letters, note-books, and other requirements of daily life.   A young

girl in a charming Pompeian wall-painting ("Museo Borbonico,"
vol. vi., Pl. 35) has in her hand a double tablet (δέλτιον
δίπτυχον), while with her other hand she holds her pencil to her
chin, as if pondering over a letter. Her nurse looking over her
shoulders tries to decipher the contents of the love-letter. Besides
these tablets, Herodotos mentions the use of paper (βίβλος) made
of the bark of the Egyptian papyrus-plant. The stalk (three or

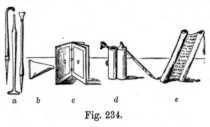

a　　b　　　c　　　　d　　　　　e

Fig. 234.

four feet in length) was cut
longitudinally, after which
the outer bark was first
taken off; the remaining
layers of bark, about twenty
in number (*philuræ*), were
carefully severed with a pin;
and, afterwards, the single
stripes plaited crosswise; by
means of pressing and perforating the whole with lime-water, the
necessary consistency of the material was obtained. The lower layers
of bark yielded the best writing-paper, while the outer layers were
made into packing-paper (*emporetica*); the uppermost bark was used
for making ropes. Names of different kinds of paper, such as *charta
Ægyptiaca, Niliaca, Saitica, Taneotica*, were derived from different
manufacturing places in Egypt, which, down to late Roman times,
remained the chief market for paper; other names, like *charta
regia* (βασιλική), *Augusta, Liviana, Fanniana, Claudia, Cornelia*,
were invented after emperors and empresses. Of at least equal
antiquity with the use of papyrus was that of hides (διφθέραι) for
writing materials. The Ionians used, according to Herodotos, the
hides of goats and sheep for this purpose from time immemorial;
but the more careful preparation of the material was invented not
before the reign of Eumenes II. (197-159 B.C.) at Pergamum,
whence the name περγαμήνη—anglicè, parchment. The leaves of
the papyrus had writing only on one side, those of parchment on
both. The latter were rolled on sticks (Fig. 234, *e*), kept in
cylindrical cases, a small piece of parchment (σίλλυβος), with the
title written on it, being fastened to the upper end of each roll
(compare § 102) for convenience sake. A case of this kind full
of parchment-rolls (κύλινδροι), with a cover to it, stands by the side
of Klio in a wall-painting of Herculaneum (Fig. 235). In her left

hand the muse holds a half-opened roll on which are inscribed the words ΚΛΕΙΩ ΙϹΤΟΡΙΑΝ (Klio teaches history). The ink (τὸ μέλαν) was made of a black colouring substance ; it was kept in an inkstand made of metal, with a cover to it (μελανδόχον or πύξις). As is proved by Fig. 234, *d*, it could be fastened to the girdle by means of a ring. Double inkstands, frequently seen on monuments, were most likely destined for the keeping of black and red inks, the latter of which was frequently used. To write on paper or parchment, the ancients used the Memphic, Gnidic, or Anaitic reeds (κάλαμος, *calamus, harundo, fistula,* Fig. 234, *d*), pointed and split like our pens. As

Fig. 235.

we mentioned before, it was the custom of adults to write either reclining on the kline, with the leaf resting on the bent leg, or sitting in a low arm - chair, in which case the writing apparatus was supported by the knee of the writer. The latter posture is exemplified by a reading ephebos in a vase-painting (Panofka, " Bilder antiken Lebens," Pl. I. Fig. 11); it was, undoubtedly, also that of the boys sitting on the rising steps used as forms (βάθρα) at the schools. After his elementary education was completed, the boy was made acquainted with the works of national poetry, particularly with the poems of Homer, the learning by heart and reciting of which inspired him with patriotic pride.

51. Musical instruction formed the second part of general education (ἐγκύκλιος παιδεία). Technical virtuosity was a secondary consideration, the ethic influence of the art being the guiding principle. The playing of one instrument, generally a stringed one, was an important subject of education. At games and meals, or in the throng of battle, the exhilarating and inspiring influence of music was felt. Into the intricacies of Greek harmony, as developed amongst different tribes, we cannot enter here, no more than into the relations of music to the sister-arts of poetry and the dance; or into the monodic and choral divisions of vocal music (μέλος). We must restrict ourselves to instrumentation proper, collectively called κροῦσις, so far as it may be illustrated by the remaining specimens of antique instruments. It ought to be remembered that the music of stringed instruments only was called κιθαριστική, or ψιλή κιθάρισις,

κιθαρῳδική being the term for vocal music accompanied by strings. In the same way αὐλητική or ψιλὴ αὔλησις signified music of wind-instruments; αὐλῳδική the combination of these instruments with the human voice. We shall mention first the stringed instruments, after them the wind-instruments, and conclude with the clanging instruments, chiefly used for orgiastic music.

a. The Greeks used no bows in playing on stringed instruments. The strings were placed all at equal distance over the sounding-board; a low, straight bridge (ὑκολύριον, μάγας, or μαγάδιον) only served to prevent the vibrating strings from touching the sounding-board. The strings were fastened at one end to the so-called "yoke" (ζυγόν or ζύγωμα) by means of pegs (κόλλοπες or κόλλαβοι); at the other they were attached to the inside, or outside, of the sounding-box. The use of the bow was thus made impossible, by the want of a curved bridge (as it exists in our stringed instruments), by means of which the relative height of the position of the single strings is modified. The stringed instruments of the ancients were played with the fingers, or with the straight or curved plectrum (πλῆκτρον), made of wood, ivory, or metal. Sometimes also both fingers and plectrum were employed severally or simultaneously. Both the shape and the use of the plectrum are illustrated by Fig. 237, c, e, g. It was held in the right hand, and fastened to a long ribbon (Fig. 237, g). Large-stringed instruments, played with both hands, or with the plectrum and the fingers of the left hand simultaneously (see Fig. 237, c, e), were held in a convenient position by means of a strap slung over the shoulder; other instruments, played only with the plectrum or the fingers of the right hand, might rest on the left arm, without being tied to it.[1] This strap, fastened by means of rings to either surface of the sounding-board, appears most distinctly on the statue of Apollo in the Museo Pio Clementino. The god wears the costume of a kithara-player, accompanying his own song on the instrument (see Müller, "Denkmäler," Part I., No. 141, a; compare a statue of Apollo in the same collection, ibid., Part II., No. 132). In vase-paintings these straps have been generally omitted; but their necessity may be easily conjectured from the position of

---

[1] In this sense the words ἐπωλένιον κιθαρίζων in the hymn on Hermes (verses 432 and 510) must be understood.

the instrument, which seems to float in the air. The numerous specimens in pictures, and the varied terms in authors, make it here again next to impossible to explain the *nuances* of nomenclature, the more so as the statements of the authors are frequently very brief, and the representations of the artists (particularly with regard to the number of strings) inaccurate. The last-mentioned feature can, for this same reason, be no criterion in classifying the different instruments; the construction of the sounding-board, as illustrated by the monuments, must be our only principle of division. Most likely the artists rendered essentially the forms of the real instruments, although the whole conception of Greek art forbade a slavish imitation of details. The rich ornamentation of some stringed instruments, as proved by the vase-paintings, is quite in accordance with the general taste of the Greeks.

Three fundamental types of stringed instruments must be distinguished—viz. the lyre, the kithara, and the harp. They are exemplified by an interesting vase-painting in the old Pinakothek of Munich (No. 805), the centre group of which consists of the three Muses, Polymnia, Kalliope, and Erato, playing respectively on the three mentioned instruments—the lyra, the kithara, and the trigonon (Fig. 236). The invention of the lyre (λύρα) is

Fig. 236.

ascribed, by the myth, to Hermes, who first drew strings across the oval hollow of a tortoise-shell, which in this way became the sounding-box of the instrument. This primitive form is still in use amongst some of the South Sea populations; in Greece it was only known traditionally. The remaining evidence, both literary and artistic, refers only to the developed form of the lyre. In this not only the back-shell of the tortoise, but also the part covering the animal's chest, was used, the whole forming a closed sounding-box, the natural openings for the

front legs of which were used for the insertion of the roots of the
curved horns of a goat.   Near their points these were joined
together by a transverse piece of wood, called the yoke.   Across
this frame the strings were drawn, being more than twice as
long as those of the mythical lyre.   On the chest part of the
shell (for only this flat part could be used for the purpose) was
placed a bridge, across which the strings were drawn, being at
one end tied· in knots and fastened to the sounding-board,
at the other, either simply wound round the yoke, or fastened to
pegs.   Figs. 237, *a, b, c, d, e,* illustrate a number of lyres, of
which *c* shows most distinctly the entire tortoise-shell.   The arms
(πήχεις) are, in *c, d, e,* made of goats' horns, which, as we shall
see in speaking of weapons, were also used for bows ; in *a* and *b*
they consist· of wood.   In *e* the construction of the sounding-

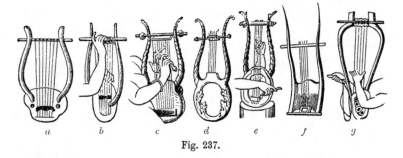

a   *b*   *c*   *d*   *e*   *f*   *g*

Fig. 237.

board is somewhat difficult to understand, showing as it does a
large round opening in the centre.   Equally difficult is the
classification of the instrument in Fig. 237, *f.*   Fig. 237, *g,* shows
an instrument nearly related to the lyre.   From the sounding-
box, consisting of a small tortoise-shell, two wooden arms issue
in divergent directions ; towards their upper ends they approach
each other, and are joined together by a yoke.   In vase-painting
this instrument appears generally in the hands of either Alkaios
or Sappho, from which circumstance archæologists have (not
without good reason) conjectured it to be the barbiton (βάρβιτον,
βαρύμιτον), a low-toned instrument, which Terpander is said to
have introduced from Lydia into Greece.   The πηκτίς and
μαγάδις, both of Lydian origin, may also have been of the nature
of lyres.   Both expressions are applied by Greek authors pro-

miscuously to one and the same, and to different instruments. In Greece Sappho is said to have played on a pektis; in Sicily it seems, at a later period, to have been used at mysteries. The magadis is said to have been one of the most perfect instruments. It comprised two full octaves, the left hand playing the same notes as the right, an octave lower. Still more perfect was the ἐπιγόνειον, the name being derived from that of its inventor, Epigonos. It had forty strings, most likely in double rows—twice as many as the magadion. Neither of the two instruments was played with a plectrum. They cannot be with certainty recognised in the pictures; but the large lyre with fifteen strings, standing before a sitting agonethis, in a marble-relief on a grave at Krissa (see Stackelberg, "Gräber der Griechen," Pl. II.), doubtlessly belongs to the same species.

The second class of stringed instruments, differing from the

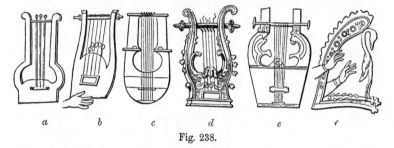

a   b   c   d   e   f

Fig. 238.

lyre both in shape and material, is called kithara (κιθάρα); it was invented by Apollo, and therefore belonged to the kitharodes, κατ᾿ ἐξοχήν. The sounding-box here consists of thin plates of wood, ivory, or metal; it is generally angular, in other cases semi-oval in shape, and is continued, in order to increase its resounding power, by two arms, also hollow, and at their base equal in thickness to the sounding-box itself. The size of the latter, as well as the length of the arms, and their distance from each other, depended on the greater or smaller number of strings, also on the desired stronger or weaker resonance, not to speak of the individual taste of the maker (λυροποιός), which, moreover, could show itself in the rich ornamentation of this particular kind of instrument. The sounding-board may have been equal in power to that of our guitars. Fig. 238, a, b, c, d, e, show a few

of the numerous variations of the kithara. Some of them
(particularly *c*) resemble perfectly the guitar (*cither*) used in
South Germany at the present day. Their forms are pleasing,
that of *d* (most likely an imitation of the ornamental kithara,
made of ivory or metal) magnificent. The distinction between
lyre and kithara, founded on the different constructions of their
sounding-boards, is not mentioned by ancient writers. The
existence of *a* distinction between these two species, however,
may be proved by written evidence, and is, moreover, confirmed
by the vase-painting in Fig. 236, where the three muses represent
the three chief classes of stringed instruments. The more complicated construction of the kithara, compared with the primitive
tortoise and goat's horns of the lyre, seems to prove its later
invention. The lyre was most likely of Thrakian origin;
Orpheus, Musaios, and Thamyris were there celebrated as masters
on it, and thence it was most likely, together with the orgiastic
worship of Dionysos, introduced into Greece. Its connection
with that particular phase of religion is sufficiently proved by
the monuments. In Greece the musical education of the youth
began with the lyre; together with the flute, it was the instrument most commonly used, for instance, at festive meals. The
kithara, on the contrary, introduced from Asia into Greece by the
Ionians, was used at musical competitions, sacrifices, and pageants,
as is proved, for instance, by the Panathenaïc procession on the
frieze of the Parthenon. The players always appeared on such
occasions in the costume of the kitharodes, *i.e.* crowned and clad
in long flowing robes. The phorminx seems not to have differed
essentially from the kithara. Homer, at least, uses the expressions
φόρμιγγι κιθαρίζειν and κίθαρις φορμίζειν as meaning the same
thing. The explanation by Hesychius of phorminx, as a kithara
carried on a ribbon over the shoulder (φόρμιγξ. ἡ τοῖς ὤμοις
φερομένη κίθαρις), is most inappropriate, seeing that a difference, if it existed at all, must have appeared in the construction of the sounding-board, or the number of strings; while, on the
other hand, the strap is common to all the forms of the kithara.

As the third form of stringed instruments, we mention an
instrument resembling our harp, called by archæologists trigonon
(τρίγωνον). It was of triangular shape, as indicated by the name,
and of Syrian or Phrygian origin. We are therefore justified in

applying to the harp-like instruments (Figs. 236 and 238, *f*), both
taken from vase-paintings, the name of trigonon, or, perhaps, that
of σαμβύκη, an instrument defined by Suidas as εἶδος κιθάρας
τριγώνου.   As in our harp, the sounding-board was on the side
turned towards the player; in the trigonon, however, the broader
side is turned upwards, differing in this from the modern instrument.   To the sounding-board the strings were fastened by
means of studs; the side of the instrument resting on the
player's lap, took the place of the yoke.   The strings, therefore,
ran parallel to the third side or arm of the instrument.   From
Fig. 238, *f*, compared with similar representations, it would appear
as if the yoke had been a double one, with double rows of strings
drawn across it, as was the case in the above-mentioned epigoneion.
The third side of the trigonon consisted either of a simple stick,
connecting yoke and sounding-board, or it was shaped like an
animal (Fig. 238, *f*).   In Fig. 236 it is wanting entirely, and the
trigonon, in consequence, resembles the harps, of different sizes,
found frequently on Egyptian monuments.[1]   An instrument with
two wooden arms and ten strings, appearing in a wall-painting
of Herculaneum (" Pitture d'Ercol."   Tav. I., Pl. 171), belongs
undoubtedly to the same class; analogous forms of this instrument
have also been found on Egyptian monuments (Wilkinson, "A
Popular Account of the Ancient Egyptians," vol. i., p. 119), and,
indeed, are still in use amongst certain tribes of the valley of the
Upper Nile.   The names of other instruments we must omit, as not
sufficiently explained by monumental evidence.   We only mention
a four-stringed instrument, with a sounding-board in the form of
a semi-globe, to which a long and narrow neck is attached just as
in the modern guitar.   It appears in a marble-relief of late Roman
origin in the Louvre, held by a muse (Clarac, "Musée," II., Pl. 119).
Instruments of this kind do not appear on Egyptian monuments.

   b. The wind-instruments (αὐλοί) may be divided into pipes
(σύριγγες), clarionets (αὐλοί proper), and trumpets (σάλπιγγες).
The oldest and simplest form of wind-instrument is the reed-pipe
(σύριγξ).   The sound was produced by blowing either into the

---

[1] Amongst the "Swanes," a tribe of the Caucasus, a harp called *Tschungi*, resembling the trigonon, is still in use.   See Radde, "Berichte über biolog.-geograph.,"
"Untersuchungen in den Kaukasusländern," I. (Tiflis, 1868), where a picture of the
instrument may be seen.

orifice of a broken reed, or, as in the fife (*Querflöte*), into a hole
made to the side of the reed.   The sound of the wind in the reeds
led most likely to the invention of the syrinx, which is ascribed to
Pan.   According to the myth, Syrinx, the daughter of the Arkadian
river-god Ladon, pursued by Pan, was changed into a reed, which
the god thereupon cut into several pieces, joining together seven
of them, decreasing in size, by means of wax.   The result received
the name of syrinx, or Pan's pipe.   The number of reeds varied
from seven to nine, as is proved both by the statements of ancient
authors and by the monuments.   Fig.
239, *b*, shows the simpler syrinx, taken
from a wall-painting at Herculaneum ;
the pipes are seven in number, and
seemingly of equal length.   Fig. 239,
a, taken from a candelabrum in the
Louvre, shows nine pipes of different
sizes.   The syrinx, together with other
wind-instruments and the lyre, appears most frequently in the
hands of Sileni and satyrs in scenes from the Bacchic myth
—for instance, on a gem in the Florence gallery (Fig. 240),
which shows two Sileni with a syrinx, an aulos, and a lyre.
In practical music the syrinx seems to have been used little,
although it appears occasionally, together with other instruments,
in pictures representing concerted music.   An
Etruscan bas-relief (Micali, " L'Italia avanti il
dominio dei Rom.," Atlas, Tav. 107) shows
three girls playing severally on a syrinx, a
flute, and a kithara ; and in another Etruscan
representation (Müller, " Denkmäler," Part II.,
No. 757) the sirens use it to allure Odysseus.
Nearest akin to the syrinx is the πλαγίαυλος
(fife), said to be invented by the Libyans.   It
was not a favourite instrument with the Greeks,
and is rarely found on monuments.   Fig. 241, *m*,
shows a youth playing on it, after a bas-relief in the Louvre
(compare the statue of a young satyr in Müller's " Denkmäler,"
Part II., No. 460).   Generally both the instruments in Fig. 241, *g*
and *h*, are also called plagiauloi ; whether rightly or wrongly we
will not venture to decide.

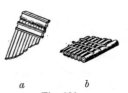

a   *b*
Fig. 239.

Fig. 240.

The αὐλός proper resembles our hautboy or clarinet, differing, however, from the latter in the fact of its lower notes being more important than the higher ones. The aulos consisted of two connected tubes and a mouthpiece, to the latter of which belonged two so-called tongues (γλῶσσαι), in order to increase the trembling motion of the air. The myth connected with the invention of the aulos illustrates, at the same time, the mutual position of wind and stringed instruments amongst the Greeks. Athene played for the first time on an aulos, made from the bone of a hart, at a feast of the gods. Here and Aphrodite rallied her on account of her blown-up cheeks, and the goddess, after having ascertained the truth of these objections by looking at her image, while playing, in the fountain on Mount Ida, threw down the instrument in disgust. It was found by Marsyas, the Phrygian Silenos, who, on the strength of it, dared to compete with Apollo, the inventor of the lyre, the Muses being appointed as umpires. The victory of the god symbolised that of stringed over wind instruments. It took a long while before the playing on the pipe was fully received in Greece; and although in Athens it formed part of the musical education, it never was there appreciated as much as in Bœotia, whose inhabitants were celebrated for this art. Perhaps the particularly fine reeds growing in the marshy plains of Orchomenos tend to explain this phenomenon.

The materials of the aulos were, besides reeds, the wood of box or laurel, the bones of the hart, and ivory; metals were chiefly used in it for ornamental purposes. At first the aulos had only three or four holes (τρήματα, τρυπήματα, παρατρυπήματα), but Diodoros of Thebes added to the number. The addition of side holes, with keys to them, completed the aulos. It was blown by means of a removable mouthpiece; which, if not used, was kept in a case (γλωσσοκομεῖον). The βόμβυξ (reed) itself was mostly straight; sometimes it was bent upwards near the opening, which was wider or narrower according to the strength of tone required. The simplest and oldest form of the aulos is seen Fig. 241, *b* and *n*; it resembles a short shepherd's pipe (*schalmei*), and the figures holding it in both cases are taken from the statues of shepherds. The form of the mouthpiece appears distinctly in Fig. 241, *a, d, e, f.* The clarinet (μόναυλος, μονοκάλαμος) with one tube only is seen also on the frieze of the

Parthenon ; but still more common was the double clarinet, called
by the Romans *tibiæ geminæ*.   It consisted of two tubes blown
simultaneously by means of one common or two separate mouthpieces (Fig. 241, *a, d, e, f, i, k, l*), and comprises as many notes as
the syrinx.   The tube held in the right hand, and blown with the
right side of the mouth, had three holes, and was called by the
Romans *tibia dextra*, by the Greeks the " male " clarinet (αὐλὸς
ἀνδρήϊος) ; the left tube had four holes, and was called *tibia
sinistra*, or "female" aulos (αὐλὸς γυναικήϊος).   The former
produced the lower, the latter the upper notes.[1]   The tubes are

Fig. 241.

either both of the same length and shape (used to accompany
revels and gymnastic exercises (Fig. 241, *a, d, f, k, l*), or of
unequal length but equal shape (αὐλοὶ γαμήλιοι) ; or, finally,
differing totally both in shape and length (Fig. 241, *e, i*).   The
pipes might be with (Fig. 241, *d*) or without keys (Fig. 241,
a, f, k, l).   The first-mentioned instrument (*d*) appears on a sarcophagus in the Vatican, in the hands of a genius displaying the

---

[1] Double shepherd's pipes, called "dutka," are still used by peasants in certain
parts of Russia.

attributes of Euterpe. Sometimes the lower opening was shaped
like a bell (κώδων) (Fig. 241, c d), as in our clarinets. The
Phrygian double-pipe (ἔλυμοι αὐλοι), with one tube straight and
the other bent downwards like a horn, shows the largest extension
of the tube-opening. Fig. 241, i, shows a female figure playing
the Phrygian double-pipe, taken from a sarcophagus in the
Vatican; the two Phrygian pipes put crosswise (e) are
taken from one side of a square altar in the Vatican, and
appear in exactly the same form in a relief representing an
Archigallus surrounded by the attributes of his dignity (Müller,
"Denkmäler," Part II., No. 817). The difference in shape
between the two mouthpieces is remarkable. Other varieties
appear frequently (see, for instance, "Museo Borbon.," vol. ix.,
Tav. 37; and Fig. 247, b, representing a dancing bacchante, from
a marble relief). Both Greek and Roman players occasionally
tied a leather bandage round their lips and cheeks (φορβειά,
στόμις, χειλώτηρ), through the hole of which, bound with metal,
the mouthpieces of the double clarinet were put (Fig. 241, l).
The purpose of this bandage was to soften the tone by preventing
violent breathing. It was used particularly at theatrical representations, sacrifices, and pomps, to play long pieces on the large
double clarinets; while the female players in representations
of symposia always appear without it. It was never used with
single clarinets. The bagpipe is of antique invention. Fig. 242,
taken from a bronze statuette, shows a bagpipe-player (ἀσκαύλης,
utricularius). His instrument resembles those used by modern
pifferari. Its squeaking notes naturally appealed only to the
taste of the lower classes.

The σάλπιγξ (trumpet) consists of a tube considerably increasing
in circumference towards the lower opening, and a mouthpiece in
the shape of a drinking-vessel. The long trumpet, unknown to
the Greeks in Homer's time, is said to have been introduced by
the Pelasgic Tyrrhenians; the Hellenic salpinx was undoubtedly
identical with it. The far-sounding salpinx was a warlike instrument, no less than the pipe and kithara, used as such chiefly
by the Spartans and Cretans; it also accompanied religious
ceremonies. By the sound of an Argive salpinx Agyrtes rouses
the warlike spirit of Achilles, hidden amongst the women of
Deïdameia in the isle of Skyros (Fig. 243, taken from a marble

relief), while Diomedes and Odysseus display shining weapons to the young hero. Of other trumpets and horn-like instruments ascribed by Greek authors to Oriental nations, but not to the Greeks themselves, we mention the Egyptian χνοῦς, used to call the people to the sacrifice; it resembled the curved salpinx (σάγπιγξ στρογγύλη), the *cornu* of the Romans (Fig. 245). We further name the trumpet called the Galatian, bronze, or shrill (ὀξύφωνος) salpinx, with a leaden mouthpiece and a kodon in the shape of an animal's mouth; by the Galatian Celts it was called κάρνυξ. The Paphlagonian trumpet was low-toned (βαρύφωνος), and larger than the Greek salpinx; from its koden, bearing the shape of a bull's head, it was called βόϊνος. The Medes used a hollow-sounding salpinx, made of a bulrush, with a wide kodon.

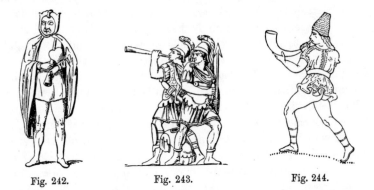

Fig. 242.   Fig. 243.   Fig. 244.

This Median trumpet seems to be depicted in two vase-paintings: in one of them (Micali, "L'Italia avanti il dominio dei Romani," Atlas, Tav. 100) we see an Asiatic archer, in a Median or Parthian dress, blowing on a very thin, long tube, with a screwed-on mouthpiece, which he has fastened to his mouth by means of a bandage in the manner of an aulos-player; the other (Gerhard, "Griechische Vasenbilder," Part II., Pl. 103) shows the same instrument in the hands of the Amazon Antiope clad in Greek armour. It appears from the position of both these figures that this instrument was turned towards the ground on being played, differing in this from the Greek trumpet. We finally mention the Tyrrhenian bronze trumpet, the kodon of which was bent upwards (κώδων κεκλασμένος); it was also called the curved

or Etruscan lituus (λίτυον), and resembled, in its shape, the
Phrygian pipe (compare Fig. 241, *i*); it was used as a signal-
trumpet in battles, and at games and ceremonies. Horns (κέρατα),
as warlike instruments, seem to have been unknown to the Greeks.
Barbarian nations frequently used them for that purpose. Fig.
244 shows a player on the horn (κεραταύλης) whose *pileus* of black
lamb's wool betrays him as an Armenian or Persian. In the
vase-painting in which he occurs, he seems to encourage Asiatic
warriors fighting with Greeks, while the latter are called to battle
by the sounds of Hellenic trumpets.

To conclude, we mention the water-organ (ὕδραυλος, ὑδραυλίς,
organon hydraulicum), invented by Ktesibios, the mechanician, and
described by his pupil, Hero of Alex-
andria. It was constructed on the syrinx
principle, and contained seven pipes made
partly of bronze, partly of reed. The
sound was produced by waving the air-
columns through the means of water. It
was played, *organo modulari*, on a keyboard.
Ktesibios' invention was afterwards considerably improved. Nero took a particular interest in it, and during his reign
hydraulic organs of a new construction

Fig. 245.

were built (*organa hydraulica novi et ignoti generis*). Fig. 245
shows an organ taken from a Roman mosaic floor at Nennig. A
man is playing on the horn to the sound of the organ.

c. We now come to the " clanging instruments " used chiefly
at religious ceremonies connected with the worship of Dionysos and
Kybele—castanets, the cymbal, and the
tambourine. They were also used as a
rhythmical accompaniment of social dances,
played by the spectators, or the dancers
themselves, as is still the custom amongst

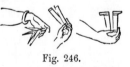

Fig. 246.

peasants in the south of Europe. The castanets (κρόταλοι),
said to be invented by the Sicilians, consisted, like our modern
ones, of small pieces of reed, wood, or metal, or of shells, tied
together with a ribbon. They were struck against each other by
the fingers at rhythmical intervals. The three pairs of castanets
seen in Fig. 246 appear in the hands of dancing-women in wall-

paintings and on vases.   Their manipulation requires no other explanation.

The cymbals ($\kappa\acute{\nu}\mu\beta\alpha\lambda\alpha$) consisted, like those of our military bands, of two metal bowls in the form of semi-globes (Fig. 247, *a*).

They were held in the hollow of the hand or by means of straps (see "Museo Borbonico," vol. xv., Tav. 47).   They were used at the above-mentioned religious ceremonies, and were also hung upon the branches of holy trees (compare Fig. 1).   Still more noisy was the tambourine ($\tau\acute{\nu}\mu\pi\alpha\nu o\nu$), a broad ring of wood or metal with a covering of hide.   Bells and pieces of brass were added to increase the noise (Fig. 248).   In vase-paintings the tympanon appears with a sound-

a   *b*

Fig. 247.

ing-bottom in the form of a semi-globe, which makes it resemble our kettle-drum.   To conclude, we mention the *sistrum* ($\sigma\epsilon\hat{\iota}\sigma\tau\rho o\nu$, Fig. 249), not used by the Greeks, but introduced to the Romans

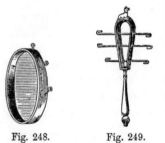

as part of the secret worship of Isis. It consisted of a sounding-box re-sembling that of the lyre, made of brass or precious metals, into which were inserted loosely small bars of metal, bent down at the end so as to prevent their sliding out.   By means of a handle the instrument was shaken, whereat the vibrating motion of the bars produced a not

Fig. 248.   Fig. 249.

inharmonious sound.

52. It was a distinguishing feature of the Greeks amongst ancient nations to consider corporeal exercise as a no less important factor of education than mental progress itself.   The harmonious development of the body, and, indeed, of every single limb, was thought to be of the utmost importance for the attainment of self-conscious determination in the practical demands of life.   This principle of acting, through means of the body, on the mind, was realised in the gymnastic and agonistic institutions of Greece.

Lucian, in his "Apology of Gymnastics," insists upon the ethic bearing of athletic exercise on the mind of young men in directing their ambition into the right channel, in preventing them from laziness and its accompanying vices, and in endowing them with that combination of good qualities which is collectively called καλοκαγαθία. The physical as well as the intellectual (for instance musical) education varied greatly amongst the different tribes of Greece. Amongst the Doric tribes, chiefly in Sparta, it consisted principally in hardening the body of the young citizen-warrior against the influence of pain and exertion; amongst Ionian tribes, and chiefly at Athens, the harmonious development of body and soul, *i.e.* grace and ease of bearing and demeanour (εὐρυθμία and εὐαρμοστία), were the objects chiefly aimed at.

The beginnings of gymnastic and agonistic exercises, although lacking at first the systematic development of later times, date back to prehistoric ages. Games were held at an early period in honour of gods and heroes; and the laws of Solon and Lykurgos only served to regulate and further develop the skill thus acquired.

To our previous remarks (§ 25) we must add a few words as to the important question of the separation of the gymnasion from the palæstra. The separation of the two localities, destined as they were for different branches of athletic exercise, seems established beyond doubt, notwithstanding the utterances of ancient writers frequently contradicting each other. Herodotos, for instance, calls both the dromos and the palæstra γυμνάσια while Vitruvius uses palæstra for gymnasion and palæstra collectively. At one time the palæstra was undoubtedly a building by itself, connected with, or detached from, the gymnasion. At the time of the emperors, but not before, this distinction seems to have disappeared; hence the mixing up of the two terms by Vitruvius. At Athens the gymnasia were public institutions, supported by private or public means, at which epheboi and men spent a part of their day in athletic exercise and in instructive and social intercourse. There were the Lykeion, the Kynosarges, the Academy, the Ptolemaion, the splendid gymnasion of Hadrianus, and the small gymnasion of Hermes. The number of palæstrai at Athens was still greater. They were all private institutes kept by single pædotribai, and destined for the athletic education of boys only.

In smaller cities, the joint practice of youths and grown-up men
in the same locality was frequently inevitable.   But it is erroneous
to suppose that the palæstra was exclusively the resort of
athletai.   The separation of youths and men from boys was
desirable both for moral and educational reasons.   For the
difficulties of the task increased in proportion to the age of the
aspirant.   Classifications according to age and abilities are
contained in the expressions παῖδες νεώτεροι and πρεσβύτεροι, or
πρώτη and δευτέρα ἡλικία—the former applying to younger, the
latter to older boys.   A more advanced stage was the τρίτη
ἡλικία, denoting the transition from the age of the boy to that of
the ephebos ; another name for these youths was ἀγένειοι.   Similar
distinctions existed undoubtedly amongst the epheboi of different
ages.   These distinctions were especially marked in Sparta, where
each age had its particular amount of sufferings and exertions
to go through.

Before entering upon the single exercises, we must try to
define the three general appellations, γυμναστική, ἀγωνιστική, and
ἀθλητική.   The first term comprises all kinds of regulated
bodily exercise for the purpose of strengthening the body or
single limbs.   The expressions ἀνταγωνιστής and ἀγών apply to
those games on which the emulation of several persons was brought
to bear.   The ἀγωνιστική comprises the gymnastic exercises
tending to prepare the athletai for the wrestling-matches, which
formed an important feature of national festivities, particularly of
the games of Olympia, celebrated once every five years, at the time
of the first full moon after the summer solstice.   Here assembled,
invited by the peace-messengers of Zeus, the delegates of empires
and cities ; not to speak of crowds of enthusiastic spectators from
the most distant shores.   The flower of Greek youth came to test
their skill in the noble competition for the crown of Zeus.   Only
he whose unstained character and pure Hellenic descent had been
certified by the Hellanodikai was allowed to approach the silver
urn which contained the lots.   A previous training of at least ten
months at a Greek gymnasion was further required for obtaining
the permission of taking part in the holy contest.   Supreme were
the honours conferred on the victor.   The umpires crowned him
with the fresh olive-wreath and the palm in the temple of Zeus ;
poets like Pindar sang his praise ; inscriptions and statues of brass
announced his fame to coming generations.

The ethic purpose of gymnastic art came to be more and more neglected when artificiality and affectation began to prevail. It was then that the noble art deteriorated into a mechanical profession; the ἀθλητική is the later signification of that term.

To the fine arts the palæstra and gymnasion yielded an inexhaustible supply of beautiful models both for youthful grace and manly strength. The national pride of the Greeks further encouraged the artist in the choice of athletic subjects; hence the innumerable plastic monuments in the native cities of the victors, and on the sites of their triumphs. Pausanias, who wrote after the wholesale spoliation and destruction of Olympia by the Roman conquerors, mentions no less than 230 bronze statues of Olympian victors adorning her streets and squares as the remnants of past glories. We possess only few specimens of this branch of Greek art, but their excellence and technical finish demonstrate the reciprocity between the feeling of the nation and its artistic expression. Scenes from the palæstra and gymnasion frequently occur in vase-paintings. There we see older or younger men clad in himatia, leaning on crooks, and looking down on the wrestlers, or directing their movements by means of peculiarly forked staffs (Gerhard, "Auserlesene griechische Vasenbilder," Taf. CCLXXI.), the destination of which, however, seems somewhat doubtful. These men are the gymnastai and pædotribai; the former having to superintend the general development and deportment of the body, the latter directing the single exercises. These were the real teachers in gymnastics, and their place was amongst the wrestlers. Amongst other officials we mention the sophronistai, who were responsible for the good behaviour (σωφροσύνη) of the boys. Their number at Athens was ten, one being selected by each phyle. During the imperial times we meet with a kosmetes, with one anti-kosmetes, and two hypo-kosmetai as assistants, who had to watch the epheboi at the gymnasia. The gymnasiarchos was the superintendent of the whole gymnasion, an honorary and, moreover, expensive post. He had to pay the expenses of the torch-races, and also for the oil used at the games, which afterwards was supplied by the State. He also had to arrange memorial processions in honour of great men.

It may be assumed that the simplest bodily exercises, viz. those that required no weapons or antagonists, were also the oldest. The most primitive of these was the foot-race (δρόμος), which always came first amongst the contests at the great Hellenic festivals. At the Olympic games, indeed, the foot-race continued for a long period the sole athletic exercise; and the Pythian, Nemean, and Isthmian games, which were modelled after them, always began with the foot-race whenever the pentathlon was enacted in its entirety. The foot-race consisted of the simple race (στάδιον or δρόμος), in which the racecourse had to be run over once from beginning to end. The race of the boys, however, comprised but half the racecourse, and those of ageneioi of two-thirds. This race of the boys was incorporated with the Olympic games in the 37th Olympiad, and the names of the youthful victors are invariably first quoted in old inscriptions. But in those states in which the *physique* of the female sex was likewise trained and developed, the foot-race was regarded as the most suitable of gymnastic exercises for maidens, the length of their course being shorter by one-sixth than that reserved for men. In the second species of race, the diaulos (δίαυλος), the competitors had to run twice over the whole length of the racecourse. The goal had to be doubled in a curve (καμπή), whence the name κάμπειος δρόμος. But the greatest exertion of strength and endurance had to be displayed in the third species of races, the long-run (δόλιχος), in which, without stopping, the course had to be measured so often that the whole distance, according to various reports, consisted of 12, 20, or 24 stadia, that is, more than half a geographical mile, if we accept the highest computation.

We can understand, therefore, that the Spartan Ladas, when crowned conqueror in the foot-race, after having, for twelve successive times, run backwards and forwards over the course, should have dropped down dead on reaching the goal. Strength of limb and breath were, according to Lucian, the necessary requisites in running this race; while the greatest possible speed, on the other hand, was required by those who took part in the shorter course. The race in complete armour (ὁπλίτης δρόμος) also belonged to these exercises. At first this was executed by young men fully equipped with helmet, shield, and greaves; but at a later period their armour for this race was reduced to the simple shield. This armed race was undoubtedly of the greatest importance as a preparation for active service; and

Plato, with a view to this military object, demanded its being practised both in the long and short running matches. For the Greeks, like the French, were wont to attack the ranks of the enemy at a running pace. This is said to have been the case at the battle of Marathon. At foot-races, as in all other exercises, the combatants used to appear quite naked, except in earlier times, when they girded their loins with a cloth. The runners who presented themselves at the agon as candidates were ranged in divisions (τάξεις) (each consisting, as may be seen from monuments, of four agonistai) and led to the starting-point, where it was decided by lot in which order the different divisions were to follow each other. Any kinds of tricks, bribery, or force, employed by racers to gain an advance upon the others, were strictly prohibited. After the various divisions had run their race, the victors of each had again to compete with each other; and only in the last race was it settled to whom the prize or garland should be awarded. Races of this description, run by four men or epheboi, are often represented on Panathenaïc vases. The runners here appear perfectly naked, and their lifted arms look as though they were to increase the swiftness of their legs.[1] The torch-race (λαμπαδηδρομία) may also be regarded as belonging to this species of athletic sports. It was held at night in honour of various gods and goddesses in different parts of Greece. The principal object at these night races was to reach the goal with one's torch alight. Two epheboi, armed with round shields, and flourishing torches in their hands, are thus depicted on a vase (Gerhard, "Antike Vasenbilder," Cent. I. 4, Taf. 63). On two other vessels (Tischbein, "Vas. d'Hamilton," Taf. III., Pl. 48, and II. 25) Nike presents the crown, in sign of victory, to one of three youthful torch-bearers competing for the prize. Other races were connected with festivals of a religious character, such as the Oschophoria at Athens, where runners, clad in female garments, bore vines covered with grapes from the temple of Dionysos to that of Athene Skiras in the Demos Phaleros. These and others, however, do not properly come under the category of races.

Leaping (ἅλμα) ranked next in the series of gymnastic exercises. Homer already introduces practised leapers in his

---

[1] "Mus. Gregorianum," II., Tav. 42. "Monum. in edit. d. Inst. di Corrisp. archeol." I. Tav. 22. Gerhard, "Antike Bildwerke," Cent. I., Taf. 6, etc.

description of the games of the Phaiakai, and the same exercises
were afterwards introduced amongst the gymnic agones; they, as
well as the foot-race, formed a part of those sports to be presently
described as the pentathlon.   The leaps upwards, forwards, and
downwards appear to have been practised at the palæstra and the
gymnasia, in a similar manner as in our modern gymnasiums.
But it is doubtful whether the Greeks were acquainted with the
long pole now habitually used in gymnastics; the poles depicted
on many vases held in the hands of leaping epheboi having rather
the appearance of spears than poles.   But if we consider that the
Greeks regarded gymnastics as a preparation for military service,
and that the spear was often employed in war to leap over ditches,
we may safely assume that poles were also used for gymnastic
purposes.   This surmise is further strengthened by the Amazon

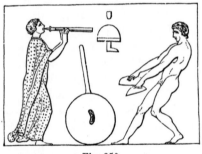

Fig. 250.

on a gem (Müller's "Denk-
mäler," I., Taf. XXXI., No.
138, *b*), who, grasping such
an instrument in her hands,
prepares for the leap.   Written and monumental evidence
proves, on the other hand,
that the Greeks, in order to
secure accuracy of motion for
the distant leap, made use of
so-called ἀλτῆρες.   The form

of this instrument, not unlike that of our own dumb-bells, though
rarely mentioned by ancient authors, appears in numerous pictorial
representations.   On a vase where an ephebos is just preparing for
the leap, a pair of these instruments is depicted (Fig. 250).   They
were either pieces of metal of semi-oval form, in the curved lines of
which orifices were left for the hands, or they consisted of short
iron bars having knobs at each end, thus resembling our dumb-bells
in shape; this latter kind was that in use at the pentathlon.   The
mode of using these dumb-bells was probably as follows.   The
person about to leap, whether first stepping back a few paces or not,
stretched his arms, laden with the dumb-bells, back in a straight
line; and then, in the very act of leaping, swung them forwards
again with a sudden motion (Fig. 250).   But as this violent
motion of the arms necessarily imparted an oblique and receding

position to the body, in coming down the person would necessarily have fallen on his back had not the equilibrium been restored by a rapid backward motion of the arms. It has, in fact, recently been proved by practical experiments that a person in the act of leaping is capable of taking a much wider leap by the aid of dumb-bells: still, even acknowledging the greater practice of the Greeks, it remains inexplicable how Phayllos could, by aid of these dumb-bells, have leaped to a distance of fifty-five feet, considering that the most practised gymnasts of our time only succeed in leaping one-third of that distance. As is the case in our gymnasiums, the ancients marked, by a line dug in the ground, or a board, the spot whence the leap had to be taken (βατήρ). Such a board, of a very lofty height, whence a palæs-trites takes the *salto mortale*, is depicted in a wall-painting in an Etruscan burial-chamber (Micali, "L'Italia avanti il dominio dei Romani," Atlas, Tav. 70), where, in fact, the most varied exercises of the palæstra are most graphically represented. The goal which had to be attained in leaping was marked either by a furrow dug in the earth (σκάμμα), or the distance to which each of the competitors leaped was marked by an incision in the ground. This drawing of furrows is probably indicated by those agonistic representations on vases, of men with hoes (Gerhard, "Auserlesene griechische Vasenbilder," Taf. CCLXXI.). Others, again, depicted in these paintings, carry long red ribbons in their hands, probably pieces of tape, by which the length of the leaps as well as other kinds of athletic exercises were determined. Although the use of the dumb-bells as weights to be held in leaping has not been introduced into modern gymnastics, its strengthening the muscles of the arms, neck, and chest has, nevertheless, been as fully recognised as it was by the ancients.

Wrestling (πάλη) was the third species of athletic exercise. The custom of preparing for this exercise by anointing the body (ἔγαιον) seems to have been introduced in post-Homeric times. It contributed to the suppleness and elasticity of the limbs, and was soon not only used in wrestling but in all other kinds of athletic exercises. But in order to obviate the too great facility of extricating the limbs from the embrace of an antagonist, the wrestlers used to sprinkle their bodies with sand. Besides, as Lucian says, this double covering of the skin prevents a too copious perspiration by closing the pores, which, owing to the violent exercise, are open, and thus more exposed to the bad effects of draughts; it also strengthens the powers of endurance generally. The duty of anointing the limbs devolved on the ἀλείπτης. At the end of the combat the body, of course, was thoroughly cleansed; and the ancients for that purpose used an instrument of the nature of a scraper, which they called στλεγγίς (*strigilis*). Both sexes were also in the habit of employing the same scraper after every bath for the cleansing of their limbs. This instrument, hollowed out in the shape of a spoon, and consisting of metal, bone, or reed, was provided with a handle, and we naturally find an instrument so constantly used in daily life depicted in various paintings (Gerhard, "Auserlesene

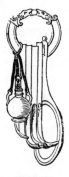

Fig. 251.

griechische Vasenbilder," Tafs. CCLXXVII. CCLXXXI. "Mus. Gregor," vol. ii., Tav. 87), the subjects of which are taken from the palæstra or from domestic life. As a rule, it appears together with a vessel of a globular shape, in which the oil was kept. Fig. 251 may assist the reader in forming a correct idea of a complete apparatus of this sort, consisting of an oil-flask suspended by cords, of scrapers of various lengths, and of a flat dish; the original is at the Museo Borbonico. The manner of using this instrument is exemplified in a particularly vivid manner by the beautiful statue of an athlete scraping himself, in the Museo Chiaramonti, Fig. 252, generally known under the name of 'Αποξυόμενος. In no other kind of contest was a professional training as necessary as in the wrestling-matches. Not only rude strength was required, but also firmness of eye in finding out an antagonist's weak points. No less useful were certain dexterous thrusts learned at the wrestling-schools, and quickness in out-witting an antagonist by feigned turns and positions, all of which had, at the same time, to be executed in a pleasing and decorous manner. Certain rules were enforced at the wrestling-school which the combatants were not allowed to transgress. They do not, it is true, harmonise with our more humane ideas; for, although the beating of an opponent was then, as now, forbidden, not so were pushing (ὠθισμός), and spraining his fingers and toes, nor grasping his throat with the hands. The combatants were also allowed to knock their heads against each other (συναράττειν τὰ μέτωπα), unless this is to be understood as a mere pressing together of foreheads, a position which is also permitted in our modern gymnasiums. This later species of combat seems depicted on a vase of the Blacas collection (" Musée Blacos," t. i., Pl. 2, compare with it a similar representation in the "Museo Pio Clemintino," vol. v., Pl. 37), where two naked wrestlers, with their heads pressed against each other, endeavour to grasp each other's arms. The Greeks had two species of wrestling. In the first the wrestlers strove to throw each other (πάλη ὀρθή, ὀρθία) while standing in an upright position, and, if thrown, to rise again to renewed contest. If the opponent was thrown three times in the same contest he had to declare himself beaten. The other species of wrestling formed the continuation of the first; the custom in this being, that as soon as one of the combatants had been thrown the other knelt down upon him to prevent his rising, the contest (ἀλίνδησις, κύλισις) being carried on in this recumbent position. In both species of wrestling certain tricks were used, by means of which the wrestlers tried to deprive their opponents of the free use of their arms and legs, by closely

Fig. 252.

embracing them. The opponents (Fig. 253) first approached each other, at the beginning of the contest, with uplifted arms, at the same time advancing the right leg, and taking a firm position with the upper body drawn back (ἐμβολαί).

The contest, then, was begun with arms and fists (Fig. 253), each antagonist try-ing to encircle the other's arms and shoulders (δράσσειν). Another, σχῆμα (the technical name for

Fig. 253.

the different tricks of wrestling) was done with the legs; Odysseus, in his contest with Aias, applies it by knocking his heel against the bend of the knee of his antagonist, and flooring him by that means (ὑπέλυσε δὲ γυῖα). Another similar trick consisted in suddenly lifting up the antagonist's leg with one's hands, and throwing him down in that manner; this is frequently depicted in

vase-paintings (" Monumenti dell' Istit.," vol. i. 22, No. 8, *b*). The encircling of the antagonist's legs, continued even after the wrestlers had fallen to the ground, also belongs to this species of combats; it is illustrated by the celebrated marble group of " The Wrestlers," at Florence. The technical name for it was ὑποσκελίζειν and it formed an important feature of the art. In the above-mentioned group (Fig. 254) the

Fig. 254.

uppermost wrestler has laid his left leg tightly round that of his antagonist; the latter endeavours to lift himself up by means of his disengaged left arm and of his right knee. But his right arm has been firmly grasped by the victor, and is being pushed upwards. Many other schemata of wrestling mentioned by ancient authors we omit as not sufficiently explained.

The fourth kind of gymnastic exercise is the throwing of the diskos (δισκοβολία). Our illustration (Fig. 255) is taken from the statue of a Diskobolos found in 1781 at the Villa Palombara, belonging to Principe Massimi. It is undoubtedly a copy of the celebrated statue by the sculptor Myron. The upper part of the body is bent down towards the right, and rests on the left arm, the left hand itself resting on the knee of the right leg, which is slightly bent. The weight of the body, therefore, is thrown on the right foot; while the left one, with the toes bent slightly, only touches the ground to keep up the equilibrium. The heavy diskos lies on the lower part of the arm and the right hand. The right arm is bent backwards up to the height of the shoulder, so as to add force to the throw. The neck and head are turned towards the hand holding the diskos, so as to control the direction of the throw. The same position is also mentioned by Philostratos (" Imag.," I., 24) in his description of a diskobolos, and was,

undoubtedly, the regular one. It somewhat resembles that of our
players at nine-pins, with the difference, however, that in our
game the ball is thrown in a straight line, while the diskos was
propelled in a curve. This game is connected with mythical gods
and heroes ; Homer mentions it as a favourite occupation of men.

The Homeric diskos (σόλος) consisted of
a heavy piece of cast iron (αὐτοχόωνος)
or of stone ; as, for instance, amongst the
Phaiakai. The historic diskos has the
shape of a lens. It resembled a small
round shield without a handle, and was,
therefore, difficult to manage. The diskobolos bent his fingers over the side
of the diskos which rested on his palm
and on the lower part of the arm (Fig.
255). A diskos found at Ægina is 7·7"
in diameter, and weighs 3 lbs. 14½ oz.
It is at present in the antiquarium of
the Royal Museum of Berlin (Bronzen,
No. 1273) ; on it are represented
two epheboi, one of them throwing
a spear, the other holding dumb-

Fig. 255.

bells.[1] The diskobolos stood on a small earth-mound (βαλβίς),
and the longest distance obtained decided the victory, whether
or not a goal had previously been marked.

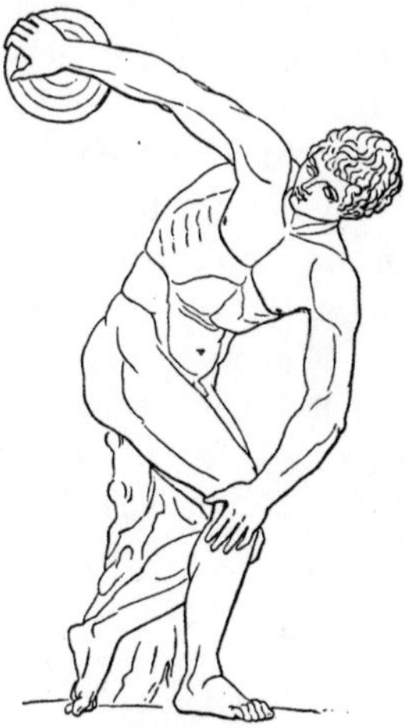

Still more than was the case with the diskobolia another
exercise, viz. the throwing of spears (ἀκόντιον, ἀκοντισμός), was
considered as a preparation for actual warfare. It was well known
in Homer's time, and afterwards counted amongst the gymnastic
and agonistic exercises. In Homer's time the game was performed
in full armour and with sharp spears ; later on, only pointless
spears were used, as is confirmed by several vase-paintings, in
which epheboi appear with one or two spears without points. In
the pentathlon light, short spears, with long, thin points, were
used either in throwing at aims or only for long distances. We
shall return to the spears in treating of Greek weapons (§ 54).

The five exercises thus described, viz. running, leaping,

---

[1] See the picture of a diskos (original size) in Ed. Pinder, "Ueber den Fünfkampf
der Hellenen." Berlin, 1867.

wrestling, throwing the diskos, and the spear, formed the so-called
πένταθλον. At the four great national festivals all these had to
be gone through on one and the same day, and the prize was
awarded to him only who had been victorious in all of them.
According to Böckh, the pentathlon began with leaping; after it
followed running; after that the throwing of the diskos and of
the spear, the last game being the wrestling. Other philologists
prefer a different order. It remains doubtful whether the whole
pentathlon was gone through each time. According to Krause
("Gymnastik und Agonistik der Hellenen"), the τριαγμός (viz.
leaping, and throwing of diskos and spears) was obligatory in all
cases, the running and wrestling being omitted occasionally.

The most dangerous of all contests was the boxing match
(πυγμή, πύξ). In order to increase the force of the clenched fist
each fighter (πύκτης) tied straps of bull's hide (ἱμάντες) round
both his clenched fists, so as to leave only the fingers uncovered.

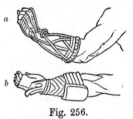

Fig. 256.

The ends of these straps were tied several
times round the wrists, so as to protect the
artery in that place. Such was the older
custom mentioned by Homer. The name
of this covering was μειλίχαι, perhaps, as
Krause remarks, because it caused a softening
of the blow dealt with it (see Fig. 256, a).
In other cases, strips of hardened leather,
or even nails and lead buckles, were attached to these coverings,
inflicting wounds at each well-aimed blow. The name of this
dreadful weapon was σφαῖραι (see Fig. 256, b, taken from the
statue of a fighter in the Villa Pamfili). The fingers there are
put through a ring of metal or leather, while round the arm
are wound numerous straps, to which is added a piece of metal
resembling a shield. A still more dangerous weapon is exemplified by the statue of a fighter in the Dresden Museum (Fig.
257); perhaps we there see what the ancients called μύρμηκες.
The fighters entered the "ring" perfectly naked. After their
straps had been adjusted by experienced men, they chose their
places. After the signal had been given, they began the
combat with the upper part of the body bent forward, but
with the throat drawn back so as to remove it from the grasp
of the antagonist. Fig. 257, and many other statues and vase-

paintings, exemplify this position. All kinds of tricks were used
by the fighter to tire out the antagonist and protect himself from
blows. Both hands were used alternately to deal blows, the
unemployed arm being used to
ward off attacks from the head,
the chest, or the belly. Quickness and agility in changing the
position were no less required than
strength of muscles. Illicit means
of gaining the victory were severely
punished, as was also the inten-
tional killing of the antagonist.
Blows were chiefly aimed at the
chest, temples, ears, cheeks, nose,
mouth, and chin. The teeth were
frequently knocked in, and the
ears squashed, as appears from
several statues. Ear-cases of wool
or leather (ἀμφωτίδες) were used
in the gymnasia and palæstrai, but
not at public fights. Fighters of
about equal strength and dexterity

Fig. 257.

sometimes used to break their combat by short intervals of rest.
Strongly contested fights, however, were generally continued
without interruption till either of the combatants confessed himself beaten by lifting up his hand.

To conclude we mention the παγκράτιον, a combination of
wrestling and boxing. It was unknown in heroic times, and does
not appear amongst public games previous to Olympiad 33. Straps
were not used in it, as these would have impeded the motion of
the hands in wrestling. According to rule in the pankration, the
blow was not dealt with the clenched fist but only with the bent
fingers. Otherwise all tricks and schemata of both wrestling and
fighting were permitted, barring illicit means of weakening the
adversary (κακομαχεῖν).

53. After having considered the gymnic agones (ἀγὼν
γυμνικός), we now come to the ἱππικὸς ἀγών, i.e. racing in
chariots and on horseback. Both these agones were considered as
the highest and noblest kinds of public games. Horses and

chariots, of course, could be owned only by the richer classes,
whence the fashionable character of these games.   Firmness of
hand and eye in directing the horses was the most important
requisite of the art.   The owners of horses, therefore, employed
frequently substitutes at the chariot races (ἁρματηλασία).   The
architectural arrangements (aphesis, goal, etc.) of the racecourse
have been described in § 28.   We add a few remarks about the
chariots themselves.   The two-wheeled chariot used by Homeric
heroes, both in the racecourse and on the field of battle, remained
in use at races during the historic period.   The charioteer alone
occupied it.   (Compare our remarks about the battle-chariot, § 54.)
The number of chariots admitted at one race most likely varied
according to the width of the hippodrome ; in large hippodromes
like that of Olympia, the aphesis of which, on each side, was about
400 feet long, it was, no doubt, considerable.   The number
of horses attached to each chariot was originally four of full-grown
size (δρόμος ἵππων τελείων), afterwards two (ἵππων τελείων
συνωρίς).   The first kind of race was introduced Ol. 25, the second
Ol. 93.   The occurrence of three horses is proved by the frieze
of the Parthenon.   After Ol. 99, the custom of using colts (πῶλοι),
either by fours or twos, was introduced.   The use of mules in the
hippodrome occurs only between Ol. 70—84.   The places of the
chariots were decided by drawing lots.   At a given signal the
horses started simultaneously, animated by the driver's shouts,
and urged on to the utmost speed by his whip (μάστιξ) or
goad (κέντρον) ; thick clouds of dust followed the wild race.[1]
Just as in the foot-race, the course was either run through
once, without returning round the goal (ἄκαμπτον), or 'the
chariots had to run back, as in the diaulos of the foot-race.   The
equivalent of the dolichos would be the running twelve times
through the whole course with grown-up horses (δωδέκατος
δρόμος), as done at the Olympia, Pythia, and Isthmia.   We
also find, analogous to the ὁπλίτης δρόμος of the foot-race, a
chariot-race at which both horses and drivers appeared in full
armour.   Usually, however, the charioteers were naked, while

---

[1] The mastix consisted of a short stick with a number of thongs attached to it
(Fig. 259) ; the kentron was a long-pointed staff similar to that used in southern
Italy and Spain at the present day.   Sometimes rattles were attached to the point of
the kentron (see Müller, "Denkmäler," Part I., No. 91 *b*).

the horses were harnessed as lightly as possible.   Great danger
of upsetting, or even smashing, the chariot was incurred in
going round the goal, not to speak of many other inconveniences
connected with the imperfect levelling of the course.   Nestor
refers to the former danger in the instruction addressed to his
son.

Chariot races have been frequently the subjects both of
sculpture and painting.   A wall-painting in an Etruscan grave-
chamber (Fig. 258) illustrates the preparation for the race. ֚ On
the left a charioteer drives his biga into the racecourse, while an
expert seems to examine the horses of the next-following chariot
before admitting it to the hippodrome.   On the right, two horses
are put to a chariot by two servants.   Other monuments show the

Fig. 258.

chariots amidst the dangers of the race.   In a vase-painting
(Panofka, " Bilder antiken Lebens," Taf. III. 10) we see a
running horse with the rein torn ; a wall-painting (Micali,
" L'Italia avanti il dominio dei Romani," Atlas, Tav. 70) shows a
chariot smashed by the kicking horses, while the charioteer is
thrown up into the air (see also the representation of Circensic
games on a mosaic floor at Lyons, § 104).

We now have to consider the races on horseback (ἱπποδρομία).
The art of riding, as applied to both warfare and racing, belongs
essentially to historic times, when the Homeric chariot began to
disappear from the field of battle.   Only barbarous nations retained
the chariot as an implement of war.   In horse-racing we also meet
with the distinction between grown-up horses (ἵππῳ κέλητι) and
colts (κέλητι πώλῳ), the race with the former dating from Ol. 33,
that with the latter from Ol. 131.   The rules of horse-racing were
most likely identical with those of chariot-racing.   The turning round
the goal in the former was much less dangerous than in the latter;
but accidents, nevertheless, were not impossible, as appears from
a vase-painting (Panofka, " Bilder antiken Lebens," Taf. III. 4),

where a rider is dragged along the ground by his horse. The
arrival at the goal is illustrated by a vase-painting (Fig. 259), in
which the umpire receives the victor; he is one horse's length in
advance of his competitors. The so-called κάλπη was a peculiar
kind of race in which the rider, while racing round the course
for the last time jumped off his horse, and, holding it by the
bridle, made for the goal. Something similar to the kalpe (which,
however, was soon discontinued) occasionally took place at chariot
races. Two persons, viz., the driver (ἡνίοχος) and the competitor,
stood in the chariot. While the course was measured for the last
time the latter jumped from the chariot and ran by the side of it,
until very near the goal, when he jumped into it again, assisted

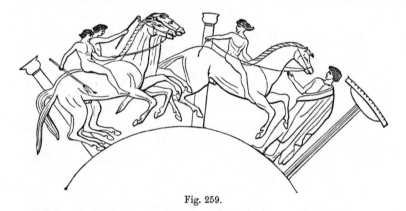

Fig. 259.

by the heniochos; hence his name ἀποβάτης or ἀναβάτης. At
the Panathenaïa this kind of race was most commonly practised,
and the frieze of the Parthenon undoubtedly contains examples of
it. There we see chariots with three horses, driven by charioteers,
while warriors, armed with helmet and shield, run by the side of
them, or are seen jumping into them.

Amongst gymnastic exercises we also name the game at ball
(σφαιριστική), greatly recommended by Greek physicians as
strengthening the limbs, and, moreover, considered by the Greeks
as a chief means of developing the grace and agility of the body.
Boys and men, girls and women, practised it. It was played
like other gymnic exercises, according to certain rules which had
to be learnt. At the gymnasia a separate place (σφαιριστήριον,

σφαίριστρα) was reserved for it, where a teacher (σφαιριστικός) gave instruction in the art. The balls were of various colours, made of leather, and stuffed with feathers, wool, or fig-seeds. With regard to size the distinctions were—small, middle-sized, and very large, empty balls. The game with the small ball (μικρά) was again divided into three classes, according as the smallest (σφόδρα μικρά), the slightly larger (ὀλίγῳ τοῦδε μεῖζον), or the relatively largest ball (σφαιρίον μεῖζον τῶνδε) was used. The chief difference between games with the larger and smaller balls seems to have consisted in the position of the hands, which in the former were not allowed to be raised above the height of the shoulders ; while in the latter they might be lifted above the head. The explanations of ancient authors are, however, not very perspicuous. Our monumental evidence consists chiefly of women, in a sitting position, playing with one or several balls. For want of a Greek representation, we have chosen a scene from a Roman sphairisterion (Fig. 260). It is taken from a wall-painting in the thermæ of Titus, in Rome. Three epheboi, superintended by a bearded teacher, are practising with six small balls. The position of their arms accords with the rule just mentioned. The ἀπόρ-ραξις was another game with small balls. In it the ball was thrown on the ground in an oblique direction, and was caught by the other player after having rebounded

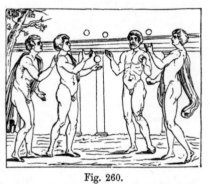

Fig. 260.

several times owing to its elasticity. These bounds used to be counted. The players altered their positions only when the ball, in rebounding, had changed its direction. Another game with the small ball was called οὐρανία, in which the little ball was thrown into the air as high as possible, and had to be caught on falling down again. In another game, of Spartan origin, called ἐπίσκυρος or ἐφηβική, the players were divided into two parties, separated by a line (σκῦρον). Behind each party was drawn another line which they were not allowed to cross in catching the ball. The ball was placed on the skyron and thrown by a member of one party towards the other party, who had to catch it, and throw it back. As soon as either party were driven back behind their boundary-line the game was ended. About the games with large and very large balls we are instructed less fully. They were thrown with considerable force, and had to be caught and thrown back by the antagonist with his arm or the palm of his hand. A similar game, played by young men in Italy at the present day, may be an antique reminiscence. Whether the game called φαινίνδα was played with large or small balls is uncertain. In it the player pretended to throw the ball towards one of his antagonists, but changed its direction unexpectedly. We know that the balls used in this game were hollow. We finally mention the game with the korykos (κωρυκομαχία, κωρυκοβολία). From the ceiling of a room was suspended, down to about the chest of the player, a rope with a balloon attached to it, which latter was filled with flour, sand, or fig-seeds. The task of the player consisted in putting the balloon in a gradually increasing motion, and in throwing it back with his hands or chest.

Bathing also may be counted amongst corporeal exercises. The warm bath as a means of refreshment after the day's labour is mentioned by Homer. In historic times, also, the beneficial influence of a bath, particularly before meals, was generally acknowledged by the Greeks, although they never cultivated bathing as a fine art like the Romans. The too frequent use of hot baths was rare amongst the Greeks. For warm baths, public and private buildings (βαλανεῖα δημόσια and ἴδια) were erected; certain rooms in the gymnasia were reserved for the same purpose (see page 106). To judge by the vase-paintings—our chief means of information with regard to the interior arrangements of baths—the ablution of the body was effected in bathing-tubs, constantly supplied with fresh spring-water (compare Gerhard's "Auserlesene griech. Vasenbilder," Taf. CCLXXVII.) In taking a sudatory or steam bath (πυρίαι, πυριατηρίαι), the bather was seated in a tub, either standing free or let into the floor (πύελοι, ἀσάμινθοι, Homer). After the bath, cold water was poured over him by the master of the bath (βαλανεύς) or his assistants (παραχύται). To the bath an anointing-room (ἀλειπτήριον) was always attached, where the body was scraped and rubbed with delicate ointment. Here, also, the bather dressed; at least, in earlier times. Separate dressing-rooms (ἀποδυτήρια) were a later addition. The peculiar arrangement of a bath for women, shown in a vase-painting, has been mentioned before.

54. The games practised at the gymnasion were, to the Greek youth, a preparation for actual warfare; this we shall now have to consider. Our chief attention will be directed towards the various weapons and pieces of armature. The different phases of Greek strategy we shall touch upon only in so far as they imply at the same time a change in the implements of war. The description of complicated war-machines, invented by the Greeks, we shall reserve for the Roman division of our work, seeing that the only illustrations of them appear on monuments belonging to the times of the emperors.

Our knowledge of Greek arms, both from written and monu- mental evidence, is considerable. The preserved specimens, on the other hand, are few in number, the weapons made of iron being almost entirely destroyed by rust, the effects of which only bronze has been able to withstand. The stone weapons of the aborigines, found in Greece, we shall omit for the present, being chiefly concerned with the classic period of Greek antiquity. Vase-paintings and sculptures, our chief means of knowledge, must be used with great caution, owing to the fantastic exaggera- tions of archaic painters, and to the ideal treatment of sculptors, both of whom were prone to sacrifice realistic truth to artistic purpose. Moreover, our written and monumental means of know- ledge are not easily applicable to each other, unless we accept the specimens on the great monuments of Roman imperial times as equally illustrative of contemporary Greek armour.

To give the reader an idea of the full armour (πανοπλία) of a Greek warrior, we will introduce him to the workshop of Hephaistos (Fig. 261), taken from a bas-relief in the Louvre. The god, dressed in a tucked-up chiton, is employed in adding the handle to a large shield which one of his satyr-assistants is scarcely able to hold. By the side of the master, another work- man is sitting on the floor, polishing a greave. On a stele near him are placed a sword and a cuirass, both in a finished condition. To the left of this group we see a furnace blazing with flames, and sitting near it a dwarfish figure, perhaps meant for Kedalion, the

faithful companion of the god. He somewhat resembles the
gnomes of northern mythology. In our picture he is looking

Fig. 261.

with the eye of a
connoisseur on a hel-
met with a crest of
a horse's mane. A
satyr standing be-
hind the furnace jest-
ingly extends his
hand towards the
pileus of the old man.
Supposing this to be
an illustration of the lines in the Iliad descriptive of Hephaistos
working at the armour of Achilles, we may consider ourselves as
perfectly informed with regard to the outfit of a Homeric hero.

As the chief weapons of defence we mention the helmet, the
coat of mail, the greaves, and the shield. The covering of the head
and the upper part of the body, to protect them from the weather
and the enemy's weapons, originally consisted of the hide of wild
animals. Thus the hunter's trophy became the warrior's armour.
Herakles, the extirpator of ferocious animals, always wears the
hide of the Nemæan lion as his attribute; other warriors appear
on the monuments with a similar head-dress. On an Etruscan
box of ashes, the relief-ornamentation of which shows the combat
between Eteokles and Polyneikes, one of the less important
figures wears a cap of lion's skin (Fig. 262, *a*). The same custom
prevailed amongst Germanic nations, and seems to have been
adopted by the Roman standard-bearers and trumpeters, as is
proved by the monuments of the imperial period. As a medium
between this primitive head-dress and the helmet of metal, we
mention the leather cap (κυνέη), made originally of the raw hide
of an animal. A cap of this kind is worn by Diomedes on his
nightly expedition with Odysseus. It was close fitting, without
crest or nob, and was made of bull's hide (κυνέη ταυρείη or
καταῖτυξ). Odysseus wore a similar head-covering on that
occasion. His cap was entirely made of leather, lined with felt,
and fastened with straps inside; on the outside it showed the
tusks of a boar, reminding one of the cap made of an animal's hide
which we mentioned before. Dolon wore a morion made of otter's

skin (κυνέη κτιδέη). According to Homer, a cap of leather was generally worn by younger warriors; Fig. 262, *b*, taken from a bronze statuette of Diomedes, may serve to illustrate its form. The casque of metal (κράνος, by Homer called κόρυς, or κυνέη πάγχαλκος) was a further development of this form. It was semi-globular in shape, and made of brass. Gradually front, back, and cheek-pieces, visors and demi-visors, were added; a crest served to protect the skull. On a hydria of Vulci, showing the taking leave of Amphiaraos and Eriphyle, the hero wears a semi-globular helmet of brass (Fig. 262, *c*).

Fig. 262, *d*, is taken from the group of the Æginetai at Munich. It represents the bowman, Teukros. His helmet protects the head to a much greater extent than that just mentioned. The semi-globular cap has been made to fit the

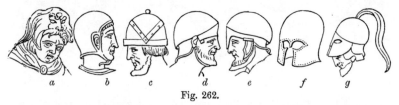

Fig. 262.

back of his head, and to it have been added a neck-piece, of about the width of a hand, and a narrow front-piece. Still more perfect is the helmet worn by Telamon in the same group (Fig. 262, *e*). The difference consists in a small piece of metal to cover the bridge of the nose being added to the front-piece. Besides this, short cheek-pieces (φάλαρα) have been attached to the sides by means of hinges, as appears from numerous vase-paintings; these cheek-pieces could be turned upwards, which gave the helmet the appearance of a winged helmet. Still more protection is offered by the helmet in Fig. 262, *f*, found in the river Alpheios, near Olympia. Front, neck, and cheek-pieces are made of one piece with the helmet, and completely cover the head down to the shoulders; only mouth, chin, and eyes remain uncovered. The αὐλῶπις was another form of the helmet, lighter and more graceful than the one just described. The neck-piece is severed from the front-piece by an incision, and the latter has been developed into a complete visor, with small slits for the eyes (Fig. 262, *g*). In the battle it was pulled down so as to cover the skull with the cap, and the face with the visor; otherwise it was worn pushed back over the neck, so that the visor rested on the top of the head (see Fig. 263, *b*; a head of Athene, from the Villa Albani). Frequently the elegant Greek helmet appears without any front-piece, and with a broad border bent upwards (στεφάνη), not unlike the open visor of a mediæval helmet (see the head of Athene, Fig. 263, *a*).

The leather cap, and frequently, also, the simple casque of metal, were without a crest (φάλος, see Fig. 262, *d, e, f*). Hence the name ἄφαλος applied to them. But Homer already mentions a heavy helmet of metal, with a crest proceeding from top to neck, and covering the seam which joins the two

a   *b*   *c*   *d*   *e*

Fig. 263.

sides of the helmet (Figs. 263, *a, c*, 264): it served to protect the head from blows, and also to fasten the crest (λόφος). Vase-paintings of the archaic kind also show this crest. To increase its power of resistance, it was frequently made of four layers of metal. Hence the name τετράφαλος, τετραφάληρος.[1] Holes or notches were made into the upper side of the phalos for the insertion of bunches of horsehair (ἵππουρις) or feathers (Fig. 262, *g*). The κύμβαχος ἀκρότατος mentioned by Homer ("Iliad," XV. 536) is, perhaps, identical with the φάλος. When the phalos was wanting the crest seems to have been fastened to the casque by means of a small tube (Figs. 262, *g*, 263, *d*).

The helmets of the common soldiers were generally without ornaments, those of the officers only being decorated with figures or patterns; the cap, visor, and stephane were frequently covered with these. The crest appears in many variations (Fig. 263, *b, c*), and sometimes was increased to overloading by the addition of feathers (Fig. 263, *d*). Decorated helmets of various kinds are generally worn by the statues of Athene, Ares, and

[1] According to Göbel's explanation; see "Philologus," 1862, p. 213.

several heroes ; we also see them on the head of Athene and various portrait-heads on coins and gems,—for instance, on cameos with the heads of Ptolemy I. and II., in the collections of St. Petersburg and Vienna. Fig. 263, *c*, shows the head of Athene from a silver coin of Herakleia ; Fig. 263, *e*, the head of Neoptolemos, taken from a bas-relief, most likely of Roman origin, published by Orti di Manara.

The second defensive weapon is the cuirass (θώραξ). Pausanias describes its older form on speaking of the lesche painted by Polygnotos at Delphi. " On the altar," he says, " lies an iron cuirass of an unusual form, such as were formerly worn by the heroes. It consists of two iron plates, connected by means of buckles (περόναι), one of which covers the chest and stomach, the other the back. The former is called γύαλον, the latter προσῆγον. They seem sufficient to protect the body, even without a shield." Pausanias here speaks of the solid cuirass (θώραξ στάδιος or στατός) worn, in Homer, by the leaders, and, in conse-quence, frequently depicted in the older vase-paintings (Fig. 264). We also refer to the figure of Teukros in the Æginetan group at Munich. This cuirass was made of strong plates, and went down only as far as the hips, where it either was cut off or had a curved border added to it. Later on the plates were made thinner, and more in ac-cordance to the lines of the muscles (see Fig. 261). The chief difference between this and the older cuirass, besides its being lighter and more elegant, consists in the prolongation of the front plate over the navel. Altogether it was more adapted to the altered warfare of later times. It was most likely worn only by officers. Round the waist was worn a belt

Fig. 264.

(ζωστήρ, ζώνη) over the cuirass, both to keep the parts of the harness together, and to protect that part of the body. It was fastened with buckles (in Homer, made of gold—ὀχῆες χρύσειοι). Odysseus wears a zoster of this kind over his jerkin, seemingly a leather one, on an Etruscan box of ashes (Fig. 265). Under the armour, but over the chiton, another broad belt, made of thin metal and lined inside (μίτρα), was usually worn. It is, of course, invisible in pictures, being covered by the armour ; but one specimen of it (Fig. 266) has been preserved to us. It was purchased by Brönsted in Euboea and described by him in his

pamphlet, "Die Bronzen von Siris." It consists of bronze, and is eleven inches long. On the inside fifteen larger and thirteen smaller indentures have been made which, on the outside, look like so many small semi-globes; the hooks at each end served to attach it to the lining of the real belt. This definition of zoster and mitra explains, at the same time, Homer's description ("Iliad," IV. 135 *et seq.*)

Fig. 265.

Fig. 266.

We mention, together with the iron cuirass, the linen jerkin (λινοθώρηξ) worn by Aias, the son of Oïleus and Amphios, in Homer; and the iron chiton (χαλκοχίτων). Both were tight-fitting, made of leather or linen, and had pieces of iron attached to them to protect the heart and the shoulders (Figs.

265, 267). A belt was added, to protect the abdomen. The shoulder-pieces tied to the belt or to the jerkin itself (Fig. 267) were, as appears from numerous representations, richly ornamented. The

reliefs on two bronze shoulder-pieces, representing Aias fighting with an Amazon, are amongst the masterpieces of Greek art. Both are in the British Museum. The incorrect statement of their having been found on the banks of the Siris has given rise to the conjecture of their having been part of a splendid armour worn by Philip in the battle on the Siris. Notwithstanding the erroneousness of this supposition, their common name, the "Bronzes of Siris," will probably remain unaltered. Both these light jerkins (said to have been introduced amongst the Athenian army by Iphikrates) and the cuirasses

Fig. 267.

modelled after the lines of the body, had longer or shorter stripes of leather or felt attached to their bottom parts. These stripes consisted frequently of two layers, and were covered with plates of metal (πτέρυγες). They served to protect the abdomen, and were, like the shoulder-pieces, frequently ornamented. (Fig. 267; compare, as an example of the older armour, the statue of a warrior on the stele of Aristion, in Overbeck's "Geschichte der griechischen Plastik," Part I., p. 98). Such πτέρυγες of smaller size were also attached to the arm-holes of the cuirass, to protect the upper arm.

The coat of mail, consisting of a linen or leather shirt covered with iron scales, occurs at an early period. The large scales were imitated from those of a fish, the smaller ones from those of a snake; hence the names θώραξ λεπιδωτός or φολιδωτός, respectively applied to the two different kinds of armour.[1] Scale-chitons are worn, for instance, by Achilles and Patrokolos on the vase known as the "Kylix of Sosias" in the Royal Antiquarium of Berlin. The Persian bowman amongst the Æginetai, generally called Paris, wears a tight-fitting armour of this kind. The cuirass of chain (θώραξ ἀλυσιδωτός) is of late Roman date, and, most likely, of Oriental invention.

The lower part of the leg was protected, even in Homer's time, by bronze greaves (κνημῖδες) covering the leg from the ankle to over the knee. They were made of flexible metal, and, in being put on, they were first bent back (Fig. 268) and afterwards placed round the leg, and their open sides bent together. They were tied across the ankle with beautifully wrought ribbons (ἐπισφύρια), as is proved by some fragments of legs belonging to the Æginetan group.[2] They do not, however, appear on other monuments. Besides this, the greaves were fastened round the calf with buckles or straps. The putting-on of greaves is frequently depicted on vases.

Fig. 268.

The principal weapon of defence was the circular or oval shield. The circular shield (ἀσπίς παντός εἴση, εὔκυκλος)—also called the Argive, or more correctly the Doric, shield (Figs. 269, *a*, *b*; 270, *b*, *c*), owing to its being first substituted for the long shield by that tribe—was the smaller of the two, covering the

---

[1] The fragments of a coat of mail have been found amongst the ruins of the old Pantikapaion. See "Antiquités du Bosphore Cimmérien," Pl. xxvii.

[2] These ribbons have been preserved on the restored figures.

soldier from about the chin to the knee. As in battle it frequently had to be raised up to the helmet, an elastic cloth, made of leather or felt, was added at the bottom (λαισήϊα πτερόεντα?)[1] sufficiently strong to ward off blows and thrusts (Fig. 269, *b*). This cloth was of Asiatic invention, but adopted by the Greeks at an early period. The oval shield (σάκος), about 4½ feet long by over 2 wide, covered the warrior almost from head to foot (ποδηνεκής ἀμφιβροτος, Fig. 264). As mentioned before, the older long shield was soon changed for the round shield; but the oval shield, although considerably shortened, occurs up to

a   b   c
Fig. 269.

a   b   c   d
Fig. 270.

a very late period. Such oval shields as had semi-circular or oval incisions in the centre were called Bœotian (Figs. 264, 269, *c*; 270, *a*). The use of these incisions is not sufficiently explained; perhaps they served as peep-holes. This form of the shield appears in the scutcheon of most of the Bœotian cities (see Fig. 270, *a*,

from a coin of the Bœotian city of Haliartos) and numerous archaic vase-paintings. The outer surface of the shields was more or less bent. The older way of carrying the shield, slung over the head and neck by means of a strap (τελαμών) fastened to the inside of the shield, must have been very inconvenient. For the left hand there was a handle (πόρπαξ) inside the shield to direct its position. The Karians, according to Herodotos, improved this weapon considerably by introducing a band of leather or metal (ὄχανον), placed in the centre of the hollow for the upper part of the arm; to which was added another handle for the arm near the rim of the shield (Figs. 264, 265, 270, *c*). Whether the τελαμών was dropped entirely, or kept by—in order to carry the shield over the back on the march, as was the Roman fashion— seems uncertain. The straps fastened to a ring which occurs, together with the two handles, on the shield of Ares, in the Villa

---

[1] Compare Aristophanes, Achon, v. 1088: τὰ στρώματ' ὦ παῖ δῆσον ἐκ τῆς ἀσπίδος.

Ludovisi (Fig. 270, *d*), is undoubtedly a telamon. In the older round shield we often see, instead of the two handles, a broad bar (κανών) reaching from one rim to the other. Through it the arm was put, the hand taking hold of the thong of leather or cloth fastened round the whole inner edge of the shield (Fig. 270, *b*). The numerous handles thus effected had the advantage of enabling the soldier to change the position of the shield in case one side of it was damaged. This mode of holding the shield belongs, most likely, to earlier times, being met with only on vase-paintings of the archaic period.

The shield was made of bull's hides, and frequently consisted of several, sometimes of no less than seven, layers, sewed one over the other, with a metal plate fastened to the top of them by means of nails. These nails protruded from the rim of the shield like buckles (ὀμφαλοί, Fig. 269, *a*); hence the epithet ὀμφαλόεσσαι applied to the shield by Homer. The centre boss, generally richly ornamented, and used to parry blows, was the omphalos κατ᾽ ἐξοχήν. The Greeks also had massive round shields of metal (πάγχαλκος ἀσπὶς), which, owing to their weight, were soon disused. The beauty of some shield-decorations appears from the verses in the " Iliad " descriptive of the shield of Achilles made by Hephaistos, and from Hesiod's description of that of Herakles. The dreadful head of the Gorgon, lions (Fig. 269, *b*), panthers, boars, bulls (Fig. 269, *a*), scorpions, snakes, anchors, tripods, chariots, etc., appear frequently in vase-paintings as emblems (ἐπίσημα σημεῖα) on shields, mostly with some reference to the character of the wearer. The shield of Idomeneus, for instance, showed a cock, in allusion to his descent from Helios, to whom that bird was devoted; Menelaos's scutcheon consisted of the image of the dragon which had appeared to him in Aulis as a divine message. A similar emblem, on the shield placed on Epaminondas's grave at Mantinea, indicated the descent of the hero from Kadmos; the shield of Alkibiades showed Eros throwing the lightnings. We also recall Æschylos's description of the shields of his seven heroes before Thebes. Besides these individual signs (οἰκεῖα σημεῖα), there existed, also, national emblems of the different Greek tribes. This custom dates from the Persian wars. The shields of the Sikyonians showed a brilliant Σ, those of the Lakedæmonians an archaic lambda ᴧ (whence their

name, lambda, or labda), those of the Mykenians a M, those of
the Athenians an owl, and those of the Thebans an owl or a
sphinx.   Inscriptions also occur; on the shield of Kapaneus was
written, πρήσω πόλιν; on that of Demosthenes, ἀγαθῇ τύχῃ.
Only *one* Greek shield has been preserved; it is in the Museum of
Palermo.

The Persian wars caused an entire change of Greek strategy.
In the heroic age the valour of the individual showed itself in
single combats; in more modern times the hoplitai, *i.e.* the heavy-

armed foot-soldiers, decided the battle.
These warriors retained the Homeric oval
shield, while the heavy iron cuirass was
changed for leather or linen jerkins with
iron plates; helmet and greaves also were
made of lighter materials.   After the
Persian wars we meet with light infantry
as distinguished from the hoplitai.   After
the expedition of the Ten Thousand, the
light infantry became an essential feature
of Greek armies; they were divided into
γυμνῆτες, γυμνοί, soldiers without any
armour, and πελτασταί, πελτοφόροι, *i.e.*
soldiers wearing a pelta as defensive
weapon.   They were destined to fight
at a distance; their weapons were,
according to their national predilec-
tions, the bow, the sling, or the javelin.
The peltastai also wore a shield in the

Fig. 271.

form of a crescent (πέλτα).   It was two feet long, made

Fig. 272.   Fig. 273.

of wood or osiers,
and covered with
leather.   It is said
to have been of
Thrakian origin.   In
vase-paintings the
pelta is generally
worn by Amazons,

and a comprehensive knowledge of its more graceful forms might
be gathered from the numerous representations of battles of

Amazons. Fig. 271, from a beautiful marble statue of the Dresden collection, may serve to illustrate not only the pelta but the whole warlike costume of the Amazons in Greek art. This Amazon appears in a noble Greek dress; more frequently, however, we meet with an Oriental costume, as worn, for instance, by an Amazon shooting with a bow (Fig. 272). Sometimes the Amazons also wear the vaulted oval shield of the Greek soldiers; on the above-mentioned bronze armour from Siris we see one with a small flat pelta in the shape of a disk with only one handle. Fig. 273 shows a peltastes from a skyphos at Athens. The figure is of particular importance to us as being illustrative of the new mode of attack for foot-soldiers introduced by Chabrias. Cornelius Nepos, in his biography of that commander, says: *Reliquam phalangem loco vetuit cedere, obnixoque genu scuto, projectaque hasta impetum excipere hostium docuit.*

The aggressive weapons of the Greeks were the spear, sword, club, battle-axe, bow, and sling. The spear (ἔγχος, δόρυ) consisted of a smooth shaft (in Homer's time generally made of ash-wood, μείλινον) about 6 to 7 feet long, over the pointed end (καυλός) of which an iron head (αὐχμή, ἀκωκή) was drawn by means of a socket (αὐλός), and fastened to it with an iron ring (πόρκης). The shape of this spear-head varies greatly; it frequently resembles a leaf or a broad bulrush (Fig. 274, *b, c, e, f*), at other times it has a barb (Fig. 274, *i*); sometimes, also, it is exactly like the spear's head used by our modern lancers. To the other end of the shaft (especially in post-Homeric times) a "shoe" (σαυρωτήρ, Figs. 273, 274, *f, g*) was added, which either served to fasten the spear in the earth when not used, or supplied the spear's head in case this was broken. Smaller spears were used for throwing, longer ones for thrusting; of the former, the Homeric heroes generally have two in their chariots. Warriors in vase-paintings also generally carry two javelins; it appears, however,

a b c d e f g h i

k

l

Fig. 274.

on comparing these two spears on numerous monuments, that they were of unequal length, whence it may be concluded that the longer was used for thrusting, the shorter for throwing (compare the lances worn by Achilles and Aias in Panofka, " Bilder ant. Lebens," Taf. X. 10, and by Peleus in Overbeck's " Gallerie heroischer Bildwerke," Taf. VIII. 6). .Something analogous to this unequal length of the spears we observe in the fact of the Roman *hastati* and *principes* being armed with the *pilum* or *vericulum.*

Besides these spears, of an average length of 5 to 7 feet, we find in vase-paintings others only 2 to 3 feet long, in which latter the iron part is equal to one-third of the entire length (see Overbeck, *ibid.*, Taf. XIII. 1, and Taf. XVIII. 3, in the latter of which the spear of Aias is still shorter, Fig. 274, *l*). The same custom of carrying several spears of unequal length was continued in historic times. The peltastai in Xenophon's army carried five shorter and one longer javelin, the latter having a strap (ἀγκύλη, *amentum*) attached to it, whence the name μεσάγκυλον, *hasta amentata* (Fig. 274, *h*). About the handling of these spears with straps opinions differed for a long time ; both written and monumental proofs with regard to this point are, indeed, very scanty. Köchly was the first to treat the question comprehensively, illustrating it at the same time by means of practical trials (see Verhandlungen der 26. Versammlung deutscher Philologen und Schulmänner," Leipzig, 1869, pp. 226-38). According to him, this weapon was adopted by the peltastai from the gymnasion. It must be considered as a javelin, $2\frac{1}{3}$ to 3 Greek yards (*Ellen*) long by $\frac{3}{4}$ inch thick, to which, in its centre of gravity, a leather strap was tied. The two ends of the strap were tied round the shaft several times and arranged in a loop,

Fig. 275.

through which the fingers were put (διηγκυλωμένοι. Ovid, " Metamorph.," XII. 326 : *inserit amento digitos*). At the moment of throwing the spear the loop was pulled violently, by means of which the strap, in being unwound, conveyed to the spear a rotating movement, similar to that of the missiles of our rifled guns. Fig. 275 is the only existing antique representation illustrative of the use of this weapon. From a passage in Plutarch's "Life of Philopoimen," it appears that the ankyle remained attached to the shaft. That commander is hit by a spear in both thighs, and, owing to the force of the throw, the strap also is pushed through one thigh, which makes the extraction of the weapon a difficult matter.

The longest of all spears, called σάρισσα, σάρισα, were used by the Makedonians. According to Greek authors they were at first 16, in later times 14 yards long, which, reckoning the Greek yard at $1\frac{1}{2}$ foot, would make 24 and 21 feet respectively. A spear of such length would have been unwieldy in the hands of the strongest soldier; we therefore agree with Rüstow and Köchly ("Geschichte des griechischen Kriegswesens," p. 238 *et seq.*) in changing the "yards" of antique measurements into feet. With this modification we will quote the description by Ælianus ("Theory of Tactics," c. xiv. *et seq.*[1]) of the Makedonian phalanx; our conjectural reductions of the measurements are added in brackets. "Every man under arms in the closed phalanx stood at a distance of 2 yards (2 feet, meaning the distance from the chest of the man in the first row to that of the man in the second row). The length of the sarissa was, according to the original pattern, 16 yards; in reality, however, only 14 yards (16 to 14 feet). From this the space between the two hands holding the spear = 4 yards (4 feet) must be deducted; the remaining 10 yards (10 feet) lie in front of the first row of hoplitai. The second row stands 2 yards (2 feet) behind the first, their sarissai, therefore, protrude by 8 yards (8 feet) from the front row, those of the third row by six yards (6 feet), of the fourth row by 4 yards (4 feet), of the fifth row by 2 yards (2 feet); those standing in the sixth row are unable to let their sarissai protrude from the first row. The five sarissai in front of every man of the first row naturally are of fearful aspect to the enemies, while, at the same time, they give fivefold strength to his attack."

Shorter than the sarissa, but still of considerable length, was the lance of the Makedonian cavalry. Representations of this

---

[1] Compare Ælianus, c. xiv., in "Griechische Kriegsschriftsteller," erklärt von Köchly und Rüstow.

weapon are scarce.   A silver coin of the Thessalian city of
Pelina may serve to illustrate the arms used in northern Greece.

On one side of the coin (Fig. 276)
we see a horseman, covered with a
Thessalo-Makedonian felt hat, and
armed with sauroter and sword; the
reverse shows a light-armed foot-
soldier with the same kind of hat,
and armed with a Makedonian round
Fig. 276.

shield, a sword, and three short spears.   The latter is perhaps
meant for one of the hypaspistai, introduced into the Makedonian
army during the reigns of Philip and Alexander; the horseman is
most likely a representative of the celebrated Thessalian cavalry,
who joined the Makedonians as allies.

The hunting-spear (ἀκόντιον) resembles, on monuments, that
used by soldiers; Fig. 274, *i*, shows one with a double barb.

The sword (ξίφος) was worn on the left side, about the height

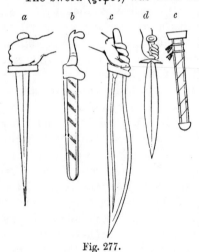

a   *b*   *c*   *d*   *e*

Fig. 277.

of the hip.   It was fastened, by
means of a loop (ἀορτήρ), to
a belt (τελαμών) which was
thrown over the right shoulder.
The hilt (κώπη, λαβή), 4 to 5
inches long, had no guard; a
cross-hilt (Fig. 277, *a*) sometimes rounded (Fig. 277, *d*)
serving to protect the hand.
Hilt and blade were frequently
made of one piece; in more
ornamental swords the blade
was let into the hilt.   The
blade, sharpened on both sides
(ἄμφηκες ἀμφίγυον), was about
16 to 18 inches long by 2 to 2½
wide[1] (Fig. 277, *d*).   A scabbard (κολεός, Fig. 277, *e*[2]), made

---

[1] A beautiful Greek sword, found near Pella in Makedonia, now in the Royal Antiquarium of Berlin, has a blade 17 inches long, and a handle measuring 4 inches.
The blade of another sword in the same collection is 19¼ inches in length, the hilt
being 4 inches long.   The latter resembles perfectly our Fig. 277, *d*.

[2] Sword and scabbard (Fig. 277, *e*, *d*) belong to one and the same figure.

either of leather or metal, covered the blade up to the hilt.[1]   The
sword of heroic times was, like most weapons, modified by the
changed mode of warfare of a later period.   According to Cornelius
Nepos, Iphikrates increased, according to Diodoros he doubled, the
length of the sword-blades of the infantry of the line ; the hoplitai,
however, retained the shorter sword of earlier times.   Besides
this straight sword, ancient writers also mention another, the
Lakedæmonian sword (μάχαιρα) ; its blade was slightly bent on
one, the sharpened, side, while the other side was blunt like the
backs of our knives ; the end was pointed obliquely towards the
back (see Fig. 277, *c*, and Fig. 277, *b*, in the latter of which the
form of the handle indicates a curved sword inside the scabbard).
A third kind of sword, the blade of which is like that of a
dagger, is repeatedly found on monuments (Fig. 277, *a*).   Artistic
ornamentation was chiefly applied to the hilt.   The sword of the
resting Ares in the Villa Ludovici has a hilt in the form of an
animal's head (Müller, " Denkmäler," Part II., No. 250).

   To conclude, we mention the sickle, the most primitive instrument for cutting grain, the form of which resembles that used at
the present day.   For pruning of vines and trees, the pruning-
knife (ἄρπη) was used.   Kronos first applied
it in the fight with his father ; the harpe
(Fig. 278, *a*) belongs to an image of
that god.   The knife used at sacrifices to
cut off the animal's head resembles the
sickle.   It consists of a straight blade with a
sickle or hook-like addition near its end
(Fig. 278, *b*).   In exactly the same form
the harpe appears in renderings of the
myth of Perseus, who with this instrument
cuts off the head of the Gorgon (compare
Fig. 278, *c*, another form of Perseus's weapon).

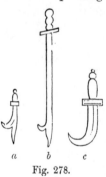

Fig. 278.

Barbarous
nations used swords shaped like sickles, as appears from the monuments of imperial Rome.   Battle-chariots with sickles attached to
the wheels and axle-trees (δρεπανηφόρον ἅρμα) were also used by
barbarians, but never by Greeks ; in the battle of Gaugamela fifty
sickle-chariots were placed in front of the centre of the Persian line.

---

[1] The Royal Antiquarium of Berlin possesses a scabbard of chased silver, belonging to a dagger-like weapon.

A wooden and an iron club (ῥόπαλον, κορύνη), the former cut by Hercules from the root of a tree, the latter made for that hero by Hephaistos, are mentioned in the "Iliad." This weapon, however, was never introduced into the Greek army. Herodotos mentions amongst the weapons of the Assyrians in Xerxes' army clubs covered with iron buckles (ῥόπαλα τετυλωμένα σιδήρῳ), reminding one of maces, clubs, and flails of the middle ages.

The battle-axe (βουπλήξ, ἀξίνη) appears chiefly in the hands of Amazons; it is also carried by some of the heroes of the "Iliad," for instance, by Peisandros in the hollow of his shield

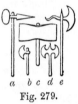

a b c d e

Fig. 279.

("Iliad," XIII. 611 et seq.) The later Greeks never used this weapon. In the East it seems to have been retained much longer; even in Alexander's time two thousand Barkanian horsemen in the Persian army use battle-axes. Fig. 279, c, shows the oldest form of the weapon as used by the inhabitants of the isle of Tenedos, and depicted by them on their coins. Fig. 279, b, shows a bill, d a double battle-axe, a and e fighting hammers combined with axes—all found in the hands of Amazons, and all resembling mediæval weapons of the same kind.

We have to distinguish two forms of the antique bow (τόξον). The one, simpler and more easy to bend, consisted of a curved elastic piece of wood, the ends of which were turned slightly

Fig. 280.

upwards, for the purpose of fastening to them the string (νευρή). This bow, called Skythian or Parthian, is frequently found on monuments. Fig. 280 reproduces a vase-painting in which three epheboi practise shooting with this bow. The aim is a cock placed on a column. Only in few Greek states archery was received amongst the gymnastic exercises, for which reason we have not mentioned it amongst the agones. Whether the just-mentioned bow, or that called the Greek bow proper, was the older of the two, is difficult to determine. The simpler construction of the former seems to indicate its greater antiquity, although the Greek bow was universally used as early as the heroic period. As to the construction and manipulation of the latter, we refer the reader to Homer's graphic description ("Iliad," IV., 105 *et seq.*)

Like the lyre, this bow was made of the horns ($2\frac{1}{2}$ feet long) of a kind of antelope ($\pi\hat{\eta}\chi\nu\varsigma$), the growing ends of which were joined together by a metal socket ($\kappa o\rho\acute{\omega}\nu\eta$); on this the arrow rested; the other ends were tipped with iron, and to them the string, made of calf-gut, was tied. Including the socket, the Homeric bow must have been about 6 feet long, which allows 16 hands for each horn. To bend a bow of this kind required considerable strength. After being disused for some time it required greasing to recover its elasticity. At a later time these horns were imitated in wood, both because of the cheapness and the lightness of the material. The arrow ($\ddot{o}\ddot{\iota}\sigma\tau\acute{o}\varsigma$, $\dot{\iota}\acute{o}\varsigma$) consisted of a shaft ($\delta\acute{o}\nu a\xi$) 2 feet in length, made of reed or light wood, and of a generally three-edged metal head 2 to 3 inches long, with or without a barb. The back end of the arrow was feathered. A notch ($\gamma\lambda\nu\phi\acute{\iota}\varsigma$) was cut into the shaft where it lay on the string. The quiver ($\phi a\rho\acute{\epsilon}\tau\rho a$, $\tau o\xi o\theta\acute{\eta}\kappa\eta$) was made of leather or basket-work. It usually held nineteen or twenty arrows (Fig. 281). It was carried on the left side by a strap slung across the shoulders (Figs. 272 and 280), and had a

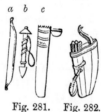

Fig. 281.　Fig. 282.

cover attached to it (Fig. 281, *b, c*). Sometimes both bow and arrows were kept in the quiver (Fig. 282), as is still the custom amongst Mongolians and Kirghis. Bending the bow the archer generally put one knee on the ground—a position taken, for instance, by the archer of the Æginetan group (compare Figs. 272, 280). As early as Homer's time the Kretans were renowned as skilful archers. Kretan bowmen formed a peculiar feature of Greek armies up to the latest times, in the same way as Makedonian archers were a separate corps of the light infantry of Alexander the Great. Amongst barbarians, the Skythians and Parthians were celebrated bowmen, both on foot and horseback.

The sling (σφενδόνη) consisted of a strap, broad in the centre and narrowing towards the two ends. The stone or leaden bullet (μολυβδίς) was placed on the broader part of the strap; in throwing, the slinger held the two ends of the strap in one hand, and, after whirling the sling round his head several times, threw the bullet by letting go one end. In the "Iliad" the sling is mentioned only once as used by a Trojan; it seems to have been

Fig. 283.

of Oriental origin. Later on it seems to have been adopted by various Greek tribes, who had experienced its efficacy in the war with Xerxes. At first the Akarnarnians, afterwards the inhabitants of Ægium, Patræ, Dymæ, Rhodes, and Melos, were renowned as slingers. According to Livy (XXXVIII. 29), the Greek sling consisted of three straps sewed together; the precision of which it was capable even surpassed that of the Balearic slingers. The coins of the Pisidian city of Selge are the only Greek sculptures which represent slingers (Fig. 283); they frequently occur on Roman monuments.[1]

The use of battle-chariots belongs to the heroic period. The warrior (παραβάτης), standing by the side of the charioteer (ἡνίοχος), was driven in front of the line to invite hostile warriors to single combat. When the strategic skill of the commander superseded the demands on his personal valour, the chariot was transferred from the battle-field to the hippodrome, where alone its original form was preserved. The description of the Homeric battle-chariot, therefore, to a great extent, also applies to the historic chariot of the racecourse. Notwithstanding the plentiful monumental evidence, many important points, as, for instance, the harnessing of the horses, remain open to controversy. The generic term for chariot was ἅρμα; its other name δίφρος is a *pars pro toto*, the denomination of the body of the chariot being applied to the whole. The body of the chariot

---

[1] Compare § 107 as to the inscriptions on the missiles of slings.

rested on two wheels (τροχοί, κύκλα) connected by an axle-tree. The small diameter (30 inches) of the former must be explained from the desire of preventing the chariot from being upset by the impediments of the battle-field, such as *debris* or dead bodies. The axle-tree (ἄξων) was about 7 feet long, which, counting 1 foot for the nave of each wheel, leaves 5 feet for the chariot; a width sufficient not to impede the movements of the warrior. The nave (πλήμνη, χοινικίς) contained in its opening (σύριγξ) an inner ring (ἄταρνον, γάρνον, δέστρον), while two other metal rings, one before, the other behind, the spokes (πλημνόδετος, θῶραξ), surrounded it on the outside. The Homeric wheels had eight, those in vase-paintings generally four, spokes (κνῆμαι, hence ὀκτάκνημα). They were let into the four feliles (ἀψῖδες) forming the rim of the wheel (ἴτυς). In order to prevent the wheel from falling to pieces a tire of metal (ἐπίσσωτρον) was added. The body of the vehicle (ὑπερτερία, or δίφρος proper) rested on the axle. To the axle a wooden frame (τόνος ἱμάντωσις τοῦ δίφρου) was fastened by means of nails and pegs, and on this frame the boards forming the bottom of the chariot (πτέρνα), elliptic in shape, were placed. Along the curved side of these boards rose the sides of the chariot (περίφραγμα τάρριον), frequently made of osiers in the manner of trellis-work (hence Homer's expression δίφρος εὔπλεκτος), and reaching on the side of the horses up to the knee of the charioteer, while towards the back it became gradually lower, Fig. 258). The upper rim (ἄντυξ), made of wood or metal, was either prolonged towards the back in a large curvature (Fig. 258), or it was doubled all along the sides of the chariot (Fig. 284). Its form varies greatly in the vase-paintings. Its destination was, most likely, twofold: the back part was grasped by the warrior on jumping on to the chariot, while the front part served for fastening the reins and the traces of the "wheel-horses"— an important point, hitherto unnoticed. The diphros was mounted from the back, which was open. The height of the sides in front was about 2 feet; in the

Fig. 284.

Roman triumphal chariot (an imitation of the Greek battle-chariot) it was increased up to about the chest of the charioteer. A cover of leather served to ward off missiles; where it was wanting the

sides were composed of strong boards. Fig. 285, taken from a
Roman relief, shows a chariot into which the corpse of Antilochos

is being lifted by his friends.
About the construction of
vehicles for everyday use
we know little. As some-
what similar to the two-
wheeled diphros, we mention
the gig. The wheels resemble those of the chariot; a
seat for two people, with
a back and sides to it, rests
on the axle (Fig. 286). In
another vase-painting (Gerhard, "Auserlesene griech.

Fig. 285.

Vasenbilder," Taf. CCXVII.) this seat resembles a chest; on it
a female figure is seated; the driver sits at her feet close to the

pole with his legs hanging down at the side, a
position similar to that of modern Neapolitan
coachmen. On a coin of the city of Rhegium we
see a one-horse vehicle on which the driver sits
in a cowering position. We are ignorant of
the names of these different forms of the gig.

Fig. 286.

'Απήνη and ἄμαξα seem both to apply to four-
wheeled vehicles of larger dimensions, used for carrying
people and goods. The ἄμαξα, for instance, served as bridal
chariot, on which the bride was seated between the bridegroom
and parachos, a circumstance which proves the greater width of
the vehicle. On journeys, or as a means of enjoyment, vehicles
were used to a limited extent; walking, and riding on horseback,
were deemed preferable.

The pole (ῥυμός) of the diphros was firmly inserted into the
axle; its other end was bound with metal, frequently shaped like
the head of an animal; the ends of the axle-tree were frequently
adorned in like manner. To the point of the pole the yoke
(ζυγόν, made of ash, maple, or beech-wood) was fastened by
means of a very long strap (ζυγόδεσμον, *Archäol. Zeitung*, 1847,
T. VI.)

The slipping off of the yoke was, moreover, prevented by

a long nail (ἔστωρ) being struck through the pole, and a ring (κρίκος) put over it. The yoke itself consisted of two wooden half-rings joined together by a tranverse bar, which were put on the necks of the animals, the inner surfaces being stuffed so as to prevent chafing. To prevent the horse from shaking off the yoke, rings were attached to the curved parts which, by means of straps, were connected with the girths and the neck-straps (λέπαδνα). Only the two horses next to the pole carried a yoke (whence their name ζύγιοι), the one or two additional horses running by the side of them being called σειραῖοι (σειραφόροι, παράσαιροι, παρήοροι), or trace-horses, because they pulled by one trace only, fastened to the antyx of the vehicle and to the neck-strap of the animal. The harnessing of these trace-horses is illustrated by numerous vase-paintings (Gerhard, "Auserlesene griech. Vasenbilder," Tafs. 107, 112, 122, 123, 125, 131, 136, and others). In one vase-painting (Taf. 102, *ibidem*) this mode of fastening the traces to the antyx has even been applied to the biga. Whether the yoke continued to be used at a later period remains doubtful; Pollux, in his description of the harnessing process, does not mention it. With few exceptions (Fig. 258, compare Gerhard, "Ueber die Lichtgott-heiten," in "Abhandlungen der Berliner Akademie der Wissen-schaften," 1839, Tafs. III. 1, and IV. 2) the yoke is invisible on the monuments, owing to the harness of the yoke-horses being covered by the trace-horse nearest the spectator. The bridle perfectly resembled that now in use. The Greeks had names for the single parts of it, as, for instance, χαλινός for the bit, and κορυφαία for the strap running from the bit upwards across the head. The reins were fastened to both ends of the bit. As is evident from vase-paintings, all the reins were drawn through a ring just above the pole; they were held by the charioteer.

About the warlike equipment of the horses and horsemen of historic times we know little: monumental evidence is almost absent, seeing that the lancers occasionally met with on coins are very imperfectly armed. The citizen-horsemen in the Pana-thenaïc procession on the frieze of the Parthenon are quite unarmed. As appears from this monument and various repre-sentations of horse-races (Fig. 259), saddles were not used in common life. Greek cavalry in battle used the saddle-cloth (ἐφίππιον), fastened to the horse's back by means of a girth (ἔποχον). The horse of Alexander the Great in the Museo Borbonico (Müller, "Denkmäler der alten Kunst.," Part I., No. 170) wears a saddle-cloth. The ends of the cloth are there joined together over the chest of the horse by means of an elegant clasp; the bridle is adorned with rosettes. Stirrups and horse-shoes were unknown to the Greeks. The rider jumped on his horse, making use occasionally of stones lying by the road, or of his lance. The horse was protected by pieces of armour for the head (προμετωπίδιον), the chest (προστερνίδιον), and the sides (παραπλευρίδια). In a fragment of a vase-painting ("Micali, Monumenti inediti," 1844, Atlas, Pl. 45) a head-armour of this kind is depicted resembling a plate, which is fastened to the horse's head by means of iron bands.

Almost all the battle-scenes on Greek monuments represent mythical subjects. Historical battle-scenes, as frequently found on Roman coins and triumphal monuments, are very rare. Of historic representations we mention the battle between Greeks and Persians on the frieze of the temple of Nike Apteros, at Athens, the mosaic known by the name of "Battle of Alexander," and the assembly of the nobles of Darius Hystaspis, painted on a vase in the Museo Borbonico (Gerhard, "Denkmäler und Forschungen," 1857, Taf. CIII.)

To conclude, we mention the trophy (τρόπαιον) which, according to international custom, was erected from pieces of the booty on the spot where the enemy had turned to flight (τρέπω, τροπή; τρόπαιον στῆσαι, στήσασθαι). Only in rare cases it was erected with a view to permanency; as, for instance, the trophy placed in the temple-grove Altis by the inhabitants of Elis, in commemoration of their victory over the Lakedæmonians. As a

Fig. 287.

rule, the trophy was temporary, and was frequently destroyed by the beaten party, in case their defeat was not decisive enough to compel them to own it. The trunk of a tree, on which a complete armour has been hung, and at the foot of which pieces of booty have been heaped, appears as a tropaion on a coin struck by the Bœotians, most likely in commemoration of some victory (Fig. 287). The commemoration of victories and victorious generals at home by means of votive offerings, monuments, and inscriptions, was of a more lasting kind, although the Greeks never indulged in the self-glorifying exaggerations of the Roman emperors.

55. We add a few remarks about Greek war and merchant vessels. Many attempts at explaining the construction of antique ships have been made, but the mutual ignorance of seafaring men and philologists with regard to the technical terms of their respective branches of knowledge has, in many cases, led to bewildering confusion and wild conjectures. Moreover, antique representations of ships—partly from the total want of perspective, partly from the omission of the most important details—are of comparatively little assistance to us. Graser has attempted a new solution of this important problem, which is amongst the most difficult tasks of antique research.[1] Following the researches of Boeckh (in his celebrated work on the Attic navy) with regard to the construction and rigging of Greek ships, Graser has expounded an entirely new theory of the dimensions and rowing apparatus of Greek vessels. His intimate knowledge of modern ships has been of considerable assistance to him. We have essentially adopted the results of his investigations in preference to all previous conjectures.

We pass over the earliest attempts at navigation in hollow trees or on rafts. The invention of the art of shipbuilding, like that of most other arts, must be placed in prehistoric times ; gods and heroes are mentioned as its originators. A bas-relief in the British Museum (Fig. 288) shows Athene supervising the building of the *Argo,* in which Jason and his companions are said to have ventured on the first long voyage. Homer's descriptions of the interior

Fig. 288.

arrangements of ships prove that at the time of the Trojan war the art of shipbuilding was considerably advanced. Rowers

---

[1] Graser, "De veterum re Navali." Berolini, 1864. "Philologus," supplementary volume iii. part ii.—"Das Modell einer athenischen Fünfreihenschiffs Penteres, aus der Zeit Alexanders des Grossen im kgl. Museum zu Berlin." Berlin, 1866.

(20 to 52 in number), sittting on benches (κληῖδες) along the
sides of the ship, beat the waves simultaneously with their
long oars (ἐρετμά) made of pine-wood. As in our sloops
(*Schaluppen*), the oars of the Homeric vessel were made fast
between pegs (σκαλμοί) by means of leather straps (ἠρτύναντο δ᾿
ἐρετμὰ τροποῖς ἐν δερματίνοισιν), so as to prevent their slipping.
In case of a calm or of adverse winds the ship was propelled by
the rowers; the mast (ἰστός) was placed in a case, or rather on
props (ἰστοδόκη), and kept in its position by means of ropes
fastened to the prow and poop of the vessel. The sail (ἰστίον)
was attached to a yard (ἐπίκριον). Wind and oars were thus
conjointly made serviceable; the helmsman (κυβερνήτης) directing
the course of the vessel by means of the rudder (πηδάλια). The
war-vessels sent against Ilion carried fifty to a hundred and
twenty soldiers, who, undoubtedly, had also to act as rowers. Of
the fifty men forming the crew of the smallest vessels, forty plied
the twenty oars by turns, the others taking care of the rigging or
acting as officers. The small draught of the vessels is proved by
the fact of their being, without much difficulty, pulled ashore,
where wooden or stone props (ἔρματα) served to keep them dry
and protect them from the waves.

The development of shipbuilding was undoubtedly due to the
Greeks. The numerous natural harbours of the Greek continent,
combined with the growing demands of intercommunication with
the islands, and the colonies of Asia Minor and southern Italy,

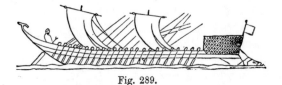

Fig. 289.

favoured the rapid growth of navigation. The continual wars
waged amongst the Greek tribes, and by them collectively against
barbarians, necessitated the keeping up of large navies. The
Homeric vessel, most likely only a transport, and unfit for
battle, was soon supplanted by war-vessels of larger dimensions.
Besides flat-bottomed vessels, called, according to the number of
rowers sitting on both sides, εἰκόσοροι, τριακόντοροι, πεντηκόντοροι

(Fig. 289), and ἑκατόντοροι, we also hear of ships of greater draught in which the oarsmen sat in two rows, one over the other. During the Persian and Peloponnesian wars the fleets consisted of τριήρεις exclusively. Vessels with more than three ranks of rowers, such as τετρήρεις and πεντήρεις, were first introduced by Dionysios I., tyrant of Syrakuse, after a Carthaginian pattern. Dionysios II. introduced ἐξήρεις. Even six rows were not always deemed sufficient. Ten and (with a modification of the system) more rows were placed one over the other, the result being a surprising velocity and handiness of the vessels thus constructed. In the battle of Actium we hear of ships with ten rows; Demetrios Poliorketes had even vessels of fifteen and sixteen rows, the seaworthiness of which is warranted by antique authors.

The construction of the war-vessel, as introduced shortly before the Persian wars, must now command our attention. The keel (τρόπις, *carina*) consisted of one horizontal beam, parallel to the longitudinal axis of the vessel; in older ships it rose from the centre to the ends in a wide curve. The large ships of a later period had keels composed of several straight beams joined together, into the ends of which stem (στεῖρα) and stern posts (ἀσάνδιον) were inserted almost in a right angle, being only slightly bent outwards. Under the keel another beam (χέλυσμα) was placed parallel to it, so as to add to its power of resistance; corresponding to this, a third beam (δρύοχον) lay on the top of the keel; into this, the ribs of the ship (ἐγκοίλια, *costæ*) were let. The upper ends of each pair of corresponding ribs forming together one curvature were joined together by means of a straight cross-beam (στρωτήρ), destined to carry the upper deck (κατάστρωμα, *constratum*). The bulwark, enclosing the two long sides of the latter, generally consisted of trellis-work. In larger vessels a second layer of boards (ζυγόν, *transtrum*), underneath the upper deck, was laid across the ribs of the vessel, destined to carry the second or lower deck (ἔδαφος, *pavimentum*). The two decks communicated with each other and the hull (κοῖλον) by means of steps, hatchways being cut in the boards for the purpose. The hull contained the ballast and the pump.

Both in the prow (πρώρα, *prora*) and poop (πρίμνα, *puppis*) of the vessel small half-decks (ἰκρίωμα), corresponding to our forecastle and quarter-deck, were placed considerably above the upper deck. They rested on the prolongation of the ribs nearest to stem and stern. The poop and prow were essentially identical in construction, differing in this from all modern vessels excepting our latest ironclads.

The planks of the vessel (σανίδες) were strengthened externally by a wooden ledge (νομεῖς) just above the water-line, corresponding to which a number of boards (ἁρμονίοι, δεσμοί) were placed along the ribs inside, so as to give firmness to the whole fabric. As a further means of increasing their compactness, war-vessels were provided with a band consisting of four stout ropes (ὑποζώματα) laid horizontally round the hull below the water-line; in case of a dangerous voyage, the number of these ropes might be increased. These hypozomata are distinctly recognisable on a small bronze in the Antiquarium of the Royal Museum, Berlin (No. 1329), representing the prow of a man-of-war (compare the small bronze statuette of Poseidon, No. 2469 of the same collection).

A little lower than the upper deck, just above the upper holes for the oars, a narrow gangway (τάροδος) runs along both sides of the vessel; in woodclad vessels (κατάφρακτοι, tectœ) this parodos is protected by strong massive boards (see Fig. 300, representing

Fig. 290.

a Roman bireme). Both stem and stern-post ended in a volute. The tent-like house (σκηνή) of the helmsman (Fig. 290) stood on the poop just underneath the volute. From this point he directed the two rudders (πηδάλιον, gubernaculum) to right and left of the stern, which are peculiar to all antique ships, by means of a rope (χαλινός) running straight across the vessel. The rudders were always kept parallel (Fig. 291). To the volute of the poop a leaf or feather ornament (ἄφλαστρον, aplustre) has been added (Fig. 290). The prow frequently shows an ornament resembling the neck of a swan (χηνίσκος), which, perhaps, at the same time, served for fastening ropes. Between these two, the flagstaff (στηλίς), with the flag (σημεῖον) attached to it, was erected. In merchant vessels the flagstaff was frequently supplied by the image of the protecting deity.   Athenian vessels, for instance, carried the image of Athene as ἀττικὸν σημεῖον.   The prow, as we said before, exactly resembled the poop.   Here, also, a strong wooden band encircled the vessel on a level with the parodos.   The point where the outer ribs crossed each other was marked by a ram's head (προεμβόλιον) made of bronze, and serving either as an ornament or as a protection to the upper part of the vessel.   Underneath this, on a level with the water-line, was the beak (ἔμβολον, *rostrum*), consisting of several rafters let into the

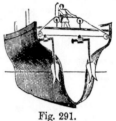

Fig. 291.

body of the vessel and ending in a point, which was made more formidable by the addition of a massive piece of iron divided into three blunt teeth of unequal length.   Two beams (ἐπωτίδες), supported by props (ἀντηρίδες), protruded on both sides of the rostrum ; on these the anchors were hung up.   They also served to protect the vessel from the attacks of the enemy's beak.   We finally mention an opening on each side of the prow, through which the cables were drawn ; these holes were bound with iron, and somewhat resembled eyes, whence their name ὀφθαλμοί.   The resemblance of a vessel thus constructed to a fish was not unnoticed by the ancients (see Fig. 289).   Something similar we meet with in the imitation of dragons in the vessels of the Norsemen, and in the construction of Chinese junks.

The beam of merchant-vessels was usually equal to a quarter, that of men-of-war to one-eighth or one-tenth, of their length. Hence the name νῆες μακραί (*naves longæ*) applied to the latter. A trireme was 149 feet long by 14 wide (at the water-line) and 19½ deep.   Her draught was 8½ feet, her tonnage 232.   In the pentere the corresponding figures were 168 feet, 18 feet, and 26½ feet ; the draught being 11½ feet, and the tonnage 534.

The main-mast (ἱστὸς μέγας) stood in the centre of the vessel. It was square-rigged (κεραῖοι, *antennæ*), and carried two sails (ἱστία μεγάλα), one above the other, answering to our course and top-sail.   Above these was another square sail corresponding to our topgallant-sail (δόλων, *dolon*), and above that two triangular sails (σίπαροι, *suppara*).   Besides the main-mast there were two

S

smaller masts (ἰστὸς ἀκάτειος), with two fore-and-aft lateen sails each, one over the other, which were important in tacking. Strong ropes supported the main-mast (stays, πρότονοι; back-stays, ἐπίτονοι; and shrouds, κάλοι) and the two smaller masts; thinner ropes served for lifting and bracing the yards, setting the sails, etc.

Besides the ropes of the rigging, collectively called σκεύη κρεμαστά, a war-vessel required various contrivances of a similar nature to protect her both against high seas and the missiles of the enemy. To this class belonged strips of tarpaulin (ὑπόβλημα) hung round the hull to cover the apertures for the oars, when these had to be pulled in owing to the roughness of the sea; as also an awning (κατάβλημα) suspended over the upper deck as a protection both from the sun and missiles; a woven stuff was also pulled over the trellis of the bulwark (παραβλήματα παραρρύματα) to ward off darts and arrows.

To conclude, we mention the anchor, the ship's ladder, the boat-hook, and the lead. The most primitive forms of the anchor (ἀγκύρα, ancora) were blocks of stone, sand-bags, and baskets filled with stones. Later, anchors in our sense, made of wood and iron, and essentially like those at present in use, were

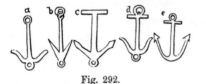

introduced. Their varieties are illustrated by Fig. 292; a, c, being taken from coins of the city of Tuder; b, from one of Luceria; d, of Germanicia Cæsarea; and e, of Pæstum. The

Fig. 292.

antique anchor, as appears from the pictures, has at the end of the stem a ring, movable or immovable (a, b, d, e), to which the cable is fastened; the cross-beam is underneath this ring (c, d, e). The flukes of the anchor appear in many varieties on the coins. Those on the coins of Pæstum (e) exactly resemble our modern ones. At the point where the flukes met a loop or staple (a, b, c, d) was attached to the anchor, to which a rope was fastened for the purpose of lifting up the flukes so as to make them catch. This could be done only where the water was not very deep. The cable (σχοινία ἀγκύρεια, ancoralia, funes ancorales) was wound round a capstan (στροφεῖον), by means of which the anchor was weighed (see "Pitture d'Ercolano," t. ii., p. 14).

The cable ran through eye-like hawse-holes on both sides of the prow. Each ship had several boat-hooks (κοντοί) and ship's ladders (κλιμακίδες, *scalæ*). Fig. 293 and other monuments illustrate their use as bridges or gangways thrown from the side of the high vessel to the shore. As appears from a vase-painting (Micali, "L'Italia avanti il dom. dei Romani," Tav. 103), these ladders were secured to the rigging by means of ropes. Fig. 294, from a bas-relief in the British Museum, shows the lead (βολίς, καταπειρατήρ, *perpendiculum*) suspended on the volute of the prow.

Fig. 293.

Fig. 295 shows a design of a triere, by means of which the mutual position in the vessel of the parts hitherto mentioned may be recognised: *a* is the periphery of the vessel at the water-line; *b*, θαλαμῖται; *c*, ζυγῖται; *d*, θρανῖται; *h*, πάροδος; *i*, ἰκρία (forecastle and quarter-deck); *k*, κατάστρωμα; *l*, ἐπω-τίδες; *m*, ἀντηρίδες; *n*, ἔμβολον; *o*, point where the stern (στεῖρα) begins; *p*, ἀσάνδιον; *q*, ἱστὸς ἀκάτειος; *r*, ἱστὸς μέγας; *s*, χαλι-νός; *t*, πηδάλιον; *u*, διαφράγματα.

Fig. 294.

The interior arrangement of the antique ship, particularly with regard to the position and manipulation of the oars, is subject to many doubts. Here, also, Graser's investigation of the original sources, combined with practical experiments, has elucidated the question to a considerable extent. The rowing apparatus (ἔγκωπον) was confined to the centre part of the hull. Poop and prow were unavailable, owing to their narrowness, and the former supposition of the uppermost rank of rowers having sat on deck has been completely abandoned, as has also the opinion that the space for the rowers was divided by horizontal partitions of any kind. The space for the rowers (ζύγωσις) was enclosed on the one hand by the long sides of the ship, on the other by two vertical partitions (διαφράγματα), with openings in them through which the rowers (ἐρέται, *nautæ*) filed off to their seats. The benches (ζυγά, *transtra*), reaching from the diaphragma to the side of the vessel, were arranged in rows of different heights.

Owing to the outward curvature of the hull, the rowers in the lower ranks naturally sat nearer to the side of the vessel than those in the higher. The width of seat necessary for each man may be counted at 8 square feet (Fig. 296). The benches were arranged so that the seats of the upper row were on a level with the heads of the lower. Fig. 297, *a*, shows the arrangement of the ranks which, in a manner, were dovetailed into each other (Fig. 297, *b*), in consequence of which the handles of the oars in one row required to be only two feet lower than those in the row above it. This arrangement, which left sufficient freedom to the movements of the rowers, explains why, in many-ranked vessels, the oars of the upper rows need not have been too long or too heavy to be plied by one man only. For Greek ships, unlike medieval galleys, had only one rower to each oar. In order to make this possible, the oar (κώπη, *remus*) was balanced as much as possible, the weight of the part inside the vessel being increased by the thickness of the handle and additional pieces of lead, so as to make it quite as heavy or even a little heavier than the outer part. Besides this, the aperture for the oar (τρῆμα, *columbarium*) was bound with metal, so as to reduce the friction to a minimum. The force of the beat of the different banks of oars on the water was made equal through the proportion of the inner to the outer part of the oar being in the same proportion in all oars (at first, 1 : 2 ; afterwards, 1 : 3).

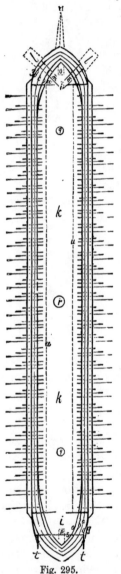

Fig. 295.

As we said before, the rowers of each bank sat horizontally behind each other, the ranks themselves lying perpendicularly over each other.

The number of these ranks determined the name of the vessel (τριήρης, *triremis;* τετρήρης, *quadriremis;* πεντήρης, *quinque-remis;* etc.) In the triere the rowers of the bottom bank were called θαλαμῖται, those of the middle ζυγῖται, those of the top row θρανῖται; in the pentere the rowers of the fourth row were called τετρηρῖται, those of the fifth πεντηρῖται. The distance between the oars of the same row was exactly 4 feet; but they were always pushed 1 foot in front of the corre- sponding oars of the upper row (see Fig. 298, *b, c, d*).

Fig. 296.

Reckoning the distance of the bottom row from the water-line, the thalamitai would have required oars of a length of $7\frac{1}{2}$ feet. This length was increased by 3 feet in each ascending row, which determines the length of the oars of the zygitai at $10\frac{1}{2}$ feet, of the thranitai (the topmost row of the triere) at $13\frac{1}{2}$ feet,

Fig. 297 *a.*

of the tetreritai at $16\frac{1}{2}$ feet, of the penteritai (the top row of the pentere) at $19\frac{1}{2}$ feet. The vertical distance of the handles of the oars was, as we said before, 2 feet (Fig. 298, *a, b*); but this distance was reduced to $1\frac{3}{4}$ feet by the curvature of the sides of the vessel (*c, d*); that between the apertures, seen from the outside, was, indeed,

Fig. 297 *b.*

only $1\frac{1}{4}$ feet (*f, g*). The distance of the top row from the surface of the water in the pentere was only 8 feet, in the triere $5\frac{1}{2}$ feet. For a ten-ranked ship this gives a distance of the apertures from the water of $14\frac{1}{2}$ feet, the length of the oar being $34\frac{1}{2}$ feet. Even in sixteen-ranked ships, such as were built by Demetrios Poliorketes, the length of the uppermost oars could be reduced to $27\frac{3}{4}$ feet, so as to make the vessel seaworthy. This was done by making the row-locks more slanting. This explains the possi-bility of the forty-ranked state-ship built by Ptolemaios Philopator; which, however, could be used only in smooth water. The uppermost oars were, according to Athenæus, 57 feet long.[1]

Fig. 298.

The celebrated state-ship of Hieron of Syrakuse was, however, not a vessel of war, but of burden.

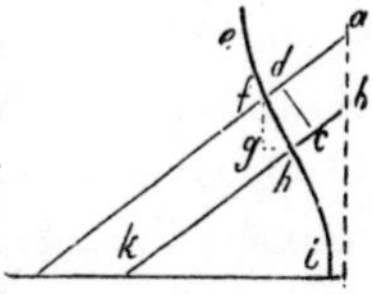

---

[1] See Graser, " De veterum re Navali," §§ 64—70, Tab. IV.

The number of rowers was increased by one in each ascending rank. The number of the thalamitai, counting both sides, was 54; of the zygitai, 58; of the thranitai, 62; of the tetreritai, 66; of the penteritai, 70. The triere, therefore, contained altogether 175 rowers; the pentere, 310. All these were under the command of the κελευστής (*hortator*) and his lieutenant, the ἐπόπτης. The rowing was accompanied by the rhythmical notes of a piper (τριηραύλης). The number of marines (ἐπιβάται) was comparatively very small. An Attic pentere contained only eighteen of them, besides twenty-four sailors (ναῦται, *nautæ*). The small number of marines is explained by the fact of a Greek sea-fight consisting chiefly in endeavours to knock a hole into the enemy's vessel by means of the above-mentioned rostrum, or, at least, to break her oars in passing close by her. Everything, therefore, depended upon skilful manœuvring.

The building and equipping of vessels was done in military harbours, of which that of Athens is in the best state of preservation.

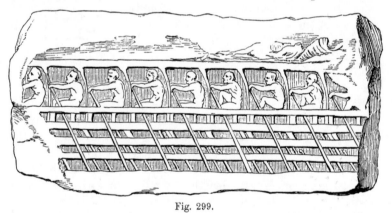

Fig. 299.

It was separated from the commercial harbour, commonly called Piraieus, and was divided into three basins, cut nearly circularly into the Piraieus peninsula. The centre one, Munychia, could hold twice as many men-of-war (viz. 200) as each of the two others, Zea and Kantharos. The docks (νεώσοικος) lay round these basins close to the water, their openings being turned towards the centres or the outlets of the basin; in them the ships, when not in use, were protected from the weather. Farther back were

situated the arsenals (σκευοθήκη), containing the fittings of the
ships not in use; the name for the whole dockyard was νεώρια.
The docks, or ship-sheds, generally contained one vessel each; as,
for instance, was the case in the celebrated harbours of Rhodes,
Korinth, and Kyzikos, the latter of which could hold two hundred
ships; in Syrakuse, however, and some other places, each dock
contained two vessels. Graser's measurements of the Athenian
harbours have fully confirmed his above-mentioned conjectures
as to the construction of the vessels themselves. Further confir-
mation is derived from the bas-relief of an Attic τριήρης
ἄφρακτος, but κατάστρωτος, in which, therefore, the uppermost
bank of oars is visible (Fig. 299).

As the Roman vessel resembles the Greek in most points, we
will here add a few remarks about the former. The Latin terms

Fig. 300.

have already been given. As long as Roman conquests were
limited to Italy, their navy consisted only of long boats (*caudices,
naves caudicariæ*) for river navigation, and of small sea-vessels as
a means of intercommunication between the maritime provinces,
not to mention the defence of the harbours. The Carthaginian wars
necessitated the building of a powerful fleet. In a space of two
months 130 penteres and trieres were constructed, after the pattern
of a stranded Carthaginian pentere. The timbers were roughly
cut, and the improvised sailors had to be trained on rowing-frames
erected on shore; but the foundation was thus laid of a fleet of
triremes, quadriremes, and quinqueremes, commonly called *naves
longæ*. The Romans, differing in this from the Greeks, transferred the mode of close fighting to their sea-battles. Two or

four towers (*navis turrita*) and catapults transformed the deck into a castle, from which the marines began the fight with missiles till the vessels approached within boarding distance. The marines, therefore, were much more numerous on board Roman than Greek vessels. The quinquereme contained 120. After the battle of Actium Roman ship building underwent a thorough change. That battle had been won against the Greek-Egyptian fleet of Antony, built according to Greek rules, chiefly by means of the ships of the Liburnian pirates, which had only two banks of oars and a very light rigging. In consequence, the Roman fleet was reorganised according to the same principle (*navis Liburna*). Besides men-of-war, larger vessels of burden were required ; these *naves onerariæ* ($\phi o \rho \tau a \gamma \omega \gamma \grave{o} \varsigma$ $\nu a \hat{v} \varsigma$ or $\sigma \tau \rho o \gamma \gamma \acute{v} \lambda \eta$) were about three or four times as long as they were broad. Many statements in ancient authors prove the quickness of voyage in those days. Balbilus went from Messina to Alexandria in six days (the French mail-steamers require $6\frac{1}{2}$ days for the same distance). Valerius Maximus sailed from Puteoli to Alexandria *lenissimo flatu* in nine days, and the voyage from Gades to Ostia took only seven days, in case the wind was favourable; that from Gades to Gallia Narbonensis (perhaps to Massilia), three days.

56. From the serious business of life we now follow the Greek citizen to scenes of merriment. We mentioned before (§ 33) that the chief difference between the customs at the meals of earlier and later periods consisted in the former being taken in a sitting, the latter in a reclining position ($\kappa a \tau \acute{a} \kappa \lambda \iota \sigma \iota \varsigma$). The Kylix of Sosias, in the Berlin Museum, where the gods appear at their meal sitting on thrones in couples, may serve to illustrate the older Homeric custom. Only the Kretans preserved this old custom up to a later period. Almost all the later representations show the men lying at their meals ; women and children, on the contrary, appear in an upright posture, the former sitting mostly on the farther end of the kline at the feet of their husbands, or on separate chairs.[1] The sons were not allowed to recline till they came of age ; in Makedonia not till they had killed a boar. The women we occasionally see in pictures (mostly of later date) are probably hetairai

---

[1] Compare the specimens collected by Welcker, "Alte Denkmäler," vol. ii. p. 242 *et. seq.*

(see Fig. 304). This, however, is different in Etruscan representations, where a man and a woman are seen reclining on one
and the same kline. Aristotle says expressly that men and their
wives used amongst the
Etruscans to lie down to
their meals under one and
the same coverlid. In
Greece, also, a kline was
generally occupied by no
more than two people. Fig.
301 shows two couches with

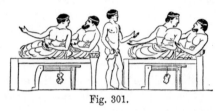

Fig. 301.

an older and a younger man reclining on each of them, talking to
each other in a lively manner. A cup-bearer is about to replenish
their emptied goblets. Where three or four persons are seen
on the same kline (see Fig. 304), we may suspect the introduction
of a Roman custom into Greece.

The gorgeous arrangement and more refined cookery of the
meals of latter days widely differed from the frugality of
Homeric times. Pieces of beef, mutton, goat meat, or pork,
roasted on the spit, were placed by the maid-servants on little
tables in front of the guests (see § 33); the bread was handed
round in baskets; and at the end of the meal wine was drunk,
which had been previously mixed with water in huge krateres.
The use of knives and forks remained unknown, whence the
custom of washing the hands (ἀπονίψασθαι) and drying them on
a towel (χειρόμακτρον) provided for the purpose. Tablecloths
and napkins were equally unknown. The latter were supplied by
a peculiar kind of dough, which served to clean the fingers from
grease. Sometimes temporary spoons were formed of the same
material, to eat the more fluid victuals. Such is still the custom
in the East. Greek cookery, even of a later period (not to
mention Spartan frugality), is described as simple, if not poor;
consisting chiefly of μᾶζα (flat round cakes of barley, still
eaten in Greece), various kinds of salad, garlic, onions, and
pulse, whence the derisive expressions μικροτράπεζοι or φυλλο-
τρῶγες applied to the Greeks. The more refined tastes of Grecia
Magna were only gradually introduced amongst the richer classes
of Greece itself. Various kinds of fish and shell-fish, and different
vegetables, gradually supplanted the huge joints of Homeric

times. The meals were prepared by cooks hired from the market, or by Sicilian "chefs," who, in Roman times, were amongst the slaves of every rich Greek family. The *menus* which might be composed from the statements of ancient authors seem little palatable according to our notions; but the rich and tasteful plate and other table-furniture described by us (§ 33 *et seq.*) give us a high idea of the elegant appearance of a Greek dinner-table.

Another characteristic of the meals of later times was the addition of the συμπόσιον to the meal proper (δεῖπνον). Deipnon was the name of the chief meal or dinner, about sunset ; ἀκράτισμα that of the breakfast ; ἄριστον that of the luncheon, about mid-day. In early times the meal was considered as finished as soon as the appetite was satisfied ; later, the drinking-bout, animated by conversation, music, mimic representations, and games, became the most important part of the meal. Wit and humour were displayed to their fullest advantage, for the Greek, differing in this from the more indolent Roman, took an active part in the various amusements.

The removal of the dinner-table (αἴρειν, ἀπαίρειν, ἐπαίρειν, ἀφαιρεῖν, ἐκφέρειν, βαστάζειν τὰς τραπέζας), and the simultaneous cleaning of the floor from bones, peelings, and other remnants of the meal, gave the signal for rising. Sosus, the artist, imitated in mosaic a floor, covered with such remnants and other rubbish for the dining-hall of the royal palace of Pergamon. At the end, as at the beginning of the meal, the hands were washed with scented soap (σμῆγμα or σμῆμα); the meal proper then was closed by a libation of unmixed wine, which was drunk by all round to the good spirit (ἀγαθοῦ δαίμονος), or to each other's health (ὑγιείας). A second libation (σπονδαί) introduced the symposion. Hymns and the solemn notes of a flute accompanied this libation, which, as it were, gave a sacred character to the beginning symposion.

The dessert, called, in opposition to the πρῶται τράπεζαι or δεῖπνον proper δεύτεραι τράπεζαι or τραγήματα, later also ἐπιδόρπια, ἐπιδορπίσματα, ἐπιδόρπιοι, τράπεζαι, ἐπίδειπνα, ἐπιδει-πνίδες, ἐπιφορήματα, ἐπαίκλια, γωγαλεύματα, etc., consisted of about the same dainties as nowadays. Piquant dishes, stimu-lating the guests to drinking, were chosen in preference ; amongst cheeses, those from Sicily and from the town of Tromileia in Achaia were particularly liked ; cakes sprinkled with salt (ἐπίπαστα) were another important feature of the Greek dessert.

Dried figs from Attika and Rhodes, dates from Syria and Egypt, almonds, melons, etc., and salt mixed with spices, were seldom wanting. Many of these dainties, as various fruits and Attic cakes shaped liked pyramids, may be recognised in pictures lying on little tables in front of the topers. The drinking began simultaneously with the appearance of the dessert; for during the meal no wine was served. Unmixed wine (ἄκρατον) was not as strictly forbidden to the Greeks as to the inhabitants of Lokri, in Southern Italy, where the law of Zeleukos made it a capital crime; still, the diluting of the wine with water was an old-established custom in Greece. This dietetic measure, made necessary by the universal custom even amongst the lower classes of drinking the fiery wine of the South, was so common in Greece that the contrary was considered as a characteristic of barbarous nations. Habitual drunkenness was exceptional amongst the Greeks, although occasional inebriation at symposia was by no means uncommon; the severe Doric customs of Sparta and Krete for that reason forbade the post-prandial drinking-bout altogether. The wine was mixed with hot or cold water; in the latter case snow was frequently mixed with the wine, or the filled vessel itself was put into a wine-cooler filled with snow. The mixture always contained more water than wine; a mixture by halves (ἴσον ἴσῳ) was very uncommon. The proportion of water to wine was generally 3 : 1 (a mixture called by Athenæus in derision "frog's wine"—βατράχοις οἰνοχοεῖν), or 2 : 1, more rarely 3 : 2. This proportion, however, was modified by the taste of the drinker and the quality of the wine. Large krateres of metal or burnt clay (see the vessels standing on the floor in Figs. 302 and 304) were used for mixing the wine. From this large vessel the wine was poured into the goblets (phiale, kylix, skyphos, kantharos, karchesion, keras, and rhyton) by means of the kyathos or oinochoë

Fig. 302.   Fig. 303.

(see the vase-painting, Fig. 302). Fig. 303 is taken from another vase-painting, in which the youthful cup-bearer there depicted approaches two girls on a kline with two kyathoi in his hands. As soon as the goblets were filled a king of the feast (βασιλεύς, ἄρχων τῆς πόσεως, συμποσίαρχος, ἐπίσταθμος) was chosen. His election was generally decided by casting the dice, unless one of the topers chose himself. This ruler had to decide the right mixture of the wine, the number of goblets to be drunk by each guest, and the general rules of the feast (τρόπος τῆς πόσεως), which he occasionally had to enforce by penalties. The drinking was begun with small goblets, soon followed by larger ones,

Fig. 304.

which had to be emptied by each guest at one draught (ἀπνευστί or ἀμυστὶ πίνειν) to the health of his right-hand neighbour. All this somewhat reminds one of the customs of German students at their drinking-bouts. The southern vivacity and wit of the Greeks gave a peculiar charm to these feasts, which, however, frequently ended in sacrifices to Aphrodite Pandemos, as is but too easily explainable from the presence of beautiful girls as singers, players of flute and kithara and cup-bearers. Frequently these feasts were held at the houses of celebrated hetairai.[1]

[1] The presence of female slaves as cup-bearers at these feasts is proved by a bas-relief (Micali, "L'It. av. il. Dominio d. Rom." Atlas pl. 107), where a female slave fills the goblets of two couples reclining on couches, while three girls are playing on a flute, lyre, and syrinx respectively.

Fig. 304 represents one of these scenes, which in later times were undoubtedly of frequent occurrence, and have often been the subjects of vase-paintings.

Jugglers of both sexes, either single or in gangs, were common all over Greece putting up their booths, as Xenophon says, wherever money and silly people could be found. These frequently amused the guests at drinking-feasts with their tricks. The reputation of this class of people was anything but above suspicion, as is proved by the verse of Manetho ("Apotheles," IV. 276), in which they are described as the "birds of the country, the foulest brood of the city." Their tricks were innumerable, and outvied in boldness and ingenuity those of our conjurors, barring,

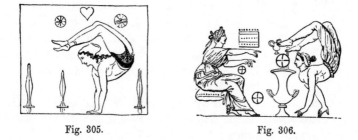

Fig. 305.   Fig. 306.

of course, such as are founded on the modern discoveries of natural science. Male and female jugglers jumped forwards and backwards over swords or tables; girls threw up and caught again a number of balls or hoops to the accompaniment of a musical instrument; others displayed an astounding skill with their feet and toes while standing on their hands. Rope-dancers performed the most dangerous dances and *salti-mortali*. In Rome even elephants were trained to mount the rope. Flying-machines of a construction unknown to us are also mentioned, on which bold aëronauts traversed the air. Alkiphron tells a story about a peasant who, on seeing a juggler pulling little bullets from the noses, ears, and heads of the spectators, exclaimed: "Let such a beast never enter my yard, or else everything would soon disappear." Descriptions of these tricks are frequent in ancient writers, particularly in the indignant invectives of the early fathers of the Church (compare § 100). Amongst the pictures of female jugglers in all kinds of impossible postures we have chosen three. Fig. 305 shows a girl in short drawers and with a cap on her head, performing the dangerous sword-dance (ἐς μαχαίρας κυβιστᾶν) described by Plato ("Euthymed.," p. 294) and Xenophon ("Symposion," § 11). It consists in her turning somersaults forwards and backwards across the points of three swords stuck in the ground. A similar picture we see on a vase of the Berlin Museum. Fig. 306 shows a female juggler dressed

Fig. 307.

in long drawers standing on her hands, and filling with her feet a kantharos from a krater placed in front of her. She holds the handle of the kantharos with the toes of her left foot, while the toes of her other foot cling round the stem of the kyathos used for drawing the liquor. A woman sitting in front of her performs a game with three balls, in which the other artiste also seems to take a part. In Fig. 307 a girl in a rather awkward position is shooting an arrow from a bow.

Of social games played by the topers we mention, besides the complicated kottabos, the games played on a board or with dice. Homer already mentions a game of the former class (πεττεία), and names Palamedes as its inventor; of the exact nature of this game we know little or nothing. Neither are we informed of the details of another kind of petteia played with five little stones, ψῆφοι, on a board divided by five lines. The so-called "game of cities" (πόλεις παίζειν) seems to have resembled our chess or draughts. The board was divided into five parts (πόλεις or χῶραι). Each player tried to checkmate the other by the skilful use of his men. Games of hazard with dice and astragaloi were most likely greater favourites with the topers than the intellectual ones hitherto described. The number of dice (κύβοι, κυβεία, κυβευτήρια, *tesserœ*) was at first three, afterwards two; the figures on the parallel sides being 1 and 6, 2 and 5, 3 and 4. In order to prevent cheating, they were cast from conical beakers (πύργος, *turricula*), the interior of which was formed into different steps. Each cast had its name, sixty-four of which have been transmitted to us by the grammarians. The luckiest cast, each of the dice showing the figure 6 (τρὶς ἕξ), was called

Aphrodite; the unluckiest, the three dice showing the figure 1, had the names of "dog" or "wine" applied to it (κύων, οἶνος, also τρεῖς, κύβοι). Another game of a similar nature was played with the so-called astragaloi (ἀστράγαλοι, *tali*), dice of a lengthy shape made of the knuckles of animals. Two of the surfaces were flat, the third being raised, and the fourth indented slightly. The last-mentioned side was marked 1, and had, amongst many other names, that of "dog" (κύων, *canis*); the opposite surface, marked 6, was called κῷος. The Latin names of the two other sides marked 3 and 4 were *suppus* and *planus* respectively. The figures 2 and 5 were wanting on the astragaloi, the narrow end-surfaces not being counted. The number of astragaloi used was always four, being the same as in the game of dice. Here also the luckiest cast was called Aphrodite, with which at the same time the honour of king-of-the-feast was connected. Young girls liked to play at a game with five astragaloi, or little stones, which were thrown into the air and caught on the upper surface of the hand (πεντελιθίζειν, πενταλιθίζειν). This game is still in use in many countries. We possess many antique representations of these various games.[1] Two vase-paintings (Panofka, "Bilder antiken Lebens," Taf. X., Nos. 10, 11) show soldiers playing at draughts. Astragaloi and dice of different sizes, some with the figures as above described on them, others evidently counterfeited, are preserved in several museums. Of larger representations we mention the marble statue of a girl playing with astragaloi in the Berlin Museum, and a Pompeian wall-painting ("Museo Borbon.," vol. v., Tav. 23) in which the children of Jason play the same game, while Medea threatens their lives with a drawn sword. The celebrated masterpiece of Polykletes, representing two boys playing with astragaloi, formerly in the palace of Titus in Rome, has unfortunately been lost. Another wall-painting (Milin, "Mythologische Gallerie," Taf. CXXXVIII., No. 515) shows in the foreground Aglaia and Hileaira, daughters of Niobe, kneeling and playing the same game.

In connection with these social games we mention a few other

---

[1] Amongst the false dice of the R. Museum of Berlin, one has the figure 4 twice over; another was evidently loaded with lead. Besides, there is a die in the shape of an octagonal prism; the surfaces show the following sequence of figures: 1, 7, 2, 6, 3, 5, 4. 8.

favourite amusements of the Greeks. The existence of cock-fights (ἀλεκτρυονομαχία) is proved by vase-paintings, gems, and written evidence. It was a favourite pastime with both old and young. Themistokles, after his victory over the Persians, is said to have founded an annual entertainment of cock-fights, which made both these and the fights of quails popular amongst the Greeks. The breeding of fighting-cocks was a matter of great importance, Rhodes, Chalkis, and Media being particularly cele-brated for their strong and large cocks. In order to increase their fury, the animals were fed with garlic previous to the fight. Sharp metal spurs were attached to their legs, after which they were placed on a table with a raised border. Very large sums were frequently staked on them by owners and spectators. Here again we see antique customs reproduced by various modern nations. The Italian game of *morra* (*il giuco alla morra* or *fare alla*

Fig. 308.

morra) was also known to the ancients. In it both players open their clenched right hands simultaneously with the speed of lightning, whereat each has to call out the number of fingers extended by the other. Fig. 308, from a vase-painting in the Pinakothek of Munich, shows Eros and Anteros playing this game. It was called by the Greeks δακτύλων ἐπάλλαξις, by the Romans *micare digitis*. (Compare similar representations in *Archæologische Zeitung*, 1871, Taf. 56.)

57. Mimetic dances were another favourite amusement at symposia. They mostly represented mythological scenes. A few words about Greek dancing ought to be added. Homer mentions dancing as one of the chief delights of the feast; he also praises the artistic dances of the Phaiakian youths. This proves the esteem in which this art was held even at that early period. In the dances of the Phaiakai, all the young men performed a circular movement round a singer standing in the centre, or else two skilled dancers executed a *pas de deux*. Homer's words seem to indicate that the rhythmical motion was not limited to the legs, as in our modern dances, but extended to the upper part of the body and the arms. Perhaps the germs of

mimetic art may be looked for in this dance. According to Lucian, the aim of the dance was to express sentiment, passion, and action by means of gestures. It soon developed into highest artistic beauty, combined with the rhythmic grace peculiar to the Greeks. Like the gymnastic and agonistic arts, the dance retained its original purity as long as public morality prevailed in Greece: its connection with religious worship preserved it from neglect. Gradually, however, here also mechanical virtuosity began to supplant true artistic principles.

The division of dances according to their warlike or religious character seems objectionable, because all of them were originally connected with religious worship. The distinction between warlike and peaceful dances, called by Plato τὸ πολεμικὸν εἶδος and τὸ εἰρηνικόν, is more appropriate. Amongst the warlike dances particularly adapted to the Doric character, the πυῤῥίχη was the oldest and that most in favour. It dates from mythical times. Pyrrhichos, either a Kretan or Spartan by birth, the Dioskuroi, also Pyrrhos the son of Achilles, are mentioned as its originators. The Pyrrhic dance, performed by several men in armour, imitated the movements of attack and defence. The various positions were defined by rule; hands and arms played an important part in the mimetic action, hence the name χειρονομία also applied to this dance. It formed the chief feature of the Doric gymnopaidia and of the greater and lesser Panathenaïa at Athens. The value attached to it in the latter city is proved by the fact of the Athenians making Phrynichos commander-in-chief owing to the skill dis-

Fig. 309.

played by him in the Pyrrhic dance. Later a Bacchic element was introduced into this dance, which henceforth illustrated the deeds of Dionysos. A fragment of a marble frieze (Fig. 309) shows a satyr with a thyrsos and laurel crown performing a wild Bacchic dance between two soldiers, also executing a dancing movement. It most likely illustrates the Pyrrhic dance of a later epoch. Of other warlike dances we mention the καρπεία, which rendered the surprise of a warrior

T

ploughing a field by robbers, and the scuffle between them.   It
was accompanied on the flute.

More numerous, although less complicated, were the peaceful
choral dances performed at the feasts of different gods, according
to their individualities.   With the exception of the Bacchic
dances, they consisted of measured movements round the altar.
More lively in character were the gymnopaidic dances performed
by men and boys.   They were, like most Spartan choral dances,
renowned for their graceful rhythms.   They consisted of an
imitation of gymnastic exercises, particularly of the wrestling-
match and the Pankration; in later times it was generally
succeeded by the warlike Pyrrhic dance.   Another dance, performed by noble Spartan maidens in honour of Artemis Karyatis,
is depicted, Fig. 310.   The chain-dance (ὅρμος) belongs to the
same class.   It was danced by a number of youths and maidens

Fig. 310.

placed alternately in a ring, and holding each other's hands ; they
each performed the softer or more warlike movements suited to
their sex, so that the whole, according to Lucian, resembled a
chain of intertwined manly courage and female modesty (compare
Fig. 310).   We pass over the names of several dances, of which
nothing is known to us beyond their connection with the worship
of Dionysos.   In this worship, more than in any other, the
symbolic rendering of natural phenomena was felt by the people.
The dying throbs of Nature in autumn, her rigid torpor in winter,
and final revival in spring, were the fundamental ideas of the
Bacchic myth.   The joy and sorrow expressed by the Bacchic
dances were in a manner inspired by these changes in nature.
This dramatic element in the Bacchic dance was the germ of
theatrical representations.   The grave and joyful feelings excited

by the approach of winter or spring found their expressions both
in hymns and choric dances.   In the intervals between two
hymns the choragos, disguised as a satyr, stepped forward, and
recited in an improvised oration the feats of Dionysos, celebrated
in the dithyrambos.   His language was either serious or jocular,
according to the facts related.   Thespis, by distinguishing the
actor from the chorus, and introducing a dialogue between him
and the choragoi, initiated the artistic drama.   The choruses sung
at the Lenaia, the Bacchic winter celebrations, were descriptive of
the death of Nature, symbolised by the sufferings of Dionysos.
Tragedy owed its origin to them, while comedy was the development of the small rural Dionysia at the conclusion of the vintage.
In the latter the phallus, the symbol of Nature's creative power,
was carried in festive procession, surrounded by a crowd, adorned
with wreaths and masks.   After the Phallic and Ithyphallic songs
had been sung, unbounded merriment, raillery, and satire became
the order of the day.   Our remarks about the Greek theatre
will be limited to the decorative arrangement of the skene (as far
as it has not been considered in § 30), and the costumes of the
actors.

58. The assembled people in a crowded theatre must have
been an imposing spectacle, in which the gorgeous colours of the
dresses were blended with the azure of a southern sky.   No
antique rendering of this subject remains.   The spectators began
to assemble at early dawn, for each wished to secure a good seat,
after paying his entrance-fee (θεωρικόν).   This, not exceeding
two oboloi, was payable to the builder or manager of the theatre.
After the erection of stone theatres at Athens, this entrance-fee
was paid for the poorer classes by Government, and formed,
indeed, one of the heaviest items of the budget.   For not only at
the Dionysian ceremonies, but on many other festive occasions,
the people clamoured for free admission, confirmed in their
demands by the demagogues.   Frequently the money reserved
for the emergency of a war had to be spent for this purpose.
The seats in a theatre were, of course, not all equally good,
and their prices varied accordingly.   The police of the theatre
(ῥαβδοφόροι, ῥαβδοῦχοι) had to take care that everybody took his
seat in the row marked on his ticket.   Most of the spectators
were men.   In older times women were allowed only to attend at

tragedies, the coarse jokes of the comedy being deemed unfit for
the ears of Athenian ladies.   Only hetairai made an exception to
this rule.   It is almost certain that the seats of men and women
were separate.   Boys were allowed to witness both tragedies and
comedies.   Whether slaves were admitted amongst the spectators
seems doubtful.   As pedagogues were not allowed to enter the
schoolroom, it seems likely that they had also to leave the theatre
after having shown their young masters to their seats.   Neither
were the slaves carrying the cushions for their masters' seats
admitted amongst the spectators.   It is, however, possible that
when the seats became to be for sale, certain classes of slaves were
allowed to visit the theatre.   Favourite poets and actors were
rewarded with applause and flowers ; while bad performers had to
submit to whistling, and, possibly, other worse signs of public
indignation.   Greek audiences resembled those of southern Europe
at the present day in the vivacity of their demonstrations, which
were even extended to public characters amongst the spectators
on their entering the theatre.

The frontage of the skene consisted in the oldest times of
only one story, to which, however, several others were added
when the development of the drama by Aischylos demanded
a greater perfection of the scenic apparatus.   According to
Vitruvius, the skene was developed architecturally, like the
façades of large buildings, and, like these, adorned with columns,
architraves, and friezes.   His statement is confirmed by the well-
preserved skene of the theatre at Aspendos, which, however, was
built after a Roman pattern (see the view and description of it,
§ 84).   According to Vitruvius, five doors were situated in the
background, the centre one being called the gate of the royal
palace (*valvæ regiæ*), most likely owing to the action of the
antique tragedy generally taking place in front of a king's palace.
The two gates to both sides of this led into buildings connected
with the palace destined for the reception of guests, whence their
name *hospitalia*.   The two remaining doors, lying near the corners
of the skene-wall and the wings of the stage, were called *aditus*
and *itinera* respectively ; the former indicating the road to the
city, the latter that to foreign countries.   In theatres where there
were only three doors, the latter names were applied to the two
doors to the right and left of the *valvæ regiæ*.   The chorus entered

the orchestra through the parodoi ; the actors coming from home or foreign parts could therefore conveniently enter and retire from the stage by means of the steps ascending from the orchestra to the logeion. Immediately before the skene-wall, perhaps only a few feet distant from it, was placed a wooden frame-work, across which the back scene was fastened. The doors in this piece of scenery corresponded to those in the stone wall. The back scene could undoubtedly be made to slide to right and left from the centre (*scena ductilis*), so as to produce a change of scenery, which, as we shall show, could be made complete by the turning of the periaktoi. Whether the back scene consisted of only two, or, as is more likely, of four or eight, movable pasteboard partitions we must leave undecided. Lohde [1] says that, in order to make the parts of the back scene, pushed behind the periaktoi, quite invisible to the public, " slight frames of woodwork, covered with painted paper-hangings, were placed at the farther end and to both sides of the pulpitum, which were immediately connected with the side wings of the stage-building." By means of these pieces of scenery the excessive length of the stage was considerably shortened—the remaining space being still quite sufficient for the few actors of the Greek drama. In order to cover the stone wall of the skene, the artificial wall alluded to had to be of considerable height. To give it firmness, a second wooden erection was placed several feet behind it, running parallel to it ; both were connected by means of cross beams, and rested on firm foundations, the remains of which have been discovered in the theatres of Herculaneum, Pompeii, Orange, and Arles, belonging, it is true, all of them to Roman times.

Besides the back scene, two side scenes (περίακτοι, μηχαναί) existed in Greek theatres. They consisted of slight wooden frames in the form of three-sided prisms, covered with painted canvas. By means of pegs they could easily be revolved on their axis, so that always one of their painted surfaces was turned towards the spectators. Each of these three surfaces was painted in a different manner, and the changed position of the periaktoi indicated a total or partial change of locality on the stage. In case the periaktos to the left of the spectator was moved, the

[1] " Die Skene der Alten." Berlin, 1860. The chief points of which investigation we have adopted in our description.

direction of the foreign road was supposed to be changed. The
revolving of both periaktoi implied a modification of the back
scene, an entire change of locality being thus indicated. The
periaktos to the right of the spectator could never be turned by
itself, for it indicated the position of home, which, as long as the
centre scene was unchanged, naturally remained the same. The
few changes of scenery occurring in the antique drama could
easily be effected. To complete the skene, a kind of ceiling of
boards was necessary, traces of which can still be distinguished
on the wall of the skene of the theatre at Aspendos. On these
boards stood the crane on which was suspended the flying
apparatus (called μηχανή in general, or more especially γέρανος,
αἰώρημα, στροφεῖον, and ἡμιστρόφιον). By means of it gods and
heroes and spectres entered and left the stage, or floated across it.
A floating-machine of this kind was also the θεολογεῖον, on which,
for instance, Zeus, with Eos and Thetis, appeared in Aischylos's
Psychotasia. The upper conclusion of the stage was effected by
means of a piece of painted canvas (κατάβλημα) hanging down,
which covered the woodwork of the ceiling and the machinery
placed there from the eyes of the spectators. The Charonic stair
we have mentioned before. Quite recently [1] a hollow, of the
shape of a coffin, has been discovered on the stage of the Greek
theatre of Azanoi in Asia Minor, just in front of the *porta regia.*
This was undoubtedly the opening of the Charonic staircase.
Whether the old Attic stage had a curtain seems doubtful : later
a curtain (αὐλαία, παραπέτασμα, originally called also προσκήνιον)
is mentioned. Perhaps it used to be parted in the middle, and
the two divisions pushed behind the sides of the proskenion.

An important part of the costume of the actors was the mask
(πρόσωπον). Its origin must undoubtedly be looked for in the
grotesque jocularities of the Dionysian worship. Disguises, the
painting of the face with the lees of wine, afterwards with minium,
or the wearing of masks made of leaves or bark, were customary
from the earliest times. Thence the drama adopted its masks of
painted canvas. It must be remembered that the antique actor
was not so much the expounder of individual passion as the
representative of the different phases and classes of society. The

---

[1] Sperling, " Ein Ausflug in die isaurischen Berge im Herbst 1862," in *Zeitschrift
für allgemeine Erdkunde.* New series, XV., 1863, p. 435.

expression of his face, therefore, was of much less importance than
in the modern drama.   K. O. Müller justly remarks that types
like Aischylos's Orestes, Sophokles's Aias, or Euripides's Medea did
not demand the *nuances* of facial expression that would be expected
from Hamlet or Tasso.   Moreover the masks could be changed so
as to render the more general gradations of passion.   Owing to the
large size of the Greek theatre, acoustical and optical means had to
be applied to convey the words and movements of the actors to
the more distant rows of spectators.   One of the latter was the
apparent increase of the actor's size by means of κόθορνοι and
high masks.   The development of the mask into a covering, not
only of the face, but of the whole head with side and front hair
attached to it (ὄγκος), was ascribed to Aischylos.   Openings were
left for mouth and eyes, the latter not being larger than the pupil
of the actor, and the former only just wide enough to afford egress
to the voice.   This was the case at least in tragedy: comic masks,
on the other hand, showed distorted features, and a mouth widely
opened, the lips serving as a kind of speaking-trumpet.   Varieties

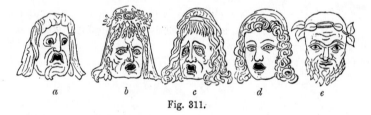

a   *b*   *c*   *d*   *e*

Fig. 311.

of modelling and painting, combined with the numerous changes
of hair and beard, tended to greatly modify the character of
the masks.   The parts of young or old men and women and of
slaves had their characteristic masks assigned to them, all of
which are enumerated by Pollux.   All this tended to some extent
to remove the stiffness of the mask.   Figs. 311 and 312 show a
number of masks found on monuments.   Fig. 311, *a, b, c, d*, are
tragic masks, *b, c* being remarkable by their high onkoi; *d* shows
a female countenance with waving locks, *e* the ivy-crowned and
nearly bald mask used in saytr-dramas.   Fig. 312 illustrates the
varieties of comic masks; it would, however, be difficult to identify
the masks described by Pollux on the monuments.   The height of
the onkos demanded a proportionate increase of the size of the

body, which was effected by the actors walking on buskins
(κόθορνος) (see Fig. 313, illustrative of a scene from a tragedy) ;

Fig. 312.

they also used to pad their limbs.   The remainder of the actors'
costumes was also to a great extent borrowed from the Dionysian

Fig. 313.

feast, both with regard to shape and colour.
Tragic actors wore chitones and himatia of
light colour richly embroidered, and embellished by brilliant gold ornaments.   In
comedy the dress of daily life was essentially
reproduced, with the difference, however, that
the old comedy caricatured this dress by
attaching to it the frequently indecent emblems of Dionysian worship, while the
later comedy retained the caricatured mask, but discontinued the
grotesque costume of older times.   The monuments contain only

Fig. 314.

few representations of scenes from tragedies ; scenes from the
satyr-drama and the older comedy are, on the contrary, very

frequent. Only in very few cases, however, are we able to trace these scenes back to the dramas preserved to us. Fig. 314 opens a view into the χορηγεῖον or διδασκαλεῖον of a poet or choragos before the performance of a satyr drama. The aged poet seems to instruct some choreutai in their parts, and to call their attention to the masks lying before them; a pipe-player is practising his music. In the background to the right an actor is putting on his costume with the aid of a servant; his mask is lying by his side. A similar rehearsal of a satyr-drama is illustrated by a large vase-painting, in the centre of which Dionysos and Ari-

Fig. 315.   Fig. 316.

adne are reclining on a couch. A second female figure, perhaps the Muse, is sitting on the other end of the couch, by the side of which stand two actors (Fig. 315), one in the dress of Herakles, the other in that of Seilenos. The third actor, in the rich costume of an unknown hero, appears on the other side of the kline. The whole group is surrounded by eleven choreutai in a similar costume as those in Fig. 314. We also discover one kitharodos and one pipe-player, and the youthful master of the chorus. Fig. 316 depicts a scene from a comedy. Herakles, in a grotesque boorish dress, presents two Kerkopes, caught and imprisoned by him in market-baskets, to the ruler, whose mask resembles the head of an ape—quite in accordance with the ape-like form of the imps.

59. Agones, hymns, and choric dances were performed in honour of the gods; sacrifices and prayers, on the other hand, established the immediate *rapport* between man and God. They were offered either to pray for a divine gift, as a successful chase,

harvest, etc., or they were intended to soften the wrath of the gods in impending or actual danger, such as illness and storms. A thank-offering eventually followed the grant of these prayers. A third sacrifice was that of expiation and atonement for a breach of the law, human or divine. The mode of prayers and sacrifices varied with their motives; but, before a man entered into intercourse with the deity, he had to undergo a symbolic process of external purification (καθαρμοί, ἱλασμοί, τελεταί). This was exacted not only from those who sacrificed, but from all who entered the precinct of a temple. Vessels with consecrated water stood at the entrances to such places, the sprinkling being done either by the person himself or by a priest. These lustrations were even performed in daily life, previous to acts in any way connected with religious ideas. The bridal bath described by us, the lustrations before feasts, the vessel with water placed at the door of a dead person for the use of the mourners on leaving the house—all these had the same significance. The contact with a dead body especially required a lustration, being considered as a taint which temporally prohibited the intercourse with the deity. Another kind of purification was that by fire and smoke. Odysseus performs a lustration with the steam of " curse-removing sulphur " (περιθείωσις) after the murder of the wooers; the fire burning on the altar, and the torches carried at religious ceremonies, had the same significance of moral purification. The carrying of the new-born infant round the flames of the domestic altar has been mentioned before. The lustration with fire and water even extended to the garments and to the utensils used at sacrifices. Herakles purified the goblet with water and sulphur before sacrificing to Zeus; Penelope took a bath, and dressed herself in clean garments, before sacrificing and praying for the safety of her son. To certain plants, such as myrtle, rosemary, and juniper, purifying qualities were ascribed. A twig of Apollinian laurel was supposed to free the murderer from his guilt. These purifications were also performed collectively by tribes and nations; in Homer, for instance, the Achaioi " purify themselves and throw their stain into the sea." In historic times collective lustrations of cities after epidemics or civil wars are mentioned repeatedly. Epimenides, for instance, purified Athens after the Kylonian massacre.

The act of purification was followed by the prayer. Plato says that it ought to precede every enterprise, great or little, and that for a virtuous man there is nothing better than keeping up the intercourse with the gods by means of offerings, prayers, and vows. Almost all important events or customs in the daily life, both of individuals and communities, were accompanied by prayers, consisting chiefly of old traditional formulas. Three gods—for instance, Zeus in conjunction with Athene and Apollo—were usually addressed together. In order not to offend the deity by omitting one of its names, certain formulas were usually added to the prayer, such as " whether you be a god or goddess;" or, " whoever you may be ; " or, "whether this or another be your favourite name." The Olympian gods were prayed to in an upright position with raised hands ; the marine gods, with hands held horizontally; the gods of Tartarus, with hands held down : the latter were also invoked by knocking or stamping the foot on the ground. Kneeling was not a custom of the Greeks : whenever it is mentioned amongst them, Oriental influence must be suspected. Only those craving protection used to embrace the statue of the god in a kneeling position, which is frequently represented on the monuments. Akin to the prayer was the curse against criminals : the Erinies were implored to execute it. Zeus Horkios, the revenger of oaths, punished the perjurer with his wrath. The solemn oath was taken on hallowed ground before the altar or statue of a god. The swearing person either touched these or immersed his hand in the blood of a sacrificed animal, calling, as in the prayer, usually on three gods as witnesses. This was the later custom : in Homer the heroes taking an oath raised their sceptre against the sky.

Prayers were always accompanied by gifts, to propitiate the gods. They were either gifts for the moment, to be deposited on the altar or consumed by fire ; or they took the shape of votive offerings, which remained the property of the sanctuary. Gifts, as an old proverb says, determine the acts of gods and kings. Offerings of the former class consisted of the first-fruits of the field, such as onions, pumpkins, grapes, figs, and olives. Prepared eatables, such as cakes (πέμματα, πέλανοι) and other pastry, frequently in the shapes of animals, and in the place of real ones, were also offered to the gods. Roasted barley (οὐλαί, οὐλοχύται)

was another common gift; it was either thrown into the flames or
sprinkled on the necks of the animals brought for sacrifice. A bloodless offering is depicted in Fig. 317. The laurel-crowned priest
stands in front of the fire on the altar, throwing into it the barley
which is presented to him by an attendant in a basket adorned
with sacred twigs. On the other side another youthful attendant
is holding a long staff resembling a torch, to the upper end of
which is fastened some wool or oakum, serving most likely to
light a fire. By other archæologists this figure is explained as
a neokoros with a besom of laurel branches; a musician accom-

Fig. 317.

panies the ceremony on the pipe. Libations formed an essential
feature of sacrifices, just as they did at the meals of mortals. To
some gods unmixed wine was offered; others, for instance the
Erinies, Nymphs, Muses, and deities of Light, received honey,
milk, and oil. A libation of this kind is represented in the
frequently repeated choragic bas-reliefs, where Nike pours the
sacred beverage into a vase which is offered to her by the victorious Kitharoidos (Milin, "Galérie mythol." Pl. XVII., No. 58).
      The choice of the animals to be sacrificed depended on the
individual qualities of the various gods. The Olympian gods pre-
ferred white animals; those of the sea and the nether world, black
ones. To Demeter a pig was sacrificed, to Dionysos a he-goat,
because these animals destroyed the gifts granted to man by
these gods. Heifers, sheep, goats, and pigs were offered in larger
or smaller numbers, according to the wealth of the worshipper;

sometimes these different animals were promiscuously offered on one and the same occasion. In Homer sometimes twelve, at others ninety-nine, bulls are slaughtered together; in later times we repeatedly hear of hekatombs of a hundred and more bulls being killed. The original custom of burning the entire animal gradually disappeared; and, even in Homer's time, the gods received only the haunches and small pieces of flesh as their share, the remainder being eaten by those present. These sacrificial meals, shared, as it were, by gods and men, became an integral part of the sacrifice; only offerings for the dead, and the sacrifices on which lay a curse, were buried entire. The animals had to be strong and healthy, and their previous use for human purposes made them inadmissible; only in Sparta, where luxurious sacrifices were altogether unusual, owing to Doric frugality, this absolute purity of the animals was less strictly insisted upon.

For a graphic account of the sacrificial ceremonies, which remained essentially unaltered in later times, we refer the reader to two passages in Homer (Od., III. 436 *et seq.*, and Il., I. 458 *et seq.*)

The custom of gilding the horns mentioned by Homer was afterwards changed into adorning them with wreaths and tainiai. It was considered a favourable omen if the animal went to the sacrifice without opposition, or even nodded its head, as if consenting to its death. According to the sacrifice being for the Olympian or nether world, the head of the animal was bent upwards or downwards. Its throat was then pierced with a knife. Vase-paintings frequently show Nike in the act of sacrificing a bull. The animals, as well as the baskets and other sacrificial utensils, were adorned with twigs or wreaths; the latter, or instead of them a woollen tie, were worn by the Greeks at all religious acts. Criminals only were forbidden to wear them, and were by that means excluded from sacrificial ceremonies. Barring a few representations not easily to be explained (*e.g.* "Museo Borbon.," vol. v., Tav. 23), Greek monuments, as a rule, illustrate only simple sacrificial acts, as the adorning of divine images or the offerings of gifts of various kinds: we therefore refrain from entering into details. To the sacrifices for the dead we shall return hereafter.

The most brilliant exhibitions of religious worship were the
festive processions. The Panathenaïa, in which the whole
Athenian population took part, are rendered, on the cella frieze
of the Parthenon, by the master-hand of Phidias. Theseus, who
united the Attic komai into one city, was also named as the
originator of this celebration of fraternity. At first only horse
and chariot races took place, to which were added in Peisistratos's
time, gymnic agones, and, since Perikles, poetical and musical
competitions. The performance of all these agones took place in
the third year of every Olympiad, between the twenty-fifth and
twenty-seventh days of the month of Hekatombaion. The climax
of the feast—the procession—was held on the twenty-eighth day
of that month. It moved through the streets of the city to
the seat of the goddess, in the Akropolis. On the morning of
that day the citizens of Athens, together with the peasants of
the neighbouring country, assembled before the chief gate of
the city, and formed themselves into a procession according to a
fixed ceremonial. Kitharoidoi and auletai opened the procession ;
the reason of this distinction being that the musico-poetical
agones were those last introduced at the Panathenaïa. After
them followed, in good order, citizens on foot, armed with spear
and shield, and others on horseback. Next came the victors in
the horse and chariot races—the former riding on their horses,
or leading them ; the latter standing on their splendid quadrigæ.
Priests, with their attendants, guarded the hekatombs to be
sacrificed ; old men, chosen for their dignified appearance, held
olive-branches, from the holy tree of the Academy, in their hands
(θαλλοφόροι) ; other distinguished persons carried the votive
offerings destined for the goddess ; a select band of citizens'
daughters carried baskets containing the utensils of the sacrifice
(κανηφόροι) ; while epheboi brought valuable plate, wrought by
the most celebrated masters. After them followed the wives and
daughters of the tribes protected by the Athenians ; the matrons
holding in their hands oak-branches, the emblem of Zeus Xenios,
so as to mark them as guests ; the maidens carrying the sunshades
and chairs of the citizens' daughters (σκιαδηφόροι, διφροφόροι).
The centre of the procession was formed by a ship resting on
wheels, which carried, by way of a sail, the peplos of Athene,
woven by Attic maidens, and richly embroidered, in which the

old Xoanon of the goddess in the Akropolis was dressed. In this order the procession moved through the most splendid streets of the city, past the most celebrated sanctuaries where gifts were offered, round the rock of the Akropolis, entering, at last, through the celebrated Propylæa. Here the procession divided, to gather again on the east side of the Parthenon. All arms were taken off, and hymns were sung to the goddess by the assembled crowd, while burnt-offerings blazed on the altars, and votive-offerings were deposited in the sanctuary.

Although the frieze of the Parthenon-cella does not systematically render the procession, we can easily reconstruct it from the indications thus offered ; indeed, all the important components of the festive crowd appear in the different groups. According to Bötticher,[1] however, the subject of the frieze is not the procession itself, but the preparations for it, such as the division, amongst the persons destined to carry them, of chairs, couches, and bolsters, which were kept in the Hekatompedon, and other preparatory arrangements. The various scenes represented are, according to him, divided both by space and time. Bötticher's conjecture was started in contradiction to all previous archæologists.

60. We now have to follow the Greek to his last place of rest, to see how the holy rites (τὰ δίκαια or τὰ νόμιμα) are duly performed for him. To watch over the rights of the dead, and to do him the last honour, so that his spirit might not wander restlessly on the banks of Acheron, excluded from the Elysian fields —this was the beautiful Greek custom sanctified by the precepts of religion. Hence the pious usage of adorning the dead for their last journey, of burying them with becoming ceremonies, and of considering their graves as holy places not to be profaned. With the same view the bodies of those who died in foreign countries were brought home, or, where this proved impossible, an empty tomb, a kenotaphion, was erected in their birthplace. It would have been disgraceful to deprive even enemies of the honour of a burial, and it was the custom, after a battle, to interrupt hostilities till both parties had buried their dead. Solon's laws discharged the son from all obligations towards his father in case the latter

---

[1] In "Königliche Museen. Erklärendes Verzeichniss der Abgüsse antiker Werke." Berlin, 1871, pp. 188-228.

had committed an immoral act against him, with the exception
only of the duty "of," to use the words of Aischines, "burying
his father according to prescribed custom in honour of the gods
and the law. For he who receives the benefit is no more able to
feel it." Only he who had betrayed his country or committed a
capital crime was deprived of the honour of a burial. His corpse
remained unburied, the prey of wild beasts, with no friend near to
throw at least a handful of earth on it. On the other hand, an
honourable burial (ὑπὸ τῶν ἑαυτοῦ ἐκγόνων καλῶς καὶ μεγαλοπρεπῶς
ταφῆναι) was, as Plato says in Hippias Maj., the most beautiful
conclusion of a life prolonged to old age, and surrounded by
wealth, health, and the esteem of men.

We first turn to the burial rites of heroic times. The closing
of lips and eyes of the dead was, as early as Homer's time, the
first service of love (τὸ γὰρ γέρας ἐστὶ θανόντων) on the part of
the surviving relatives or friends. After it the body was washed,
anointed, and clothed in white thin garments; only the head
remaining uncovered. Thus arranged, the body was placed on a
kline, the foot end of which was turned towards the door of the
house. Thereupon began the lament, for a specimen of which we
refer the reader to the passage of the " Iliad," in which the death of
Patroklos is announced to Achilles. The ceremonies performed
at the couch of the slain Hektor prove the existence of a regulated
lament for the dead at that time. We there hear of singers
intoning chants of complaint (θρῆνοι) interrupted by the loud
lamentations of Andromache, Hekabe, and Helen. The corpse
was exhibited for several days (*e.g.* that of Achilles seventeen
days, that of Hektor nine), during which time the lamentations
were renewed incessantly; ultimately it was placed on the funeral
pile to be given to the flames, numerous sheep and heifers being
sacrificed simultaneously round the pyre. As soon as the funeral
pile was consumed by the flames, the fire was extinguished with
wine. The ashes, after having been sprinkled with oil and wine,
were collected into urns or boxes of valuable materials. The urn
itself was covered with gorgeous purple draperies, and deposited
in the grave.[1] On this grave was heaped a high earth-mound, as

---

[1] Ross states that in the large graves of the Isle of Rhenæa ("Archæolog. Aufsätze,"
i. p. 62) two different kinds of vessels containing ashes (ὀστοθῆκαι) have been discovered. The first kind consists of semi-globular vases (κάλπις) of thin bronze, 10

examples of which custom we mention the grave-mounds raised in
honour of Achilles and Patroklos by the Greek army.   Agones
and a festive meal concluded the ceremonies, as described by
Homer.

In early times the Attic burial rites are said to have been very
simple.   The grave was dug by the nearest relatives, and the
corpse buried in it ; whereupon the mound was sown with corn, by
means of which the decaying body was supposed to be pacified.
A meal, at which the *real* worth of the deceased was extolled by
the survivors (*nam mentiri nefas habebatur*), concluded the ceremony.   The more luxurious habits of a later period made the
great funereal pomps originally reserved for heroes a common

Fig. 318.

custom amongst all classes.   Solon had to prescribe distinct burial
regulations, by which the protracted exhibition of the dead and
other abuses were forbidden.   Upon the whole, however, the
ceremonies described by Homer remained essentially unaltered.
An obolos, being the ferriage (ναῦλον, δανάκη) for Charon, was put
into the mouth of the corpse ; the body then was washed and
anointed by the relatives (particularly the women), and clothed in
a white shroud.   It was crowned with flowers and wreaths, also
provided by the relatives, and thus prepared for the customary
lying-in-state (πρόθεσις, προτίθεσθαι).   This adorning of . the
corpse is illustrated by an interesting Apulian vase-painting
representing the crowning of the body of Archemoros (Fig. 318).

to 12 inches in diameter, which, owing to their brittleness, have been fitted into marble
cases with covers to them. Such marble shells, containing bronze vases covered with
rust and partly destroyed, have been discovered in the graves of Peiraieus. The
second kind consists of square or round boxes of lead, also with covers to them.

On a kline covered with bolsters and cushions is lying the body of Archemoros, who, when little more than a boy, had been killed by a dragon. Hypsipyle, the careless nurse of the boy, stands by the side of the bier about to put the myrtle-wreath on the curly head of the dead; another, younger, female, standing at the head of the kline, holds a sunshade over the bier, in allusion, as Gerhard thinks, to the old notion that the light of Helios should accompany the dead to his dark house, a night-burial being considered dishonourable (compare Euripides, Troad., 446: ἡ κακὸς κακῶς ταφήσῃ νυκτὸς, οὐκ ἐν ἡμέρᾳ). At the foot of the bed we observe the pedagogue, recognisable by his dress and the inscription over his head. In his left hand he is holding a lyre, in order, perhaps, to add it to the gifts destined to adorn the chamber of the dead. Under the kline stands a pitcher, the contents of which had undoubtedly served as a libation. Next to the pedagogue are standing two attendants, carrying on their heads tables, on which various vessels adorned with tainiai are placed. All these, as well as the splendid amphora standing on the ground, and the krater carried by an ephebos on the left, belong to the vessels which a pious custom deposited in the grave or on the funeral pile. At the lying-in-view of the corpse, which by Solon was considerably shortened, and of which Plato approved only as a means to prevent burying alive, the relatives and friends assembled to begin the lamentation. To avoid violent outbreaks

Fig. 319.

of grief, such as described by Homer, Solon forbade a demonstrative behaviour, particularly on the part of women: the severe law of Charondas even prohibited all kinds of complaints at the bier of the dead. Frequently women were paid on such occasions for singing woful songs accompanied by the flute. Fig. 319, taken from a bas-relief on an Etruscan ash-box, shows three women, most likely of this kind, at the kline of a deceased person; a fourth seems to lacerate her face with her hands; a smaller figure, standing near the bier, whose raised arms indicate deep grief, seems to be the son of the deceased.

After the lying-in-view of the corpse, the burial proper (ἐκφορά) took place early in the morning of the following day.

The *cortège* was opened by a hired chorus of men chanting mourning songs (θρηνῳδοί), or by a number of females playing on flutes (καρίναι), who were followed by the male mourners in grey or black garments and with their hair cut off. All these preceded the corpse, generally carried by relations or friends. The female mourners walked behind the bier; by Solon's law, however, women under sixty, unless the nearest relatives, were excluded. The old custom of burying those fallen for their country at the public expense is thus alluded to by Thukydides (II. 34) :— "According to custom, the Athenians prepared a public funeral for those fallen in battle in this manner: three days previously they erected a tent, in which the remains of the killed lay in view; every one there might bring offerings for his deceased relatives. At the funeral, the coffins of cypress-wood are placed on carts, one being assigned to each phyle; in the coffin of each phyle the remains of those belonging to it are laid. An empty covered kline is carried for those missing, whose bodies have not been recovered. Citizens and friends follow the procession, the women attending at the funeral with lamentations. The remains are buried in a public grave lying in the most beautiful suburb of Athens. This place is always used for burying those fallen in battle, with the exception of those killed at Marathon, who were buried on the spot, their courage being deemed worthy of that distinction. After the bones have been covered with earth, a wise and respected man, chosen by the citizens, pronounces the eulogium of the slain, standing on a tribune erected for the purpose." Funeral orations of this kind at the grave were in classic times usual at public funerals only.

The choice of a place for the burial, and the ceremonies accompanying it, varied according to the means of the deceased and the customs among different tribes. In the earliest times the burial-places seem to have been in the houses of the deceased themselves. This immediate contact with the dead, however, being considered unclean, burial-grounds were prepared outside the city walls both at Athens and Sikyon. Sparta and Tarentum had burial-grounds in the city in order (as the law of Lykurgos has it) to steel the minds of the youths against the fear of death. Such burial-grounds lie along the roads outside the gates of almost every city, and yield the most important specimens of the grave-monuments

described in §§ 23 and 24.   The Athenian law forbidding monuments of greater splendour than could be completed by ten men in
three days must have been often infringed.   Private persons were
allowed to bury their dead in fields belonging to them instead of
in the nekropolis.   That the burning of the bodies—at least, of
the Greek nobles—and the preserving of their ashes were customary in the heroic age, is sufficiently proved by Homer.
According to Lucian, the same practice continued to be the most
usual amongst the Greeks;   recent investigations of numerous
graves in the Attic plain, however, seem to prove that the
burial of unburnt bodies in wooden or earthen coffins (λάρναξ,
σορός), or in grave-chambers cut from the living rock, was at least
equally frequent; according to Cicero (De Legg. 2, 22), the latter
custom was even the older of the two.   Most likely the wish of the

Fig. 320.   Fig. 321.

deceased or his relatives, and also the greater or less abundance
of timber in a country, decided the matter.   The rocky soil of
Attika, bare of trees, necessitated the burial in grave-chambers
for the majority of the inhabitants.   The expression θάπτειν
applied to either kind of burial; καίειν signified cremation;
κατορύττειν, interment in particular.   Cremation became necessary particularly when the accumulation of bodies after a battle,
or, for instance, after the plague of Athens, caused dangerous
evaporations.   The same process facilitated the transfer home of
the remains of a person dying in a foreign country.

    After the burial the *cortège* returned to the house of the deceased
and sat down to a meal (περίδειπνον), they being considered, in a
manner, as the guests of the dead person.   The first (τρίτα), second

(ἔνατα), and third (τριακάς) sacrifices at the grave took place on the third, tenth, and thirtieth days after the funeral. The last concluded the mourning period at Athens, that at Sparta being still shorter. The tomb adorned with flowers was a hallowed spot where on certain days of the year oblations and libations were offered in memory of the deceased (ἐνάγισμα, ἐναγίζειν, also χοαί used chiefly of libations).

Representations of this pious custom are common, particularly on the lekythoi, which, in a more or less preserved condition, are frequently found by the side of stelai, or amongst the remains of funeral piles. For it was the custom, particularly of the Athenians, to throw behind them the vessels used on such occasions, no utensil used at funerals being allowed to serve the wants of the living. Figs. 320 and 321 are pictures taken from Athenian lekythoi. The former represents a stele adorned at the top with a

"meandering" ornamentation and crowned by a capital of coloured acanthus-leaves. A blue tainia has been wound round the stele. On either side a woman is approaching. She to the right of the spectator carries a large flat dish, on which stands a lekythos, with a tainia laid round it. The figure on the left carries a similar dish in her left hand, while her right

Fig. 322.

hand holds a large flat basket, destined most likely for carrying flowers and cakes. The second picture, only partially reproduced here (Fig. 322), represents the adorning of the tombstone. A crown of ivy and a lekythos containing the sacred oil are seen on the steps of the simple stele, round which a woman is employed in tying red tainiai, with lekythoi attached to them. Fig. 322 shows Hermes Psychopompos gently leading a female shade to the boat of Charon, on her way to the thrones of Hades and Persephone, where stern judgment awaits her.

LIST OF ILLUSTRATIONS.